EPISTLES ON WOMEN AND OTHER WORKS

broadview editions
series editor: L.W. Conolly

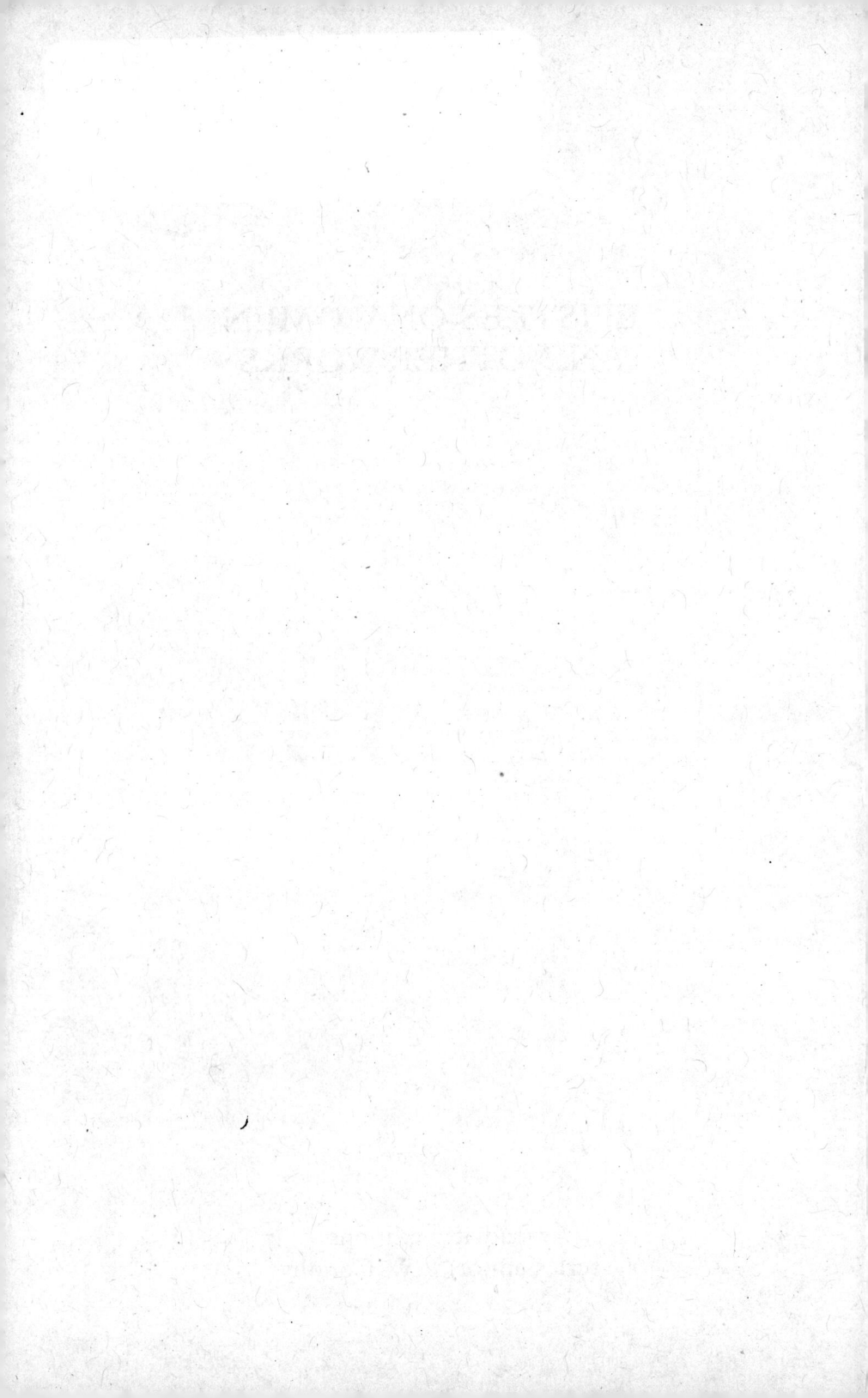

EPISTLES ON WOMEN
AND OTHER WORKS

Lucy Aikin

edited by Anne K. Mellor and Michelle Levy

b

broadview editions

Library and Archives Canada Cataloguing in Publication

Aikin, Lucy, 1781-1864
    Epistles on women and other works / Lucy Aikin ; edited by Anne K. Mellor and Michelle Levy.

(Broadview editions)
Includes bibliographical references.
ISBN 978-1-55111-713-3

    I. Mellor, Anne Kostelanetz.   II. Levy, Michelle Nancy, 1968-   III. Title.
IV. Series: Broadview editions

PR4001.A7A6 2010   828'.7   C2010-904862-8

Broadview Editions

The Broadview Editions series represents the ever-changing canon of literature in English by bringing together texts long regarded as classics with valuable lesser-known works.

Advisory editor for this volume: Juliet Sutcliffe

Broadview Press is an independent, international publishing house, incorporated in 1985.

We welcome comments and suggestions regarding any aspect of our publications—please feel free to contact us at the addresses below or at broadview@broadviewpress.com.

North America
Post Office Box 1243, Peterborough, Ontario, Canada K9J 7H5
2215 Kenmore Avenue, Buffalo, NY, USA 14207
Tel: (705) 743-8990; Fax: (705) 743-8353
email: customerservice@broadviewpress.com

UK, Europe, Central Asia, Middle East, Africa, India, and Southeast Asia
Eurospan Group, 3 Henrietta St., London WC2E 8LU, United Kingdom
Tel: 44 (0) 1767 604972; Fax: 44 (0) 1767 601640
email: eurospan@turpin-distribution.com

Australia and New Zealand
NewSouth Books
c/o TL Distribution, 15-23 Helles Ave., Moorebank, NSW, Australia 2170
Tel: (02) 8778 9999; Fax: (02) 8778 9944
email: orders@tldistribution.com.au

www.broadviewpress.com

Broadview Press acknowledges the financial support of the Government of Canada through the Canada Book Fund for our publishing activities.

This book is printed on paper containing 100% post-consumer fibre.

Typesetting and assembly: True to Type Inc., Claremont, Canada.

PRINTED IN CANADA

To

Eric Abraham Mellor

Ethan Levy Jasny

and

Nate Rydal Jasny Levy

"Hope of the world, the rising race"

– John Aikin and Anna Barbauld,
Evenings at Home (1796)

Contents

Please note that additional selections and appendix materials for this edition are available on an auxiliary website, located at <<www.sfu.ca/~mnl/aikin/epistlesonline.pdf/>>.

Acknowledgements

Many people have assisted us in the preparation of this edition. We would like to thank our diligent and skilled research assistants: Helen McManus, for her work on the bibliography; Heather Ritzer, for her help in preparing the manuscript and her many contributions to the appendices; and Hal Gladfelder, for many of the annotations to the *Epistles on Women*. Also instrumental to the project were librarians from several institutions, including the Osborne Collection of Early Children's Books, Toronto Public Library; Simon Fraser University Library; University of California, Los Angeles; and the Department of Rare Books and Special Collections, University of Rochester Library. We would like particularly to thank Sonny Wong, of Simon Fraser University's Interlibrary Loan department, for his help in securing many of Aikin's works and with the microcard reader, and Mary Huth, of the Department of Rare Books and Special Collections, University of Rochester Library, for permission to reproduce and refer to several of Lucy Aikin's letters held in their Aikin Family Collection.

We are also grateful for the generous assistance provided by a Simon Fraser University Publications Fund Grant, and the Carl H. Pforzheimer Collection of Shelley and His Circle, the New York Library, Astor, Lenox and Tilden Foundations, for permission to reproduce the poem "Written in an Alcove at Allerton."

Introduction

Lucy Aikin was the most eminent feminist historian and poet of her day. As the product of two of the leading dissenting Unitarian families in England, she fully embraced the principles of the Enlightenment: a profound conviction in the capacity of right reason to discover the truths of both human nature and the physical world, the belief that souls have no sex and that moral virtues and intellectual capacities are available to both sexes in equal measure, and that history is a process that moves by uneven developments towards higher levels of human civilization. Her *Epistles on Women* (1810) is the first text in English to rewrite the entire history of western culture, from the Creation of Genesis through the eighteenth century, from a feminist perspective, explicitly defining the practices and consequences of a patriarchal social system.

Aikin was born in the very heart of the dissenting community, at Warrington Academy,[1] Cheshire, on 6 November 1781. On her maternal side as well as her paternal side, she traced her descent through her mother Martha Jennings and her paternal grandmother Jane Jennings to her great-grandfather John Jennings (1687/8–1723), an Independent minister and tutor who trained for the nonconformist ministry at Timothy Jolly's academy at Attercliffe in Yorkshire and then founded his own academy to prepare students for the dissenting churches, promoting above all a belief in "the greatest freedom of inquiry" (according to his most devoted pupil Philip Doddridge) combined with a commitment to commercial progress and scientific innovation.[2] On her paternal side, she came from a long line of Aikins who had been at the center of the Unitarian movement in Britain. Her grandfather John Aikin (1713–80) had run a dissenting school at Kibworth Harcourt, Leicestershire, based on the principles of Philip Dod-

---

1 For an excellent study of the Warrington Academy and the emergence of the dissenting public sphere in the late eighteenth century, see Daniel E. White, *Early Romanticism and Religious Dissent* (Cambridge: Cambridge UP, 2006).

2 David L. Wykes, "John Jennings (1687/8–1723)," *Oxford Dictionary of National Biography*, www.oxforddnb.com. See also David L. Wykes, "The Contribution of the Dissenting Academy to the Emergence of Rational Dissent," in Knud Haakonssen, ed., *Enlightenment and Religion: Rational Dissent in Eighteenth-Century Britain* (Cambridge: Cambridge UP, 1996), 99–139.

dridge, and then in 1758 accepted the position of classics tutor at the new dissenting academy in Warrington where he taught not only Greek and Latin, but also French, grammar, logic, criticism, and history. In 1761 he became the head of the Warrington Academy, which Joseph Priestley later recalled as a time of "the most perfect harmony. We drank tea together every Saturday, and our conversation was equally instructive and pleasing.... We were all likewise Arians; and the only subject of much consequence on which we differed respected the doctrine of Atonement, concerning which Dr. Aikin held some obscure notions."[1] A modest man, John Aikin was known for his impartiality in presenting evidence, his lack of censorship of new ideas, and the wide breadth of his learning. As Lucy Aikin later described the Warrington dissenting community to William Ellery Channing,

> Long before my time ... my kindred—the Jennings' [sic], the Belshams, my excellent grandfather Aikin, and his friend and tutor Doddridge—had begun to break forth out of the chains and darkness of Calvinism, and their manners softened with their system. My youth was spent among the disciples or fellow-labourers of Price and Priestley, the descendants of Dr. John Taylor, the Arian, or in the society of that most amiable of men, Dr. [William] Enfield. Amongst these there was no rigorism. Dancing, cards, the theatre, were all held lawful in moderation: in *manners*, the Free Dissenters, as they were called, came much nearer the Church than to their own stricter brethren, yet in *doctrine* no sect departed so far from the Establishment.[2]

Aikin's son, also John Aikin, born at Kibworth in 1747, attended Warrington Academy where he developed a lifelong love

---

1 H.A. Bright, "A Historical Sketch of Warrington Academy," *Christian Reformer, or, Unitarian Magazine and Review*, new ser., 17 (1861): 733. On the history of Warrington Academy, also see Herbert McLachlan, *Warrington Academy: Its History and Influence* (Manchester: The Chetham Society, 1943). Arians were followers of the theological teaching of Arius (c. 250–336 CE), who rejected the doctrine of the Trinity (God as three separate but equal entities, the Father, the Son and the Holy Spirit) and instead believed that Christ was created by—and is therefore distinct from and inferior to—God the Father. As Unitarians, the Aikins believed in the unity of God, and denied Christ's divinity. The "doctrine of atonement" relates to the belief that Christ willingly offered himself up as a sacrifice to be punished for the sins of humankind.

2 Anna Letitia Le Breton, ed., *Correspondence of William Ellery Channing, D.D., and Lucy Aikin, from 1826 to 1842* (Boston, 1874), 28–29.

of literature. He then trained for a career in medicine at Edinburgh University and the University of Leiden, but he combined his medical studies with a continuing commitment to the study of the classics and English literature, translating Tacitus' *Life of Agricola* and *Germania*, writing a life of Sir Thomas Browne, and publishing essays on the impact of natural history on poetry and the first volume of his *Medical Biography* (1780). He married Martha Jennings in 1772 and had three sons (the scientist Arthur Aikin, the surgeon Charles Rochemont Aikin, and the architect Edmund Aikin) and one daughter while they lived in Warrington, moving his family and medical practice to Great Yarmouth in 1784 when Lucy was three. His outspoken defense of the rights of the poor and of the French Revolution and his public opposition to the Corporation and Test Acts (which prevented Dissenters from voting for members of Parliament) and to the slave trade eventually forced him to give up his practice in the more conservative community of Yarmouth in 1792.[1] He then moved into the more congenial Dissenting community in Hackney, London. Here he was warmly welcomed for both his medical and literary skills, continuing to publish essays on literature, biography, and topography. Lucy Aikin thus grew up in a household frequented by such notable thinkers and writers as Gilbert Wakefield the religious controversialist, Erasmus Darwin the natural philosopher, Thomas Pennant the naturalist, James Montgomery the anti-slavery poet, and John Howard the philanthropist and prison-reformer. Even the poet Robert Southey came on occasion.[2] Dr. John Aikin became increasingly well known for his literary efforts, as the author of *Evenings at Home* written with his sister Anna Letitia Barbauld,[3] as well as a number of other well-received works for children,[4] for his numerous biographies, for his critical essays on classical authors and British poets, and for his extensive editorial efforts for such important liberal periodi-

---

1 Lucy Aikin, *Memoir of John Aikin, M.D. with a Selection of his Miscellaneous Pieces, Biographical, Moral, and Critical*, 2 vols. (London: Baldwin, Craddock, and Joy, 1823), I: 122–45.
2 Marilyn L. Brooks, "John Aikin (1747–1822)," *Oxford Dictionary of National Biography*, www.oxforddnb.com.
3 The Latin diphthong found in Barbauld's middle name ("æ" in "Lætitia") is now conventionally replaced with the single letter "e," as it is throughout this work.
4 Including *Miscellaneous Pieces in Prose* (1773), *Letters from a Father to his Son on Various Topics relative to Literature and the Conduct of Life* (1793), and *Letters to a Young Lady on a Course of English Poetry* (1804).

cals as the *Monthly Magazine*, the *Monthly Review*, the *Annual Review*, *The Athenaeum*, and Dodsley's *Annual Register*.

Lucy Aikin was educated at home by her parents. Although her grandmother had failed to teach her to read at the age of three and thereafter called her the "little Dunce," this did not stop Lucy Aikin from talking non-stop. As a frequent visitor later reminded her, "my voice was always heard in [our house at Warrington] and ... my papa never checked me, because he was so fond of me."[1] At six she knew the details of the Trojan War. When sent to a local day school, she so far surpassed the other students that her mother decided to home-school her, with the aid of a governess and her doting father, who referred to her as "so wise, so young."[2] She also received instruction from her aunt Anna Letitia Barbauld, who had become the leading literary critic of her day. Barbauld was the author of numerous poems for children and for adults, trenchant political essays, a biography of Samuel Richardson together with an edition of his correspondence, and prefaces to editions of Mark Akenside, William Collins, and Addison and Steele.[3] In 1810 Barbauld initiated the first canon-forming collection of British fiction, the 50 volumes of *The British Novelist* (1810), for which she wrote individual prefaces, documenting a lifetime of familiarity with these novels and making the case for the superiority of fiction as a genre over poetry and drama. Lucy's studies, beginning with her aunt's *Lessons for Children* (four vols., 1778–79), focused primarily on history, biography, and literature. She was taught Latin, French and Italian, and encouraged to read both the classics and fiction. Her early move from Warrington to Yarmouth led to an enduring love of the sea and a passion for nature. When ill health forced her father to retire altogether from his medical practice in 1797, he moved his family from Hackney to Stoke Newington, Middlesex (now part of London), where they lived until 1822.

---

1   Philip Hemery Le Breton, ed., *Memoirs, Miscellanies and Letters of the Late Lucy Aikin: Including those Addressed to the Rev. Dr. Channing from 1826-1842*, (London: Longman, Green, Longman, Roberts & Green, 1864), xi.

2   *Memoirs of Lucy Aikin*, xi.

3   Mark Akenside (1721–70), physician and poet, best known for his long poem *The Pleasures of the Imagination*, which influenced several Romantic poets; William Collins (1721–59), another mid-century poet well-known for his Odes; Joseph Addison (1672–1719) and Richard Steele (1672–1729), best known for their editorship of the popular and influential periodical *The Spectator*.

It was primarily under her father's guidance that Lucy Aikin's mental acuity and extensive learning developed. When he was composing his *General Biography*, a series of essays on the most famous men of western civilization, he habitually discussed his research and opinions with his family. As Lucy Aikin later recalled,

> I can speak with all the certainty of personal experience to the pleasures and benefits derived to his family from his social and communicative habits of study. From witnessing so closely the progress of his various works, they insensibly acquired a lively interest in the subjects of them; these again became favorite topics of domestic discussion, and often led on to references to books and facts which from these associations were impressed indelibly on the memory. Nor could the reasoning powers fail of being strengthened and matured by these inquiries, carried on under the indulgent guidance of one who did not desire even from his own children a blind and prejudiced adherence to his opinions; but, on the contrary, never ceased to impress upon them as the most important of all maxims, that their reason was given to them for the discovery of truth, and that there were no subjects on which it was not allowable, and even laudable, to exercise it independently, within the limits of modesty and candour. For myself,—if I may be pardoned the egotism,—I must ever regard it as the most important of many intellectual privileges for which I am grateful, to have grown up to maturity under the eye of my father during the time that he was engaged upon so many "fair designs," and especially on this; by virtue of which the illustrious of all ages were made to pass as it were before us in a long and leisurely procession, while we questioned each of his title to a pedestal in the Temple of Immortality. This was indeed philosophy teaching by example; and to the lessons then received, to the principles thus imbibed, I am bound, not in duty and affection alone, but in the strictest justice, to ascribe whatever favour any biographical attempts of my own may since have found with an indulgent public.[1]

Lucy Aikin also reports how her father's practice was "never to commit a single page to the printer without causing it to be previously read aloud by one of his family in his own presence," and "not only permitted, but invited and encouraged, the freest stric-

---

1 Aikin, *Memoir of John Aikin, M.D.*, I: 201-02.

tures even from the youngest and most unskilful of those whom he was pleased to call his *household critics.*" To this habit Lucy Aikin attributed her father's lucid style, so perfect that "no one ever found it necessary to read a sentence of his a second time to find the meaning"; a clarity she endeavored to bring to all of her own writing.

During this period, Lucy Aikin became a productive and widely published author. Encouraged to write at an early age, she published her first periodical contributions in *The Athenaeum* and the *Annual Register* when she was barely 17. Her earliest works were aimed primarily at a juvenile audience (selections from which can be found in Section VII). *Poetry for Children: Consisting of Short Pieces, to be Committed to Memory. Selected by Lucy Aikin,* and including some original compositions, appeared in 1801, and was reprinted repeatedly until the 1840s. *Juvenile Correspondence, or, Letters, Designed as Examples of the Epistolary Style, for Children of Both Sexes* was published by Joseph Johnson in 1811. Later in her life, she is believed to have written under the pseudonym of Mary Godolphin, returning to her work as a children's book writer, producing versions of famous books (Aesop's *Fables,* John Aikin's *Evenings at Home,* Bunyan's *Pilgrim's Progress,* Defoe's *Robinson Crusoe,* Thomas Day's *Sandford and Merton,* and Johann David Wyss's *Swiss Family Robinson*) all in one syllable, for beginning readers. In her early years at Stoke Newington she also published two major translations, of L.F. Jauffret's *The Travels of Rolando: Containing, in a supposed tour round the world, authentic descriptions of the geography, natural history, manners and antiquities of various countries translated from the French* (published by Richard Phillips in 1804) and of Jean Gaspar Hess's *Life of Ulrich Zwingli* (published by Joseph Johnson in 1812). She also is known to have contributed reviews and verse to different periodicals (see Section V, Literary Criticism and Biography).

By far Lucy Aikin's most important and highly respected work during her lifetime was as a historian. Her first original work for adults was her poetic analysis of the roles of women in western civilization, her *Epistles on Women, Exemplifying their Character and Condition in Various Ages and Nations,* which appeared in 1810 and was widely, and for the most part favorably, reviewed. This was followed by her only novel, *Lorimer* (1814), the story of a young man seduced by a bigamous prostitute into marriage, only to fall in love with Bertha Fermor, the daughter of his father's best friend and executor. When Fermor is imprisoned in Italy, Lorimer marries Bertha in order to protect her, but suffers numerous pangs of conscience over his earlier marital commitment. Finally he discovers that his first marriage was invalid and all is well; the novel is notable primarily for its interesting reversal of gender roles, in which a man rather than a woman suffers dreadfully for having been seduced into marriage by a promiscuous fortune-hunter. (An excerpt from the novel is in Section III, Fiction.)

Aikin's contemporary intellectual reputation came to rest, however, on the lengthy histories that she began to publish in 1818: *Memoirs of the Court of Queen Elizabeth* (1818), *Memoirs of the Court of James the First* (1822), and *Memoirs of the Court of Charles the First* (1833) (see Section II, Histories). In these memoirs, Aikin developed a new historical genre, what Rosemary Ann Mitchell calls "court history," the study of the manners and morals of the royal family and their aristocratic companions.[1] Aikin focused on the family dynamics, the psychological conflicts, and the kinship networks that determined court policy, rather than on military, religious, or parliamentary events and policies, because, as she put it, "it is from the intimate views of private life in various ages and countries that the *moral* of political history is alone to be derived."[2] In writing such "domestic history,"[3] Aikin gave greater prominence than earlier historians to the women at court and their influential roles in the creation of the political, social, literary, and artistic culture of the day. In doing so, as Kathryn Ready has shown, she endorsed the stadialist theory of the Scottish Enlightenment historians,[4] the argument that the advance of civilization occurred in four stages and was promoted by the improvement of manners and morals, an improvement that John Millar[5] at least attributed primarily to

---

1 Rosemary Ann Mitchell, "'The busy daughters of Clio': Women Writers of History from 1820 to 1880," *Women's History Review* 7 (1990): 121.
2 Le Breton, ed., *Correspondence of Channing and Aikin*, 79.
3 Speaking of her *Memoirs of the Court of Queen Elizabeth*, her nephew-in-law asserted that her plan for this work "comprehended the private life of the queen, and the domestic history of the period." Le Breton, ed., *Memoirs, Miscellanies and Letters of the late Lucy Aikin*, xix.
4 Kathryn Ready, "The Enlightenment Feminist Project of Lucy Aikin's *Epistles on Women* (1810)," *History of European Ideas* 31 (2005): 435–50.
5 In his *The Origin of the Distinction of Ranks* (1771) the Scottish jurist and historian John Millar (1735–1801) offered a history of women's roles in various societies and claimed that as soon as women came to be the companions of men and not their slaves or idols, they rapidly improved morally and intellectually, and soon were instrumental in promoting the prosperity and happiness of all society (84–85).

women. Widely and enthusiastically reviewed, Aikin's memoirs of Elizabeth I, James I and Charles I created a new form of social history, one that admittedly neglected the lives of the working and middle classes, but nevertheless opened a path explored by other women historians, from Aikin's peers, Mary Berry and Elizabeth Benger (whom Aikin later celebrated in a biographical memoir) to the mid-Victorian writers Agnes and Elizabeth Strickland. By focusing as much on the emotions and private motivations of the ruling classes as on their public diplomacy and military strategy, Lucy Aikin subtly called into question the sexist biases of earlier historical writing. As Greg Kucich has rightly claimed, Aikin's historiography is feminist, not simply because it reclaims the lives of women from obscurity, but also because it "entails the interrogation and dismantling of fundamental structures of historical representations in patriarchal versions of the past."[1]

At the same time, Aikin's histories demonstrate her keen support for Parliament (and the rights of the people) in her study of monarchical governance. Although she is always even-handed towards her subjects, and sympathetic to the pressures and limitations they faced, she is clearly hostile towards the abuse of power and the denial of due process that was so prevalent in the reigns of the late Tudors (Henry VIII, Mary I, Elizabeth I) and the early Stuarts (James I, Charles I). In an attempt to generate sympathy for the fate of the political and religious victims under these regimes, the memoirs are punctuated with indignant accounts of wrongful imprisonment, torture, and death. Her three histories, and in particular the latter two, read as a narrative of struggle between Parliament and the Monarchy for what is known as a mixed monarchy, wherein the monarch's powers are limited by the will of the people, as she rejects without hesitation the doctrine of divine right espoused by James I and his son and holds in contempt their efforts to rule without the people's consent. Her histories are also highly attuned to the spiritual controversies so central to the period, where again she condemns the persecution of religious minorities that were widespread. Aikin's memoirs represent a unique contribution to historiography, in the combined attention to the large transformations of public history—above all the ongoing struggle to reform both church and state—and to the small "concrete, personal details" of individual lives—as she depicts the domestic history of the court as

---

1   Greg Kucich, "Romanticism and Feminist Historiography," *Wordsworth Circle* 24.3 (1993): 134.

well as the lives of those affected by the repressive regimes under consideration. Her commitment to toleration and religious freedom, to representative government and the rule of law, inevitably reflect her own political values as well as the particular struggles of dissenters and radicals awaiting the repeal of the Test and Corporation Acts and the reform of Parliament (finally achieved, respectively, in 1828 and 1832).

In 1823, after her father's death in 1822 after a long illness during which Lucy devotedly cared for him, Lucy Aikin and her mother, "finding the dullness and seclusion of Stoke Newington oppressive,"[1] moved to their own small house, Milford House, on Church Row, Hampstead, next door to Joanna Baillie, and her sister and mother. Baillie, a successful playwright and poet, the author of *A Series of Plays on the Passions*, soon became one of Aikin's dearest friends. As Aikin recorded in her "Recollections of Joanna Baillie" (1864), after praising Baillie for her humility, tolerance, moral courage and "perfect self-possession," Joanna Baillie "was the only person I have ever known, towards whom fifty years of close acquaintance, while they continually deepened my affection, wore away nothing of my reverence."[2] At Milford House, Aikin regularly entertained leading members of Whig society who shared her progressive views. Thomas Malthus (political economist), Henry Hallam and William Smyth (both historians, the latter the Regius Professor of Modern History at Cambridge University), Thomas Whishaw (a Commissioner of Audit), and Sydney Smith (the liberal politician and founder of the *Edinburgh Review*) were regular visitors and correspondents.[3] The leading poets and writers of the day were among her guests: she met Crabbe, Moore, Wordsworth, Samuel Rogers, and Charles Lamb.

She also sought out the acquaintance of the most prominent women writers of her day. On a visit to Edinburgh in 1812, she frequently visited the housebound novelist and essayist, Elizabeth Hamilton, recording that Hamilton's "good sense, her cheerfulness, her knowledge of the world, and her great kindness of heart,

---

1 Anna Le Breton (Mrs. Herbert Martin), ed., *Memories of Seventy Years by One of a Literary Family* (New York: Griffith & Farran, 1884), 103.

2 Lucy Aikin, "Recollections of Joanna Baillie," in *Memoirs of Lucy Aikin*, ed. Le Breton, 10. An excerpt is reproduced in Section V, "Literary Criticism and Biography. [ONLINE]"

3 Anonymous reviewer, "Three Women of Letters," *The North British Review* LXXXIV (June 1865): 167.

make her a delightful companion."[1] She met Maria Edgeworth, one of the period's leading novelists, in 1830, who recalled the encounter:

> Miss Aikin I saw one evening and one morning and got acquainted with her and thought her very entertaining; though she has some primnesses and *suavities* of manner now and again caught or imitated from Mrs. Barbauld and that odious way of softening the voice below natural and contradicting in the mildest of all possible slow obstinate ways when she is vexed in argument. But upon the whole she is more agreeable than Mrs. Barbauld. She is a merry soul and has humour and tells good stories and is not overgrand.[2]

Harriet Martineau frequently came to her for advice. Aikin was especially impressed by the rhetorical skill and intelligence of Martineau's *Illustrations of Political Economy* and by her "extraordinary talent and merit, and a noble independence of mind";[3] she hailed her as a "champion" of women, and "zealously" supported her efforts to educate working-class girls on the dangers of prostitution.[4] Although she disagreed with some of Martineau's views, she firmly endorsed her campaign for the political rights of women, asserting that

> I certainly hold, and it appears to me self-evident, that, on the principle that there should never be taxation without representation, women who possess independent property *ought* to vote; ... the Reform Bill, by affixing the elective franchise only, and in all cases, to the possession of land, or occupancy of house of a certain value, tends to suggest the idea that a single woman possessing such property as unrestrictedly as a man, subject to the same taxes, liable even to some burdensome, though eligible to no honourable or profitable, parish offices, ought in equity to have, and might have without harm, or danger, a suffrage to give. I vote for guardians of the poor of this parish by merely signing a paper; why might I not vote thus for members of Parliament?[5]

---

1 Le Breton, ed., *Memoirs of Lucy Aikin*, xxiii.
2 Maria Edgeworth, *Maria Edgeworth: Letters from England, 1813-1844*, ed. Christina Colvin (Oxford: Clarendon P, 1971), 455.
3 *Correspondence of Channing and Aikin*, ed. Le Breton, 156.
4 *Correspondence of Channing and Aikin*, ed. Le Breton, 300.
5 *Correspondence of Channing and Aikin*, ed. Le Breton, 299–300.

Lucy Aikin was widely known for her intelligence and her relish for the latest literary, religious and political news. She received frequent visits from American Unitarians sent by Dr. Channing. Aikin's liberal and cosmopolitan attitudes even attracted frequent visits from the Hindu reformer Rajah Rammohun Roy during his year in England in 1831; she regarded him as "a true sage, ... with the genuine humility of the character, and with more fervour, more sensibility, a more engaging tenderness of heart, than any *class* of character can justly claim."[1] As her close friend the Reverend John Kendrick commented, Aikin "possessed in a remarkable degree that art of conversation.... Whether in intercourse with a single friend in a small circle, or an assembly of persons of intellectual attainments equal to her own, there was the same flow of anecdote, quotation and allusion, furnished by a most retentive memory, and enlivened by wit and humour."[2]

And she continued to write: her memoir of her father was published in 1823, her memoir and editions of the works of her aunt Anna Letitia Barbauld in 1825 and 1826 (which were instrumental in securing her aunt's posthumous reputation) (see Section IV, Family Memoirs), and her biography of the poet and historian Elizabeth Benger in 1827, her biography and edition of the letters of Joseph Addison in 1843 (whom she celebrated as "a great reformer of manners"[3]). She also carried on a voluminous correspondence with friends, relatives and Unitarian dignitaries. Her 20-year correspondence (which fills a volume of over 400 pages) with the leading Unitarian minister in America, William Ellery Channing, published in 1864, kept him apprised of the latest intellectual, literary, and religious movements in Britain. At the same time, Channing helped Aikin clarify her own positions on matters of church doctrine. (Aikin's letters, when published with Channing's in 1874, were highly praised by leading American novelist and critic Henry James, who admired Aikin's style and her "vigorous intellectual temperament" and wondered why her work had "not attracted independent notice": see Appendix B7). As this correspondence makes clear, Aikin remained to the end of her life a staunch believer in the existence of a benevolent, just and all-wise God, in the role of a mortal Christ as the model of human goodness, in the power of independent, free enquiry and rational

---

1 *Correspondence of Channing and Aikin*, ed. Le Breton, 87; her eulogy of Rammohun Roy appears on pp. 196–97.
2 Le Breton, *Memoirs of Lucy Aikin*, xxvii.
3 *Correspondence of Channing and Aikin*, ed. Le Breton, 413.

thought, and in a personal moral integrity committed to a life of active virtue. She was an ardent supporter of the Reform movement in Victorian England. She continued to promote an improved educational system for all classes and both sexes, complete religious freedom (as opposed to an established national religion, "that great engine of civil and intellectual tyranny,"[1]), the reduction of class hierarchy and the elimination of poverty (or what she called *pauperism*[2]), and greater civil rights for women. Selections from Aikin's letters are to be found in Appendix A.

In 1844, at the age of 62, Lucy Aikin joined the household of her niece Anna Letitia Aikin, the daughter of Charles Rochemont Aikin and his wife Anne Wakefield (the daughter of the eminent biblical scholar and Unitarian controversialist Gilbert Wakefield), and her husband, the barrister Philip Hemery Le Breton. She lived with them in Wimbledon for six years, and then returned with them to Hampstead in 1852. Their daughter, Anna Le Breton (Mrs. Herbert Martin) later recalled that her Aunt Lucy was always the life of their domestic party: she

by no means hid her light under a bushel. Her lively, sparkling, versatile talents were essentially social ones; she had mind

---

1 *Correspondence of Channing and Aikin*, ed. Le Breton, 4.
2 On the treatment of the poor, Aikin was opposed to the extremely successful campaign of Hannah More, who had urged women of the middle and upper classes to consider the care of the poor as their profession. As Aikin sardonically observed, "Ever since Hannah More published her *Coelebs* [*in Search of a Wife* (1809), a very successful novel that read like a conduct manual for women] it has been held by a large party the indispensable duty of ladies, girls even, to spend much of their time in visiting the dwellings of the poor, inquiring into and ministering to their spiritual and temporal wants. Apparently, great good would result from these charitable offices to all parties; but you well know our national propensity to run everything to a fashion—a rage—and the result has been a great and pernicious excess. A positive *demand* for misery was created by the incessant eagerness manifested to relieve it. In many places, the poor, those amongst them especially who have known how to put on a little saintliness, have been actually pampered and rendered like the indoor menials of the wealthy: lazy, luxurious, discontented, lying, and worthless. Men have been encouraged in squandering their wages in drink and dissipation, by the assurance that the good ladies would not suffer their families to want; women have slackened their efforts to provide decent clothing for their children—improvidence has become characteristic of both." *Correspondence of Channing and Aikin*, 90–91.

enough to be quite happy through long solitary hours, with no other company but her beloved books, reading Latin with the zest with which a modern girl devours a novel, but in society she shone and loved to take the lead. I have never met any one in the least like her, the race of conversationalists of her stamp seeming extinct.[1]

Lucy Aikin also took in hand the education of her great nieces, introducing them to Latin grammar and the works of Addison, Steele, Pope, Dryden, Milton and Spenser.

Lucy Aikin died of influenza on 29 January 1864, aged 82 years, having "to the last retained her memory and her faculties."[2] Throughout her life, Lucy Aikin was devoted to her family, her social circle, and her writing. Like many of her female counterparts, including her aunt, Charlotte Smith, and Joanna Baillie, and unlike many of the male Romantic poets, Lucy Aikin enjoyed a long life and diverse literary career. She was at once a public intellectual and professional author, writing for commercial publication and public instruction, with a keen understanding of the demands of readers and the workings of the literary marketplace. While it is difficult to ascertain her precise sources of income, we know that she lived a comfortable existence during her many years in Hampstead, and it is likely that her historical writing published by the leading firm of Longman, her memoirs and editions of the works of her aunt and father, and her children's writing, all contributed to this prosperity. It is likely as well that she received an inheritance from her father, and may also have received assistance from her three successful brothers, with whom she remained intimate: Edmund (1780–1820), an architect and architectural historian; Arthur (1773–1854), a geologist and mineralogist; and Charles (1775–1847), a surgeon known for his long involvement with smallpox vaccination.

She is buried next to her beloved Joanna Baillie in the churchyard at Hampstead. Shortly after her death, Aikin's niece Anna Letitia Le Breton co-edited with her husband the *Memoirs, Miscellanies and Letters of Lucy Aikin* (1864). Anna Le Breton then edited Aikin's correspondence with William Ellery Channing and wrote a memoir of her great-aunt Anna Letitia Barbauld. Her daughter, also Anna Le Breton (Mrs. Herbert Martin), finally summed up her own and her mother's memories of this distin-

---

1   Anna Le Breton (Mrs. Herbert Martin), ed. *Memories of Seventy Years*, pp. v-vi.
2   Le Breton, ed. *Memoirs of Lucy Aikin*, xxvii.

guished dissenting family, "whose names are still held in honour," in her *Memories of Seventy Years by One of a Literary Family* (1883), celebrating them for their "almost Spartan simplicity and temperance, an austere morality, and, with all the Puritanic reserve of their habits, a warm affection and great benevolence towards their fellow-creatures."[1]

Epistles on Women, Exemplifying Their Character and Condition in Various Ages and Nations (1810)

In her first major literary production, her long poem *Epistles on Women*, Aikin took up the gauntlet thrown down by Mary Wollstonecraft, to bring about a "revolution in female manners."[2] Her poem rewrites all of western history from an explicitly feminist position. As she later told William Ellery Channing,

> If you will turn to one of Mrs. Barbauld's *Characters*, beginning, "Such were the dames of old heroic days ..." you will fully understand what kind of spirit I long to inspire into my sex. Almost all my life this desire has been one of my strongest feelings. When a little girl I used to battle with boys about the Rights of Woman. Many years ago, I published *Epistles on Women*, all to the same effect; and ... it contains many sentiments which I still cherish, and would give much to be able to disseminate.[3]

In taking up the cudgels for the *Rights of Woman*, Aikin occupied a different position from Wollstonecraft in the feminist debates of the early nineteenth century. Whereas Wollstonecraft argued that the sexes were in all significant respects equal and should be educated to do the same work in society, a position we now call liberal feminism or equality feminism, Aikin insisted that the female sex is in one all-significant way superior to the male sex. Her Introduction to *Epistles* begins with a brilliant stroke of feminist irony: "Let me in the first place disclaim entirely the absurd idea that the two sexes ever can be, or ever ought to be,

---

1 Le Breton, *Memories of Seventy Years*, iii, v.
2 Mary Wollstonecraft, *Vindication of the Rights of Woman and The Wrongs of Woman, or Maria*, in Anne K. Mellor and Noelle Chao, eds. (New York: Longman, 2006), 65, 230.
3 Le Breton, ed. *Correspondence of Channing and Aikin*, 128.

placed in all respects on a footing of equality" (p. 51[1]). She readily acknowledges that the "bodily constitution of the species" accords to the male sex superior physical strength and thereby "authority," while the female's physical inferiority has "allotted" her, in her domestic and private occupations, "a certain degree of subordination." Aikin agrees that it would be foolish of women to try to gain physical superiority over men. She then turns the tables, arguing that "the impartial voice of History" would document that women are capable of all the "worthy" efforts of men: "let the daily observation of mankind bear witness, that no talent, no virtue, is masculine alone; no fault or folly exclusively feminine.... That there is not an endowment, or propensity, or mental quality of any kind, which may not be derived from her father to the daughter, to the son from his mother" (p. 52). Having established that women are capable of possessing all the talents and virtues of men, Aikin saves for the poem itself her final feminist salvo, namely that the female maternal instinct transforms women into beings even nobler and more virtuous than men. As we shall see, Aikin finally aligns her poem with what we might now call radical feminism, a belief in the innate *moral* superiority of the female sex, the position embraced in her lifetime by Hannah More and in later days by Virginia Woolf.

Turning back to the behavior of the males of the species, Aikin suggests that their greater upper-body strength enables them to perform certain tasks (physical labor, warfare) that women cannot. But she immediately calls the value of this physical superiority into question by suggesting that, historically, men have used their physical strength primarily to oppress women, urging them, as does John Gregory in his *A Father's Legacy to his Daughters* (1774), "to conceal their wit, their learning, and even their good sense" and to submit to the ideological construction of the female gender as one of "*natural malignity*" (p. 52). The grand purpose of her poem, the "moral of my song," she asserts, is to show that in all ages and nations, whenever man degrades woman, he simultaneously degrades himself. She thus appeals to the self-interest (or "policy") of her male readers: only by improving the education and condition of women can they advance their own greater "dignity and happiness" (p. 54).

Her plan for this poem, she explains in her Introduction, is to survey all the periods of western history, from the most savage to the most civilized. She is adhering to the stadialist conception of

---

1   All page references are to this Broadview edition of the text.

history promoted by Scottish Enlightenment historians and derived from the earlier work of Vico and Montesquieu.[1] As developed in the 1760s and 1770s by Adam Smith, Adam Ferguson, John Millar, and Henry Home, Lord Kames, stadialist theory argued that societies develop through four clearly demarcated states or stages from the most primitive to the fully civilized, from (1) hunter gatherer to (2) herder of animals to (3) agrarian communities requiring some system of laws to (4) highly complex urban or commercial societies with sophisticated legal systems.[2] These can be uneven developments, as Lord Kames asserted in his *Sketches of the History of Man* (1778): "Some nations, stimulated by their own nature, or by their climate, have made a rapid progress; some have proceeded more slowly; and some continue savages."[3] These Scottish historians often compared societies on the basis of what stage of civilization they had reached; alternatively, they engaged in what Dugald Stewart first called "conjectural history,"[4] speculating about their own origins by observing "primitive" societies such as those of the African Hottentots, the American Indians, or the New Hollanders (Australian aborigines), to take Aikin's examples. This teleological theory of the inevitable progress of civilization was eagerly embraced by the Dissenting Whig culture in which Aikin was reared. All-important to the argument of her *Epistles* is the work of John Millar, who alone among these stadialist historians attributed the advancement of civilization to the improvement of *manners*, an improvement he attributed directly to the superior refinement of *women* in his *Observations concerning the Distinction of Ranks in Society* (1773).[5]

By titling her 1200-line poem *Epistles*, Aikin first positioned this work within a culturally feminine genre. Epistles, or letters,

---

1 On Aikin's knowledge of and commitment to stadialist theory, see Ready, "The Enlightenment Feminist Project of Lucy Aikin's *Epistles*," 435–50.

2 On stadialist theory and the Scottish Enlightenment, see Ronald L. Meek, *Social Science and the Ignoble Savage* (Cambridge: Cambridge UP, 1976).

3 Henry Home, Lord Kames, *Sketches of the History of Man* (2nd edition; Edinburgh: Creech, London, Strahan and Cadell, 1778), I: 84.

4 Dugald Stewart, "Account of the Life and Writings of Adam Smith, L.L.D.," in W.P.D. Wightman and J.C. Bryce, eds., *Adam Smith: Essays on Philosophical Subjects* (Oxford: Clarendon P, 1980), 293.

5 John Millar, *Observations concerning the Distinction of Ranks in Society* (2nd edition; London: John Murray, 1773), see especially Chapter 5.

had long been the work of literate women who were primarily responsible for keeping up family and kinship ties through epistolary correspondence. And many have argued that this epistolary practice in turn gave rise to the novel, which in the eighteenth century often took the form of epistolary exchange between self-revealing characters. An epistle or letter implies a recipient: such a literary performance is thus inherently dialogic, leading to what Bakhtin has called the novel's "heteroglossia," referring to the multiple voices and viewpoints, often in direct conflict, that are found within most works of fiction. An epistle also implies that the writer conceptualizes herself as existing in relation to another person, the recipient. The epistle thus implies the existence of a *relational subjectivity*, as opposed to an autonomous subjectivity; such a relational identity has been theorized by Nancy Chodorow, Carol Gilligan, and many others, as characteristic of the historical and cultural production of the feminine gender.

More explicitly, Aikin's title identifies her poem as a direct challenge to Alexander Pope's misogynist "Epistle II: To a Lady—Of the Characters of Women" (1735) (see Appendix C4). Pope had here famously endorsed the claim that "Most Women have no Characters at all" (l. 2), asserting that women were composed of "Matter too soft a lasting mark to bear, / And best distinguished by black, brown, or fair" (ll. 3–4). Attacking females as incapable of consistency and constancy ("Ladies, like variegated Tulips, show / 'Tis to their Changes half their charms we owe" [ll. 41–42]), as lacking chastity ("A teeming Mistress, but a barren Bride" [l. 72]) and intelligence ("Her Head's untouched, that noble Seat of Thought" [l. 74]), Pope insists that women are motivated by only two desires, "The Love of Pleasure, and the Love of Sway" (l. 210). The very concept of an ideal woman is, Pope concludes, impossible: "Woman's at best a Contradiction still. / Heav'n, when it strives to polish all it can / Its last best work, but forms a softer Man" (ll. 270–72).[1] Not only does Aikin's poem contest Pope's construction of the "character" of women, it also challenges his *Essay on Man in Four Epistles* (1733–34). Aikin's *Epistles* are written in the heroic couplets employed by Pope; her poem is composed of four epistles; both poems are roughly 1200 lines long. Aikin in effect is writing an *Essay on Woman*, one that directly attacks Pope's view that "WHATEVER IS, IS RIGHT" (IV: 394).

---

1 Alexander Pope, *Selected Poetry and Prose*, ed. William K. Wimsatt, Jr. (New York: Rinehart, 1951), 180–89.

Aikin is also challenging the implicit misogyny, not only of the classics (she singles out Juvenal's vicious attack on all women as unchaste "monsters" in his *Satire VI*), but more immediately of orthodox Christianity. Her *Epistles* are intended to remind us of St. Paul's *Epistles to the Corinthians*, in which the Apostle, railing against the lust inspired by women, had advocated celibacy but agreed that if the unmarried and widows "cannot exercise self-control, let them marry. For it is better to marry than to burn *with passion*" (I Corinthians 7:9). She takes explicit aim at Milton in her Introduction, who in his *Paradise Lost* had insisted that Eve must obey Adam: "He for God only, she for God in him" (IV: 299) (see Appendix C3). Her intention, in her *Epistles on Women*, is nothing less than to overthrow the legacy of both the Greek and Roman classics and the Christian fathers insofar as they constructed a patriarchal gender system in which women were systematically devalued, degraded, and abused.

Epistle I

Prefacing each of her *Epistles* with an "Argument," as Milton had done before her in *Paradise Lost*, Aikin begins her poem proper by asserting the "primary equality" of the two sexes in heaven. She then invokes her Muse, not the "divine" Urania of *Paradise Lost*, but rather a living woman and dear friend, her sister-in-law Anne Wakefield, the highly educated daughter of the Unitarian minister and propagandist Gilbert Wakefield and loving wife of Charles Rochemont Aikin. Lucy Aikin later described Anne Wakefield as possessing "the high-souled integrity and noble ingenuousness which marked her for the child and pupil of such a parent, in union with 'all that cultured taste approves, / Or fond affection dearly loves.'"[1] By invoking a living female muse, Aikin implied that her poem was inspired by an ongoing conversation, a dialogue, rather than by a "heavenly voice." As she then insists, hers is a "Historic Muse" (I: 71): her poem will tell the truth about the character and condition of women both now and in the past.

---

1 Aikin, *Memoir of John Aikin*, I: 253. Aikin later eulogized Anne Wakefield's father in her "To the Memory of the Late Rev. Gilbert Wakefield" as "a high undaunted soul, / That spurned at palsied Caution's chill controul, / A mind by Learning stored, by Genius fired, / In Freedom's cause with generous zeal inspired" (ll. 5–8); see her *Miscellaneous Poems* in the online supplement to this volume.

By invoking a muse, Aikin also signals that her poem lies within the tradition of the epic. She deliberately echoes Virgil's *Aeneid*—"Arma virumque cano" ("Of arms and the man I sing")—in her third line, "I sing the Fate of Woman." And that fate, as she immediately explains, has been to be the naive victim of a male practice which constructs her as a delicate, helpless being, denigrates the "beauteous mind" (I: 15), only to then "contemn the trifler he has made" (I: 24) with the "headlong rage" of a Juvenal or Pope (I: 27–28). Aikin then hastens to assure her male readers that she is no Amazon, no "unsex'd female" (in Richard Powhele's notorious phrase from the poem of the same name, see Appendix C), no militant feminist who, in an allusion to her aunt Anna Letitia Barbauld's unpublished poem "The Rights of Woman," "rashly bold" claims "an equal's name" (I: 37–38). No, she insists in a fine piece of feminist sarcasm, she dare not assert such a claim since the "superior force" of men would immediately punish her for doing so; she therefore involuntarily and resentfully submits to that "Right Divine in man and king," those male-created laws that define a king as possessing two bodies (one mortal, one immortal) and a woman as "a plaything and a slave" (I: 41, 40, 58). She subtly echoes Sir John Harington's famous dictum—"Treason doth never prosper, what's the reason? / For if it prosper, none dare call it treason."[1] Or as Aikin puts it, "For who gainsays the despot in his might, / Or when was weakness ever in the right?" (I: 43–44). Her Historic Muse can dare only to describe the consequences of this social construction of gender through the ages, unfolding the store of "old Experience" with hard-earned "Thought" (I: 74).

Aikin begins her account of the condition of women at the very beginning, in the garden of Eden. In a brilliant rewriting of both Genesis and *Paradise Lost*, Aikin provides us with a new version of the creation of Eve. Adam falls asleep, pressing his body against the "lonely earth, ..." (I: 75)—everything happens in those three coy ellipses. Adam has a wet-dream and impregnates Mother Earth—both Adam and earth are thus the "Unconscious parent of a wondrous birth" (I: 76). Eve is born from earth, simultaneously infant and woman—note that Aikin never mentions God in this passage, nor a rib. The angels immediately foretell the doom of Woman: her fragile body and tender mind will inevitably be conquered by "ruder" man's "pride of power," his need "to bruise, to slay, to ravage, to devour"

---

1 Sir John Harrington, *Epigrams* (1618; fac. repr. Menston: Scolar Press, 1970): Bk. I: no.5.

(I: 87–88). But their prophecy goes unheard: Eve cannot yet understand their words. And thus the alternative history that might have been written, the "sublime" account of Eve's ability to "bind willing man" and elevate him from earth to heaven, goes untold (I: 106-15).

Eve then wanders innocently, freely, in nature, gradually learning to speak by imitating the sounds of her mother, Nature. Meanwhile Adam too wanders—but since he cannot speak, since he has no mother, he walks "listless," "joyless," with "fix'd infantile stare," a mere "moping idiot" (I: 118-19, 129, 132). Eventually Eve and Adam meet—and at that moment, as Eve shapes Adam, dilating his stature, informing his countenance, and kindling his eye, Adam gains a heightened consciousness, a "new soul" (I: 132). It is Eve who teaches Adam to speak the language of Nature—"his glances speak. / So roll the clouds from some vast mountain's head" (I: 136). Again, Aikin eliminates God; she tells no tale of Adam naming the animals, of a divine origin of language, of a *logos*. Instead it is the newborn passionate love felt by both Adam and Eve that enables Adam to speak: "the youth, as love and nature teach, / Breathes his full bosom, and breaks forth in *speech*" (I: 150–51). His words, too, like those of Milton's Satan (cf. *Paradise Lost*, IX: 734–35*)*, pierce Eve's "unguarded heart"—Eve trusts Adam, and out of their mutual love, "sweet converse" and "kindred" minds is born a *primary equality*. This is the "mighty Maker's plan" (I: 154)— He, "beneficent and just," is no "partial God"; He (contra Milton's version) does not favor one sex at the expense of the other. Aikin here invokes the Priestly version of Genesis rather than the older Jahwist version (incorporated as Genesis 2:4–3:24), alluding to Genesis 1:27—"So God created man in His own image; in the image of God He created him; male and female He created them."[1] Together, equal, Adam and Eve are completely happy. No serpent appears to beguile them, no tree of the knowledge of good and evil is forbidden to them.

Since Aikin has eliminated both Satan and God's taboo, what in her version of the Creation causes the Fall? "*Equal* they trod till want and guilt arose, / Till savage blood was spilt, and man had foes" (I: 168–69). The natural love of Adam and Eve produces children; among those children are Cain and Abel. What

---

1 According to the view that the Old Testament was a composite work, compiled by many hands over time; Genesis is believed to have derived from two texts, known as the Priestly and the Jahwist.

Aikin calls the male "pride of power," what we might call testosterone, inevitably leads to male competition, greed, and conflict. Cain's "want" or need for preeminence produces Cain's "guilt" or curse; Cain kills Abel. Thus males create the foes they fight, and the heavenly pleasures and peace of Eden are lost forever.

Epistle II

In her second *Epistle*, Aikin begins her rewriting of western history, from the so-called "primitive" societies of pre-recorded history to the most "advanced" societies of eighteenth-century Europe. Her copious footnotes function first to establish her wide learning, from the Greek and Roman classics to modern historical, philosophical, literary, and scientific texts, granting her an intellectual and cultural authority rarely acceded to a woman. Secondly, they give her a textual space from which to contest the correctness of received opinion, mainly based on male-authored texts. For instance, in her lengthy footnote to *Epistle II*, l. 75, she not only quotes William Robertson's *History of America* (1777) and Samuel Hearne's *A Journey from Prince of Wales's Fort, in Hudson Bay, to the Northern Ocean, in the Years 1769, 1770, 1771, and 1772* (1795) to support her account of Native American cultural practices, but also takes the opportunity to denounce Rousseau's concept of the "Noble Savage" in his *Discours sur l'origine de l'inégalité* (1755): "Certainly Rousseau did not consult the interests of the weaker sex in his preference of savage life to civilized."

Her argument in her second *Epistle* directly challenges the classical notion that a "Golden Age" or Arcadia preceded subsequent more "fallen" periods (the Elizabethans called them the Silver, Bronze, and Iron Ages) as well as the Judaeo-Christian concept that civilization reached its peak in the idyllic pastoral society along the Tigris and Euphrates Rivers of Chaldea celebrated in King David's Psalms in the Old Testament. Instead, Aikin asserts, in every earlier or "primitive" society, women have been brutally abused, exploited, and degraded. The Australian aborigines or New Hollanders, Aikin claims, citing David Collins's *An Account of the English Colony in New South Wales* (London, 1798-1802), are "half-humanized" monster-men who "advance With brandisht club" upon their females and "drag the bleeding victim bride away" (II: 46). Ruled solely by "headlong passions" (II: 55), this "Savage Man"—also found among the Native Americans—treats his squaw so cruelly that mothers choose to kill their infant daughters rather than subject them to a life of "intolerable bondage" (II: 75 fn). Even where Nature has provided "lavish plenty" to ease the condition of mankind, as in Tahiti, Aikin observes, men have destroyed the possibility of an earthly paradise by seeking "Lawless Love"—multiple wives, unending sexual orgies, resulting both in infant sacrifice and the "poison" of venereal disease (II: 113-14). Wherever one might seek an Arcadian pastoral life, one is foiled by the reality of female suffering. The African sells his own wives and daughters into colonial slavery (II: 170–76). David's account of a pastoral paradise in Chaldea is undercut by the fact that the Tartar tribes of Asia Minor reduce their women to "homely drudges" (II: 210). The existence of Arcadia, of a lost Golden Age, is nothing but a myth, Aikin concludes, for "the hunter's cave, the shepherd's tent, / And *lawless* man, or cold, or fierce, or rude, / Proves every mode of female servitude" (II: 233–35).

Indeed, Aikin claims, the male of the species—from the human to the animal—is so neglectful of, even opposed to, the care and protection of the young that the species as a whole would have perished had it not been for that "thrice holy Power," "Maternal Love" (II: 119, 123). This is Aikin's most radical feminist claim, namely that the very survival of the species, including the human race, depends on the female biological maternal instinct. Everywhere, she insists, "from zone to zone," from the brooding hen to the she-fox to the female bear to the tigress, the female fiercely fights to protect her young, even against the attacks of their biological father: that "jealous stag" who would "gore his offspring with relentless horn" (II: 150). Everywhere maternal love—created and supported by nature—survives, excepting only among the "cursed" Tahitian groves and the "polisht scenes" of Europe (II: 135–36), where French aristocratic mothers, for instance, have been known to play football with their swaddled infants.[1]

Epistle III

Aikin's third *Epistle* turns to the "dawn of civilization," classical Greece, Troy and Rome. Here she invokes stadialist theory, arguing that the progress of history through the four stages of

---

1 A.R. Colon, with P.A. Colon, *A History of Children: A Socio-Cultural Survey across Millennia* (Connecticut: Greenwood P, 2009), 132; also see Philippe Aries, *Centuries of Childhood* (trans. Robert Baldick, New York: Vintage, 1962).

society is explicitly promoted by what she calls "the dear charities of social life," here fed by "the daughter, mother, wife" (III: 14–15). Civilization is advanced by sympathy ("human tears" or the devotion of the species to the care of its young, sick, and elderly), by intellectual efforts (the creative acts of bards and sages), by freedom, and above all by reason and virtue: "The fierce barbarian checked his headlong course, / And bent to Wisdom's hand his yielded force: / Each loftier Virtue bowed to meet the brave, / And clasped, a freeman, whom she scorned, a slave" (III: 10–13). We might note that Aikin genders her personifications of both Reason and Virtue as female (III: 23, 12), thereby subtly endorsing John Millar's claim that it is primarily women who refine manners and promote both rational and moral behaviors, a claim that has been more recently promoted by Norbert Elias in his magisterial *The Civilizing Process* (1939; trans. 1978). Her bards, sages, and patriots "sublime" or elevate—not the autonomous self, as Wordsworth does in *The Prelude*—but "the expanding heart" (III: 8), the dear charities of social life. Aikin thus suggests that it is only as women gain freedom and equality that civilization truly advances. As Kathryn Ready has argued, she is drawing on the "commercial model of femininity" proposed by David Hume, Lord Kames, and John Bowles, the assumption that only in a commercial society did women and men have the leisure to develop polite manners, a civilizing process promoted by the "softer" and "gentler" behavior of females.[1]

Aikin then retells the history of western culture, beginning with the classical era, as a history in which masculine values of competition, conquest, war, and domination (both of enemies and of women) have prevailed. Throughout her account, cities (gendered female) are destroyed by "Slaughter" (gendered male)—these personifications here function, as John Sitter has suggested in an unpublished paper, as social forces or Althusserian ideological state apparatuses, as embodiments of a larger political and cultural system. Beginning with the fall of Troy, Aikin focuses on the consequences for women and children of male-initiated wars. She makes no mention of the celebrated "heroes" of the Trojan War—no references to Achilles, Hector or Ulysses. Instead, she recounts the fate of Hector's wife Andromache, seized by Neoptolemus as his trophy bride, forced into exile as a prisoner of war and slave, and still "envied and hated for the love she hates" (III: 45). In such

---

1   Ready, "The Enlightenment Feminist Project of Lucy Aikin's *Epistles*," 440–44.

a militaristic era, the only culturally supported definition of female nobility was to become, like the women of ancient Sparta, woman warriors or Amazons, women who gladly sacrificed their sons to battle, and themselves, if taken in battle, to death (III: 69 fn). In Aikin's fiercely sarcastic comment, they thereby "scorned the Woman's for the Patriot's name" (III: 67). Such women receive no praise from Aikin; to her, they are like the dinosaurs of the past, frozen into stone (III: 81).

Fifth-century BCE Athens, so often invoked by the Neoclassical writers and artists of eighteenth-century Europe as the height of human civilization and the seat of democracy, appears to Aikin rather as the time when men preferred the company of a courtesan (the *hetaera* Phryne) to that of a Pallas Athene or chaste learned woman. Even though one of those courtesans, Aspasia, was renowned for her wisdom and philosophical sophistication, she could gain access to learning only by sacrificing her role as a respectable wife and mother. And those Athenian wives, as Aikin emphasizes, were "fettered and debased, / Listlessly duteous, negatively chaste ... They sew and spin, they die and are forgot" (III: 98–101).

Ancient Rome, whose glory, in Aikin's Dissenting Protestant view, has in the present day been far diminished by the superstitious bigotry of its dominant Roman Catholic culture (III: 116–20), nonetheless offers to her eyes positive images of heroic republican femininity. Aikin singles out for praise the Sabine women who fought valiantly to preserve their infants (III: 163), Lucretia who preferred death to dishonor after being raped by Tarquin (III: 172), Volumnia who persuaded her son Coriolanus to die rather than destroy his city (III: 181), Cornelia the model of Roman motherhood (III: 191), Portia who inspired her husband Brutus to stab the tyrant Caesar by first stabbing herself (III: 192), and finally Arria who showed her condemned husband how to die honorably by committing suicide (III: 198). But all these noble Roman women finally committed acts of violence, either against themselves or others, and thus, in Aikin's view, merely followed with "tardier tread" (III: 142) the downward way of their male consorts.

Christianity triumphed in Europe after the decline and fall of Rome. From Aikin's perspective, the early Christian era signaled a marked advance for women. The values espoused by Jesus—love, compassion, an ethic of care, fidelity, duty—were values Aikin conceptualizes throughout her poem as feminine. Moreover, early Christianity embraced the female martyr as equal to the male: "proud man shall own / As proud a mate on Virtue's loftiest throne;

/ On to the death in joy ... for Jesus' sake / Writhed on the wrack, or blackening at the stake" (III: 242–45). Most important, Christianity insisted on a monogamous marriage, raising women to the level of comrades, equals, "partners of glory and coheirs of life" (III: 249). But Aikin's dream that primary equality between the sexes might restore Eden to earth is historically thwarted in later years by the triumph of "Superstition," by the institutionalization of Christianity as the papal church of Roman Catholicism and its Pauline creed of priestly celibacy, a creed that in her eyes condemns its most ardent believers to "the yawning cloister" and "its living grave" (III: 284), to "the convent hymn, the convent prayer, / The languid lip-devotion of despair!" (III: 297–98). Admittedly, the Roman Catholic Church did admit women as well as men to sainthood—but in Aikin's eyes, these female saints are all damaged: St. Theresa gave up rationality for her mystical ecstasies; St. Clara's rigid rules for her religious order only institutionalized her "bloodless heart" and "thirst of sway" (III: 308–10); and St. Catherine of Siena exemplified "ambition" as well as "bigot pride, / Distorted virtue, talent misapplied" (III: 315–16).

Epistle IV

In her final *Epistle*, Aikin surveys the development of European culture from the birth of Christ to the eighteenth century. She first explores the possibility that there might have been societies outside the Christian culture of Europe that accorded to women both equality and respect. But the "Asiatic Man" imprisons his women in harems, in "soul-degraded thralls" (IV: 42), or condemns his widow to *sati* ("The victim widow laves in Ganges' tide," IV: 10). Meanwhile, he, "proud, each manly virtue wreckt, / Truth, science, freedom lost in base neglect," is nothing more than a "pampered slave ... / By senses cloyed of sensual bliss bereft, / And a dull drug his only refuge left" (IV: 55–60). Aikin is here endorsing the dominant Orientalism of her culture, the nineteenth-century European view, as Edward W. Said has famously analyzed it in his *Orientalism* (1978), of the East as the site of decadence, decay, and savage brutality.

Aikin then looks to the past for a historical moment when women were treated with dignity—and finds one, but only one, culture in which women attained a measure of equality, namely that of the first century German Goths described in Tacitus' *Germania* (98 CE; see Ch. 8 and 18–20), a work that she knew well through her father's 1777 translation (see Appendix C2). Rejected by the Romans as "barbarians," these Goths nevertheless were wise enough to respect, protect, and even revere their women:

> But this he knew; to woman's feeling heart
> Its best its dearest tribute to impart;
> Not the cheap falsehoods of a flattering strain,
> Not idle gauds, vain incense to the vain;
> But such high fellowship, such honoured life
> As throws a glory round the exulting wife,
> Sets her revered, sublime, on Virtue's throne,
> Judge of his honour, guardian of her own. (IV: 85–92)

Because the Goths were committed to chastity, monogamy, and a life of virtue, they were able to defeat the by then decadent, corrupt, mercenary, and tyrannical Romans, in Aikin's view (as also in Edward Gibbons's *Decline and Fall of the Roman Empire* [1776–88][1]). But by the Middle Ages, the Goths had converted to Christianity and its culture of chivalry and courtly love. In Aikin's day, a debate raged among historians and feminists as to whether the codes of chivalry increased the moral authority and political power of women—the Lady to whom the knight pledged his life-long fealty and service—or only created a fantasy of female empowerment. Such stadialist Scottish Enlightenment historians as John Millar, William Alexander, and Lord Kames hailed the Middle Ages as a time when the spirit of chivalry advanced civility by elevating the status of women and inducing men to regard themselves as subservient to the superior refinement and moral virtue of the aristocratic lady. Aikin's contemporary female historians Mary Berry and Elizabeth Benger strongly endorsed this view that the medieval lady benefited from the rituals of courtly love and exercised moral and political influence over the court.[2]

---

1 Edward Gibbon, "General Observations on the Fall of the Roman Empire in the West," in David Womersley, ed., *The History of the Decline and Fall of the Roman Empire* (London: Penguin, 2000), 434–43.

2 Karen O'Brien analyzed the ways in which Mary Berry and Elizabeth Benger promoted the culture of chivalry as empowering for women in her unpublished paper, "The History Women," delivered at the International Conference on Women's Writing 1660–1830, Chawton House Library, 17 July, 2003; also see her "Sexual Distinctions and Prescriptions: An Introduction," in Sarah Knott and Barbara Taylor, eds., *Women, Gender and Enlightenment* (London: Palgrave, 2005), 6, for her observation that this view was also endorsed by Elizabeth Montagu, Susannah Dobson, Clara Reeve, and Hannah More.

But Lucy Aikin, like Catherine Macaulay and Mary Woll-
stonecraft before her,[1] was skeptical, insisting here that such
"love" was fed only on appearances, and that the concept of the
Lady of Courtly Love celebrated in medieval troubadour poetry
was pure illusion, a fiction created only by poets: "But say, this
paragon, this matchless fair, / Trod she this care-crazed earth?
No;.... born of air, / A flitting dream, a rainbow of the mind, / ...
She blooms in Fairy land the grace of Spencer's page" (IV:
161–63, 166). Her extensive footnote here lays out the grounds of
her attack, not only on the Scottish historians, but also on
Edmund Burke's invocation of the "age of Chivalry" in his *Reflec-
tions on the Revolution in France* (1790) and on Spenser's idealiza-
tion of the Middle Ages in his *The Faerie Queene* (1596): the cele-
brated Age of Chivalry was in fact a time of corrupt morals,
widespread adultery, and gross manners. As she warns the women
of her own day who might be tempted to see themselves as the
idealized lady of courtly love and to welcome the gallantry of their
male suitors, the "love" and "fealty" of such knights is but a sham,
a performance that never lasts: "Ah! feigned humility to scorn
allied, / That stoops to conquer, flatters to deride! / Learn,
thoughtless woman, learn his arts to scan, / And dread that fearful
portent.... kneeling Man!" (IV: 177–80). (Excerpts from Aikin's
contemporary historians are included in Appendix D.)

The values and virtues of Goth culture survived only in
Switzerland, argues Aikin, where women joined the ranks of the
freedom-fighters William Tell and Arnold Winkelreid, even up to
the present age where, her footnote observes, "many females were
found" among those slain by the invading Napoleon (IV: 243 fn).
Elsewhere, in revolutionary France, the heroic republican ges-
tures of Charlotte Corday and Madame Roland have been
eclipsed by the imperial ambitions of Napoleon Bonaparte (IV:
245–57).

But what about England? Aikin ends her *Epistles* with an overview
of British history from the Roman conquest in 62 CE to the early
eighteenth century. She insists that England has long been the site
of "domestic virtue" (IV: 262), first enforced by the warrior-queen

---

1   See Catherine Macaulay, *Observations on the Reflections of the Right Hon.
Edmund Burke, on the Revolution in France, in a Letter to the Right Hon.
The Earl of Stanhope* (London and Boston, 1791), 22–23. On the femi-
nist resistance to the "spirit of chivalry" in the 18th century, see Barbara
Taylor, "Feminists versus Gallants: Manners and Morals in Enlighten-
ment Britain," in Sarah Knott and Barbara Taylor , eds., *Women, Gender
and Enlightenment* (London: Palgrave, 2005), 30–52.

Boudicca (Boadicea, Bonduca) who led the revolt of the Iceni against the Romans in 62 CE and then, defeated in 61, killed herself. She is followed by Ethelfleda, the military commander and ruler of Mercia from 914–20 CE. But their heroic example of republican femininity inspired no female followers until the Elizabethan period, where Aikin confronts the troubling case of Queen Elizabeth I. On the one hand, Aikin deeply admires the military victories achieved by Elizabeth. She preserved the Protestant Church of England, she defeated the Spanish Armada, and she sustained peaceful treaties with France and Belgium. And she created a court culture unparalleled for its support of the arts: Spenser, Shakespeare, Bacon all flourished under her patronage: "Queen of the' ascendant, whose propitious ray / Wisdom and wit, and arts, and arms obey" (IV: 392–93), Aikin enthuses. But Aikin cannot forgive the "dread Eliza" (IV: 366) for executing her rival Mary Queen of Scots, a deed that will forever "Brand her base envy, blaze each treacherous art, / And bare the meanness of her selfish heart" (IV: 384–85).

Throughout the *Epistles* Aikin has argued that men cannot degrade women without degrading themselves, and that the development of "civil society" can occur only when the values associated with women triumph. It is women, Aikin insists, who promote the domestic affections and the refinement of manners. It is their learning and moral virtue that have, by the eighteenth century, insisted that the practice of dueling among men of honor be replaced by "the bloodless contests of a nobler field / And courteous Wisdom" (IV: 335–36). Aikin therefore looks back to English history for examples of illustrious learned women who have carried the practice of Maternal Love, what Carol Gilligan has called an "ethic of care," into the public realm.[1] She singles out for praise the daughter of Sir Thomas More, the highly educated Margaret More Roper, who publicly condemned the king for unjustly executing her father and passionately consoled his final dying moments (IV: 338–56). She celebrates the magnanimity of the learned Lady Jane Grey who withstood her trial and execution with grace and dignity. She invokes Lucy Hutchinson as the "high historian of the dead" (IV: 409), the loyal and accomplished recorder of her husband's achievements in her *Memoirs of the Life of Colonel Hutchinson* (first published in 1806).[2] And she

---

1 Carol Gilligan, *In a Different Voice—Psychological Theory and Women's Development* (Cambridge and London: Harvard UP, 1982), 174.
2 For an excellent account of Lucy Hutchinson's career as a historian, see Devoney Looser, *British Women Writers and the Writing of History, 1670–1820* (Baltimore and London: Johns Hopkins UP, 2000), Chap. 2.

accords to Rachel Wriothesley, Lady William Russell, the accolade of the ideal wife, so recognized by her husband at his execution by Charles II for treason in 1683. Lady Russell devoted the rest of her life to vindicating her husband's innocence. Her *Letters, with An Introduction Vindicating the Character of Lord Russell* were transcribed and published by Thomas Sellwood in 1773.

With these examples, Aikin contrasts the violent and deadly nature of a public sphere ruled by men with the public loyalty, love, and self-sacrifice of women. She implicitly introduces what we might call a "competing" public sphere, one dominated by an ethic of care rather than an ethic of justice, one in which the needs of every member of the body politic are met. She thus reconciles, as Kathryn Ready has shown, the eighteenth-century republican with the commercial models of femininity.[1] Aikin equates the progress of civilization itself with the increasing *feminization* of political life. She urges the "Sons of Albion" to recognize this fact, to "be generous," unloose the shackles that bind the female body and mind, and benefit from their shared wisdom. She ends with a call to arms to her female readers to first reject the competitive and militaristic values of men, secondly to affirm the domestic affections as the model for all public and private relationships, and thirdly, to educate themselves in order to empower "mothering" as a *political* as well as a private practice. She ends with a passionate exhortation. If women "self-endowed, thus ... Improve, excel, surmount, subdue" their fate (IV: 478–79), then men will be inspired to embrace them as full partners in all of life's enterprises:

"Rise," shall he cry, "O woman, rise! be free!
My life's associate, now partake with me:
Rouse thy keen energies, expand thy soul,
And see, and feel, and comprehend the whole;
My deepest thoughts, intelligent, divide;
When right confirm me, and when erring, guide;
Soothe all my cares, in all my virtues blend,
And be, my sister, be at length my friend." (IV: 487-94)

One final point. Lucy Aikin recognizes that her new politics requires a new poetics. Embedded in her *Epistles on Women* is her own "Defense of Poetry," one that contests the claims both of Philip Sidney's *Defense of Poesie* and of Percy Bysshe Shelley's *Defense of Poetry*. Aikin, whose essay "Words upon Words" (see

---

1 Ready, "Enlightenment Feminist Project of Lucy Aikin's *Epistles*," 447.

Section VI, Essays), presents a similarly sophisticated under-
standing of the origins of language, nevertheless emphatically
rejects the romantic concept that poetry originates from a
"godlike power," the "divine" Imagination celebrated by Blake,
Coleridge, and Shelley. "Were mine the godlike power, / By
Genius snatched in some propitious hour, / To bid the fleeting
airy forms be still, / Or move, or change, obedient to my will; / ...
It may not be" (IV: 19–22, 27), Aikin asserts, here declining the
art of Shakespeare's Prospero. She then invokes the Platonic
concept of the visual arts as a shadow, a "reflection" or passive
imitation of reality, retelling the classical story of the origin of
painting: the Corinthian maid who traced her departing lover's
silhouette on the wall in the firelight and then filled in the outline
with colors. As opposed to the Corinthian maid, who found her
lover's image so persuasive that she then fell in love with it, Aikin
insists that her imitations of nature cannot deceive her into think-
ing them real: "Me such bright dreams delude not" (IV: 35).
Having rejected the concept of poetry both as the creation of an
original genius and as the imitation (however successful) of
reality, Aikin then defines her own concept of what poetry is. Her
work is rational and realistic, based on empirical observations
and extensive research; it is history in verse, "thoughtful, cold"
(IV: 35). All important, it depends on the response of the reader
to understand and extend its meaning; it is "fostered" by "friend-
ship," here, specifically the "partial heart" of Anne Wakefield.
Aikin is promoting a concept of poetry as a *conversation*—poetry
originates in and its meaning is defined by an ongoing dialogue
with the reader, in an act of what we might call *linguistic mother-
ing*, like that performed by Aikin's Eve in Eden, learning her
mother tongue from the sounds of Nature. Her poem is thus
engaged in the creation of a social intercourse; it is constructing
what Habermas called the "public sphere." Her title, *Epistles on
Women*, thus registers in yet another sense: it is participating in
the newly emerging, eighteenth-century discourse of public
opinion, the new Republic of Letters. Remember that Burke's
Reflections on the Revolution in France was a letter addressed to
Charles Depont. The published letter had become one of the
major genres in which public opinion was expressed and shaped
in Aikin's day. Her overtly feminist *Epistles* were thus a calculated
effort to bring about social reform.

Appropriately, Aikin both dedicates her defense of the female
sex and of the female poet to a female muse and ends with a call
to arms to that same muse, Anne Wakefield Aikin, who has

throughout the poem been invoked as the ideal *reader* of the poem. Aikin thus acknowledges that she must work together with her female readers to bring about Wollstonecraft's "Revolution in female manners." At the same time, Aikin recognizes that if poetry is a dialogue, a conversation, an act of linguistic mothering, then the meaning of a poem depends as much on the reader's interpretation as on the poet's intentions. Aikin may have been among the first to promote the concept of literary criticism as "reader-response," the theory we now associate primarily with its twentieth-century proponent Norman N. Holland (see his *The Dynamics of Literary Response*, 1968). But Aikin is confident that *her* Epistles will not only be read but will be warmly embraced and endorsed through a life of feminist action by her "judge" and "sister," who responds with love to Aikin's own "heart's farewell."

How *did* the readers of Aikin's *Epistles on Women* respond to her feminist call to arms? Aikin must have been pleased by the overwhelmingly positive reviews that her *Epistles on Women* received (see Appendix B). After doing her the compliment of taking her arguments and historical reflections seriously and at length, albeit with several quibbles, the anonymous Reviewer for *European Magazine* (July 1811) concluded that "These Epistles possess much merit, considered either as a poetical or literary performance; and therefore the patronage from the public to which they are entitled, we hope they will obtain" (39). The *Monthly Review* reviewer confessed himself "anxious to assist" Aikin in her efforts to convince man how "impossible it is for him to degrade his companion without degrading himself; or to elevate her without receiving a proportional accession of dignity and happiness" and added that "we know not one feminine attraction or accomplishment which may not co-exist with the greatest cultivation of the female mind; nor one duty, peculiarly belonging to the softer sex, of which the fulfillment will not be farthered secured by such cultivation" (April 1811: 381). He concluded by "expressing the warmest wish that the good, the philosophical, and the patriotic design of its writer may not be wholly frustrated: but that the great truth, to the support of which her pen has devoted itself, may impress some few out of the many who will peruse these epistles, with its importance, stamping the moral of her song on every intellect that is vigorous enough to receive and tenacious enough to retain it" (392). The review in the *Belfast Monthly Magazine*, after summarizing the poem at length, concluded: "We highly recommend this book to the perusal of our readers, confident that they cannot read it without having a more exalted idea of the female sex" (August 1810: 135). The *Poetical Register* singled out Aikin's prosody for praise: "We have received great pleasure from the perusal of these epistles. They are, in no common degree, pointed, polished, and energetic. The versification, too, is of the best kind. It is flowing, without being insipid; and varied, without being harsh" (1810–1811: 553). The male reviewer for *Critical Review* emphatically supported Aikin's goals: "we are happy to see a woman asserting the proper dignity of her sex, and evincing by her own example that female pretensions are well-founded" (August 1811: 419). Only one dissenting voice appeared in print: the male reviewer for the *Eclectic Review* lamented that Aikin had not written a very different poem, one that focused on the love of two parents for their children and that depicted the mother exclusively in her home, caring for her family (November 1810: 425). What is most remarkable in these reviews in the degree to which *male* readers endorsed Aikin's efforts to improve the condition of women and to recognize their all-important contributions to the advancement of civilization itself.

Lucy Aikin: A Brief Chronology

1781   Born in Warrington on November 6, to the Unitarian physician and writer John Aikin (1747-1822) and his wife Martha Jennings (c. 1746–1830). The youngest of four children (Arthur Aikin, 1733-1854, Charles Rochemont Aikin, 1775-1847, and Edmund Aikin, 1780-1820), and the only girl. Her aunt (John Aikin's sister) was Anna Barbauld. Except for a brief attendance at a day school in Yarmouth, Lucy Aikin was entirely educated at home. In infancy, Aikin was called a "little dunce" because she did not learn to read as quickly as her brothers. She did, however, later come to read widely in English, French, Italian, and Latin.

1784   Aikin family moves to Yarmouth, on the east coast of England.

1790   Meets the prison reformer John Howard.

1792   The family moves to Broad Street Buildings in London as a result of John Aikin's fall into disfavor upon the publication of his anonymous pamphlet *An Address to the Dissidents of England* (1790).

1797   LA moves with her family to Stoke Newington, Middlesex, just outside London, immediately following her father's retirement. During this period Lucy cares for her father, who had been somewhat physically disabled from a stroke. They live here until after her father's death in 1822.

1798   At 17, LA begins to write for reviews, including the *Annual Register* and *Athenaeum*.

1801   LA publishes her first book, a small-format anthology: *Poetry for Children: Consisting of Short Pieces, to be Committed to Memory. Selected by Lucy Aikin.*

1802   Arthur Aikin, LA's brother, founded and edited the first six volumes of the *Annual Review*, published between 1803 and 1808.

1803   A second edition of *Poetry for Children* is published.

1804   LA's translation from French of Louis François Jauffret's *The Travels of Rolando* published by Phillips (March).

1810   LA publishes the first edition of her first major work *Epistles on Women, Exemplifying their Character and Condition in Various Ages and Nations* (April).

1811   *Juvenile Correspondence, or, Letters, Designed as Examples of the Epistolary Style, for Children of Both Sexes.*

1812   The *Critical Review* lists the publication of a translation from French, by LA, of *The Life of Ulrich Zwingli*, the Swiss leader of the Protestant Reformation (January). Meets Elizabeth Hamilton while visiting Edinburgh. Meets Henry Crabb Robinson and William Wordsworth (May 13).

1814   LA anonymously publishes her only novel, *Lorimer, a Tale* (February). Henry Crabb Robinson, visiting LA with Charles and Mary Lamb, reported Aikin as admiring "both the wit and the fine face of Lamb" (May 28).

1815   LA, dining with Walter Scott, is pleased that though she herself went unnoticed, Scott devoted considerable attention to her aunt Barbauld (May).

1818   With the publication of her *Memoirs of the Court of Queen Elizabeth* LA launches her work in the particular style of history for which she is best known (January). Aikin tells her cousin that her publishers are encouraging her to write for children, but she admits her reluctance to do so. Meets Hester Lynch Piozzi in or near Bath (July).

1822   *Memoirs of the Court of King James the First* (January).

1822   Death of John Aikin (7 December).

1823   After her father's death, LA and her mother live in Hampstead where Joanna Baillie is among their neighbors.

1823   LA publishes a biography of her father entitled *Memoir of John Aikin, M.D.* (February). His prefaces to *Select Works of the British Poets* appear with a supplement by her at Philadelphia, 1831, and London, 1845.

1825   Anna Letitia Barbauld dies (March 9). Aikin edits *The Works of Anna Lætitia Barbauld*, including her memoir of her aunt (June).

1826   LA's correspondence with the New England Unitarian theologian William Ellery Channing begins. These letters, as printed, are likely her best known. This correspondence would continue until Channing's death in 1842.

1827   LA's biography of Elizabeth Ogilvy Benger, the primary account of this writer, is published with Benger's *Memoirs of the Life of Anne Boleyn*.

1828   *An English Lesson Book for the Junior Classes.*

1830   LA's mother, Martha Jennings, dies.

1833   *Memoirs of the Court of King Charles the First.*

1835   LA dines with Crabb Robinson, Wordsworth, Henry Coleridge, and her niece Anna Letitia Le Breton and nephew-in-law Philip Hemery Le Breton (April 18).

1837   *The Juvenile Tale Book: A Collection of Interesting Tales and Novels for Youth.*

1843   Publishes *The Life of Joseph Addison*, the first biography about Addison, which includes a number of previously unpublished letters.

1844   Joins the household of her niece Anna Letitia LeBreton in Wimbledon.

1852   Returns to Hampstead.

1858   *Holiday Stories for Young Readers* (a re-issue of *An English Lesson Book*).

1864   Dies, at age 82, of influenza, at Milford House, her home in Hampstead (January 29). LA is buried in Hampstead, and her grave lies next to that of Joanna Baillie, her beloved friend.
Philip LeBreton publishes *Memoirs, Miscellanies, and Letters of the Late Lucy Aikin, Including those Addressed to the Rev. Dr. Channing from 1826-1842* (October). This work marks the first time some of her shorter essays and many of her letters, including her correspondence with Channing are printed.

1868   *Aesop's Fables in Words of One Syllable*, and several other one-syllable texts, published under the pseudonym Mary Godolphin.

1874   LA's niece Anna Letitia Le Breton edits her correspondence with Dr. Channing, entitled *Correspondence of William Ellery Channing, D.D., and Lucy Aikin, from 1826-1842.*

A Note on the Text

All copy texts for Lucy Aikin's works are noted in the introductory headnotes to each section. Wherever possible, we have used the earliest printings, and have reproduced the spelling and punctuation of the original texts without alteration.

EPISTLES ON WOMEN AND OTHER WORKS

I. Poetry

1. *Epistles on the Character and Condition of Women, in Various Ages and Nations. With Miscellaneous Poems.* London: J. Johnson, 1810. iii–viii; 1–98

TO MRS. CHARLES ROCHEMONT AIKIN,[1] THE FOL-
LOWING EPISTLES, ORIGINALLY ADDRESSED TO
HER BY THE SOLE APPELLATION OF FRIEND, ARE
NOW INSCRIBED, TOGETHER WITH THE REMAINING
CONTENTS OF THIS VOLUME, BY HER AFFECTION-
ATE FRIEND AND SISTER LUCY AIKIN.

INTRODUCTION

The poetical epistles occupying the principal part of this volume
are presented to the public with all the diffidence and anxiety of
a literary novice conscious of a bold and arduous undertaking. As
I am not, however, aware of any circumstances in my own case
which peculiarly appeal to the indulgence of the reader, I shall
decline any further exposure of feelings purely personal, and
proceed to the proper business of this introduction,.... to offer
such preliminary remarks on the plan of the work as may be nec-
essary to prevent misapprehension.

Let me in the first place disclaim entirely the absurd idea that
the two sexes ever can be, or ever ought to be, placed in all respects
on a footing of equality. Man when he abuses his power may justly
be considered as a tyrant; but his power itself is no tyranny, being
founded not on usurpation, but on certain unalterable necessi-
ties;.... sanctioned, not by prescription alone, but by the funda-
mental laws of human nature. As long as the bodily constitution of
the species shall remain the same, man must in general assume

---

1 Charles Rochemont Aikin (1775–1847) was Lucy Aikin's brother; the
 second son of John Aikin, Charles was adopted by his aunt, Anna Bar-
 bauld, and her husband Charles Rochemont Barbauld, at the age of
 two. Charles married Anne (d. 1821), the daughter of Gilbert Wakefield
 (1756–1801). Charles became a well-known surgeon. Charles and
 Anne's first child was the writer Anna Letitia Le Breton (1808–85); she
 co-edited Lucy Aikin's *Memoirs, Miscellanies, and Letters* (1864), edited
 her correspondence with Dr. William Ellery Channing of Boston
 (1874), and wrote a *Memoir of Mrs Barbauld, Including Letters and Notices
 of her Family and Friends* (1874).

those public and active offices of life which confer authority, whilst to woman will usually be allotted such domestic and private ones as imply a certain degree of subordination. Nothing therefore could, in my opinion, be more foolish than the attempt to engage our sex in a struggle for stations that they are physically unable properly to fill; for power of which they must always want the means to possess themselves. No! instead of aspiring to be inferior men, let us content ourselves with becoming noble women:.... but let not sex be carried into every thing. Let the impartial voice of History testify for us, that, when permitted, we have been the worthy associates of the best efforts of the best of men; let the daily observation of mankind bear witness, that no talent, no virtue, is masculine alone; no fault or folly exclusively feminine;.... that there is not an endowment, or propensity, or mental quality of any kind, which may not be derived from her father to the daughter, to the son from his mother. These positions once established, and carried into their consequences, will do every thing for woman. Perceiving that any shaft aimed at her, must strike in its recoil upon some vulnerable part of common human nature, the Juvenals[1] and Popes[2] of future ages will abstain from making her the butt of scorn or malice. Feeling with gratitude of what her heart and mind are capable, the scholars, the sages, and the patriots of coming days will treat her as a sister and a friend.

The politic father will not then leave as a "legacy" to his daughters the injunction to conceal their wit, their learning, and even their good sense, in deference to the "*natural malignity*" with which most men regard every woman of a sound understanding and cultivated mind;[3] nor will even the reputation of our great

---

1 Juvenal was a Roman poet of the first century CE, author of sixteen poetic satires. His work was admired and imitated by poets of later ages, especially the neoclassical writers of the eighteenth century. A selection from his satire on women, from his sixth satire, is included in Appendix C1, below.

2 Alexander Pope (1668–1744), poet and man of letters, whose *Moral Essays* and verse epistles imitate the meter and subject of Juvenalian satire. Excerpts from Pope's satire on women, "Epistle II: To a Lady on the Characters of Women" (1735), are included in Appendix C4, below.

3 John Gregory (1724–73), physician and author, wrote *A Father's Legacy to his Daughters* after the death of his wife in 1761, in an attempt to record her opinions about the education of their two surviving daughters. Though not intended for publication, it was published by his son after his father's death in 1774. It was immediately successful and was

Milton[1] himself secure him from the charge of a blasphemous presumption in making his Eve address to Adam the acknowledgement, "God is thy head, thou mine"; and in the assertion that the first human pair were formed, "He for God only, she for God in him."

To mark the effect of various codes, institutions, and states of manners, on the virtue and happiness of man, and the concomitant and proportional elevation or depression of woman in the scale of existence, is the general plan of this work. The historical and biographical authorities from which its facts and many of its sentiments are derived, will easily be recognised by the literary reader, who will know how to estimate my correctness and fidelity: for the use of other readers a few notes are subjoined.[2]

With respect to arrangement, I may remark, that as a strictly chronological one was incompatible with the design of tracing the progress of human society not in one country alone, but in many, I have judged it most advisable to form to myself such an one as seemed best adapted to my own peculiar purposes, moral and poetical. We have no records of any early people in a ruder state than some savage tribes of the present day; and it would be in vain to seek amongst the ancient writers for such distinct and accurate delineations of the customs of Lotophagi and Troglodytes as we now possess of the life and manners of New

---

frequently reprinted. Gregory advised women to "[b]e even cautious in displaying your good sense. It will be thought you assume a superiority over the rest of the company.—But if you happen to have any learning, keep it a profound secret, especially from men, who generally look with a jealous and malignant eye on a woman of great parts, and a cultivated understanding" (31–32). Vehement attacks against displays of learning on the part of women were widespread, as for example in Richard Polwhele, from *The Unsex'd Females, A Poem* (1798). Nevertheless, many voiced opposing views; in *A Vindication of the Rights of Woman* (1792), Mary Wollstonecraft issued a withering attack against Gregory, arguing that he urged women to dissemble. Excerpts from both Polwhele and Wollstonecraft are to be found in Appendix C, below.

1   John Milton (1608–74), English poet, see his *Paradise Lost* (1667), IV, 637, 299. Excerpts from *Paradise Lost* relevant to Aikin's retelling are included in Appendix C3, below.

2   All of Lucy Aikin's original notes are retained; to distinguish them from the editor's notes, they are followed by her initials as follows: [L.A.]

Hollanders, American Indians and Hottentots.[1] From these latter, therefore, my first descriptions have been borrowed. Of the tribes of ancient Germany, indeed, we possess an unrivaled portraiture; but in the age of Tacitus[2] most of them had already risen far above the lowest stage of human society; and the progenitors of the noblest nations of modern Europe ought not to be classed with families of men whose name has perished from the earth, or wandering hordes of which we do not yet know whether or not they contain a living seed of future greatness.

In the way of explanation I have little more to add. I make no specific claims for my sex. Convinced that it is rather to the policy, or the generosity, of man, than to his justice that we ought to appeal, I have simply endeavoured to point out, that between the two partners of human life, not only the strongest family likeness, but the most complete identity of interest subsists: so that it is impossible for man to degrade his companion without degrading himself, or to elevate her without receiving a proportional accession of dignity and happiness. This is the chief "moral of my song";[3] on this point all my examples are brought to bear. I regard it as the Great Truth to the support of which my pen has devoted itself; and whoever shall rise from the perusal of these epistles deeply impressed with its importance, will afford me the success dearest to my heart,.... the hope of having served, in some small degree, the best interests of the human race.

With respect to the Miscellaneous Poems, I have only to announce, that they comprise such pieces of mine contained in *The Athenæum*, and the earlier volumes of *The Monthly Magazine*,[4] as appeared to me in any respect worthy of preservation; and that to these two others have been added.

---

1   Lotophagi: "Lotus eaters," a mythical island race who attempt to lure Odysseus and his men into a life of forgetful indolence. See Homer, *Odyssey*, 9.82–97. Troglodytes: primitive cave dwellers, possibly of Ethiopian origin. New Hollanders: Australian aborigines. (The Dutch colonized Australia in the seventeenth century.) Hottentots: a southwest African tribe.

2   Roman historian, born around CE 55, chronicler of the latter days of the Empire. Lucy Aikin's father, John Aikin, translated Tacitus' *Germania*, a text that influenced the composition of the *Epistles*. For a selection from John Aikin's translation, see Appendix C, below.

3   From Edmund Spenser's (c. 1552–99) *The Faerie Queene*: "Fierce wars and faithful loves shall moralize my song," Introduction, 1.9.

4   John Aikin was the literary editor of *The Monthly Magazine* from 1796–1806. He edited *The Athenæum* for two and a half years thereafter, when the *Monthly* was discontinued, according to Lucy Aikin because

EPISTLE I

ARGUMENT OF EPISTLE I

Subject proposed—the fame of man extended over every period
of life—that of woman transient as the beauty on which it is
founded—Man renders her a trifler, then despises her, and makes
war upon the sex with Juvenal and Pope. A more impartial view
of the subject to be attempted. Weakness of woman, and her con-
sequent subserviency. General view of various states of society
undertaken. Birth of Eve—Angels prophesy the doom of the
sex—description of Adam before he sees her—a joyless, hopeless,
indolent creature. Meeting of Adam and Eve—Change produced
in both—their mutual happiness and primary equality. Reflec-
tions. Conclusion.

HEAR, O my friend, my Anna,[1] nor disdain
My sober lyre and moralizing strain!
I sing the Fate of Woman:.... Man to man
Adds praise, and glory lights his mortal span;
Creation's lord, he shines from youth to age,   5
The blooming warrior or the bearded sage;
But she, frail offspring of an April morn,
Poor helpless passenger from love to scorn,
While dimpled youth her sprightly cheek adorns
Blooms a sweet rose, a rose amid the thorns;   10
A few short hours, with faded charms to earth
She sinks, and leaves no vestige of her birth.[2]

"the elegant style in which it was printed ... rendered it considerably
more expensive than any other monthly publication" (*Memoir of John
Aikin* I: 252).

1 Anne Wakefield, the subject of the poem's dedication.
2 It was a commonplace in the writing of many of the period's female
   authors that women and their experiences had not formed part of the
   historical record. The heroine of Jane Austen's last novel, Anne Elliot in
   Persuasion (1818), rejects the argument that women's inconstancy might
   be proven by documentary sources: "'Yes, yes, if you please, no refer-
   ence to examples in books. Men have had every advantage of us in
   telling their own story. Education has been theirs in so much higher a
   degree; the pen has been in their hands. I will not allow books to prove
   anything'" (Chapter 23). In her *Records of Women* (1828), Felicia
   Hemans (1793–1835) attempts to rectify this deficiency   (*continued*)

E'en while the youth, in love and rapture warm,
Sighs as he hangs upon her beauteous form,
Careless and cold he views the beauteous mind,　　　　　15
For virtue, bliss, eternity designed.
"Banish, my fair," he cries, "those studious looks;
O! what should beauty learn from crabbed books?
Sweetly to speak and sweetly smile be thine;
Beware, nor change that dimple to a line!"　　　　　20

Well pleased she hears, vain triumph lights her eyes;
Well pleased, in prattle and in smiles complies;
But eyes, alas! grow dim, and roses fade,
And man contemns the trifler he has made.
The glass reversed by magic power of Spleen,　　　　　25
A wrinkled idiot now the fair is seen;
Then with the sex his headlong rage must cope,
And stab with Juvenal, or sting with Pope.
Be mine, while Truth with calm and artless grace
Lifts her clear mirror to the female face,　　　　　30
With steadier hand the pencil's task to guide,
And win a blush from Man's relenting pride.

No Amazon,[1] in frowns and terror drest,
I poise the spear, or nod the threatening crest,
Defy the law, arraign the social plan,　　　　　35
Throw down the gauntlet in the face of man,
And, rashly bold, divided empire claim,
Unborrowed honours, and an equal's name:
No, Heaven forbid! I touch no sacred thing,

---

by providing historical examples of women's experience. However, by
the later Victorian period, George Eliot (1819–80) concludes her mas-
terpiece *Middlemarch* (1871–72) by reiterating the belief that women's
lives are essentially recordless. The final paragraph includes the follow-
ing summation of the life of her heroine, Dorothea Brooke: "Her full
nature, like that river of which Cyrus broke the strength, spent itself in
channels which had no great name on the earth. But the effect of her
being on those around her was incalculably diffusive: for the growing
good of the world is partly dependent on unhistoric acts; and that things
are not so ill with you and me as they might have been, is half owing to
the number who lived faithfully a hidden life, and rest in unvisited
tombs."

1　In Greek mythology, an all-female nation of warriors.

But bow to Right Divine in man and king;[1]   40
Nature endows him with superior force,
Superior wisdom then I grant, of course;
For who gainsays the despot in his might,
Or when was ever weakness in the right?
With passive reverence too I hail the law,   45
Formed to secure the strong, the weak to awe.
Impartial guardian of unerring sway,
Set up by man for woman to obey.
In vain we pout or argue, rail or chide,
He mocks our idle wrath and checks our pride;   50
Resign we then the club and lion's skin,
And be our sex content to knit and spin;
To bow inglorious to a master's rule,
And good and bad obey, and wise and fool;
Here a meek drudge, a listless captive there,   55
For gold now bartered, now as cheap as air;
Prize of the coward rich or lawless brave,
Scorned and caressed, a plaything and a slave,
Yet taught with spaniel soul to kiss the rod,
And worship man as delegate of God.   60

Ah! what is human life? a narrow span
Eked out with cares and pains to us and man;[2]
A bloody scroll that vice and folly stain,
That blushing Nature blots with tears in vain,
That frowning Wisdom reads with tone severe,   65
While Pity shudders with averted ear.
Yet will I dare its varying modes to trace
Through many a distant tribe and vanisht race;
The sketch perchance shall touch the ingenuous heart,

---

1 In determining whether these and subsequent lines should be read iron-
    ically, consideration should be given to Lucy Aikin's highly critical treat-
    ment of the doctrine of divine right in her court memoirs, particularly
    those of James I and Charles I. Relevant excerpts from these histories
    are included in the online supplement to this volume. Aikin was also
    familiar with her aunt's similarly ambiguous use of irony in "The Rights
    of Women," a poem that Aikin first published in *Works of Anna Letitia
    Barbauld* (1825). Barbauld's poem is included in Appendix C6, below.
2 These lines contain strong echoes of Anna Barbauld's poem "Life,"
    which was first published in Lucy Aikin's *Works of Anna Letitia Barbauld*.
    "Life" became one of Barbauld's best-known poems, widely antholo-
    gized throughout the nineteenth century.

And hint its moral with a pleasing art. 70
Aid me, Historic Muse! unfold thy store
Of rich, of various, never-cloying lore;
Thence Fancy flies with new-born visions fraught,
There old Experience lends his hoards to Thought.

When slumbering Adam pressed the lonely earth,.... 75
Unconscious parent of a wondrous birth,....
As forth to light the infant-woman sprung,
By pitying angels thus her doom was sung:
"Ah! fairest creature! born to changeful skies,
To bliss and agony, to smiles and sighs: 80
Beauty's frail child, to thee, though doomed to bear
By far the heavier half of human care,
Deceitful Nature's stepdame-love assigned
A form more fragile, and a tenderer mind;
More copious tears from Pity's briny springs, 85
And, trembling Sympathy! thy finest strings:
While ruder man she prompts, in pride of power,
To bruise, to slay, to ravage, to devour;
On prostrate weakness turn his gory steel,
And point the wounds not all thy tears can heal. 90
Poor victim! stern the mandate of thy birth,
Ah dote not, smile not, on the things of earth!
Subdue thyself; those rapturous flutterings still!
Armed with meek courage and a patient will,
With thoughtful eye pursue thy destined way, 95
Adore thy God, and hope a brighter day!"
In solemn notes thus flowed the prescient strain,....
But flowed on Eve's unpractised ear in vain;
In smiling wonder fixt, the new-born bride
Drank the sweet gale, the glowing landscape eyed, } 100
And murmured untried sounds, and gazed on every side. }
With look benign the boding angels view
The fearless innocent, and wave adieu:
"Too well thy daughters shall our strain believe;
Too short thy dream of bliss, ill-fated Eve." 105

Prophetic spirits! that with ken sublime
Sweep the long windings of the flood of time,
Joyless and stern, your deep-toned numbers dwell

On rocks, on whirlpools, and the foaming swell,
But pass unmarked the skiffs that gaily glide   110
With songs and streamers down the dimpling tide:
Else rapturous notes had floated on the wind,
And hailed the stranger born to bless her kind,
To bear from heaven to earth the golden ties,
Bind willing man, and draw him to the skies.   115

See where the world's new master roams along,
Vainly intelligent and idly strong;
Mark his long listless step and torpid air,
His brow of densest gloom and fixt infantile stare!
Those sullen lips no mother's lips have prest,   120
Nor drawn, sweet labour! at her kindly breast;
No mother's voice has touched that slumbering ear,
Nor glistening eye beguiled him of a tear;
Love nursed not him with sweet endearing wiles,
Nor woman taught the sympathy of smiles;   125
Vacant and sad his rayless glances roll,
Nor hope nor joy illumes his darkling soul;
Ah! hapless world that such a wretch obeys!
Ah! joyless Adam, though a world he sways!

But see!.... they meet,.... they gaze,.... the new-born pair;.... 130
Mark now the wakening youth, the wondering fair:
Sure a new soul that moping idiot warms,
Dilates his stature, and his mien informs!
A brighter crimson tints his glowing cheek;
His broad eye kindles, and his glances speak.   135
So roll the clouds from some vast mountain's head,
Melt into mist, and down the valleys spread;
His crags and caves the bursting sunbeams light,
And burn and blaze upon his topmost height;
Broad in full day he lifts his towering crest,   140
And fire celestial sparkles from his breast.
Eve too, how changed!.... No more with baby grace
The smile runs dimpling o'er her trackless face,
As painted meads invite her roving glance,
Or birds with liquid trill her ear intrance: 145
With downcast look she stands, abasht and meek,
Now pale, now rosy red, her varying cheek;
Now first her fluttering bosom heaves a sigh,

Now first a tear stands trembling in her eye;
For hark! the youth, as love and nature teach,   150
Breathes his full bosom, and breaks forth in *speech*;
His quivering lips the winged accents part,
And pierce, how swift! to Eve's unguarded heart.

Now rose complete the mighty Maker's plan,
And Eden opened in the heart of Man;   155
Kindled by Hope, by gentle Love refined,
Sweet converse cheered him, and a kindred mind;
Nor deem that He, beneficent and just,
In woman's hand who lodged this sacred trust,
For man alone her conscious soul informed,   160
For man alone her tenderer bosom warmed;
Denied to her the cup of joy to sip,
But bade her raise it to his greedy lip,
Poor instrument of bliss, and tool of ease,
Born but to serve, existing but to please:....   165
No;.... hand in hand the happy creatures trod,
Alike the children of no partial God;
Equal they trod till want and guilt arose,
Till Savage blood was spilt, and man had foes:
Ah! days of happiness,.... with tearful eye   170
I see you gleam, and fade, and hurry by:
Why should my strain the darkening theme pursue?
Be husht, my plaintive lyre! my listening friend, adieu!

EPISTLE II

ARGUMENT OF EPISTLE II

The subject resumed. Sketch of savage life in general—The sex oppressed by slaves and barbarians, but held in honour by the good and the brave.—New Holland—brutality of the inhabitants—their courtship. North American Indians—one of their women describes her wretched condition and destroys her female infant. Hardening effect of want on the human mind. Transition to Otaheite—Licentious manners of those islanders—Infanticide. Address to maternal affection—exemplified in the hind—fawns destroyed by the stag. Coast of Guinea—a native sells his son for a slave—agony of the mother—her speech. Pastoral life—Chaldee astronomers—King David. Tartars—removal of a Tartar camp—their gaiety and happy mediocrity of condition relative to the gifts of nature—yet no refined affection between the sexes—female captives and women sent in tribute preferred to the natives—No perfect Arcadia to be found on earth—Caffres[1] and Hottentots sprightly and harmless—but all pastoral and hunting tribes deficient in mental cultivation—hence the weaker sex held by all in some kind of subjection.

ONCE more my Muse uplifts her drooping eye,
Checks the weak murmur and restrains the sigh;
Once more, my friend, incline thy candid ear,
And grace my numbers with a smile and tear.
Not mine the art in solemn garb to dress   5
The shadowy forms of *delicate distress*;
With baleful charms to call from Fancy's bower
Vain shapes of dread to haunt the lonely hour;
In feverish dreams to feed the pampered thought
With heavenly bliss.... on earth how vainly sought!   10
Fan with rash breath the passions' smouldering fire,
Whet the keen wish, the thrilling hope inspire,
Woo the young soul its blossoms to unfold
Then leave it chilled with more than wintry cold.

No;.... rude of hand, with bolder lines I trace   15
The rugged features of a coarser race:
Fierce on thy view the savage world shall glare,
And all the ills of wretched woman there;
Unknown to her fond love's romantic glow,
The graceful throbs of sentimental woe,   20
The play of passions and the feelings' strife
That weave the web of finely-chequered life.
But thou possest, unspoiled by tyrant art,
Of the large empire of a generous heart,
Thou wilt not scorn plain nature's rudest strain,   25
Nor *homely* misery claim thy sighs in vain.

Come then, my friend; my devious way pursue;
Pierce every clime, and search all ages through;
Stretch wide and wider yet thy liberal mind,
And grasp the sisterhood of womankind: 30

---

1 A name denoting various Bantu-speaking peoples living in much of
   southeastern Africa. The term is now regarded as offensive.

With mingling anger mark, and conscious pride,
The sex by whom exalted or decried;
Crusht by the savage, fettered by the slave,
But served, but honoured, by the good and brave.

With daring keel attend yon convict train   35
To new-found deserts of the Southern Main;[1]
Beasts of strange gait there roam the trackless earth,
And monstrous compounds struggle into birth;
A younger world it seems, abortive, crude,
Where untaught Nature sports her fancies rude,   40
By slow gradations rears her infant plan,
And shows, half-humanized, the monster-man.
Mark the grim ruffian roll his crafty glance,
And crouching, slow, his tiger-step advance,
With brandisht club surprise his human prey,   45
And drag the bleeding victim bride away,
While shouts triumphant wake the orgies dire,
And Rage and Terror trim the nuptial fire.[2]

E'en such is Savage Man, of beasts the worst,
In want, in guilt, in lawless rapine nurst.   50
To the dumb tribes that plod their even life
Unbruised by tyranny, unvext by strife,
Instincts and appetites kind Nature gave,
These just supplying what the others crave;
The human brute the headlong passions rule,   55
While infant Reason flies the moody fool,
Hope, Fear, and Memory play their busy part
And mingle all their chaos in his heart;
Hence Vengeance fires, hence Envy's stings infest,
Hence Superstition goads his timorous breast.   60
O! not for him life's healthful current flows;
An equal stream that murmurs as it goes;
As rage and torpor hold alternate rule,
It roars a flood, or stagnates in a pool,

---

1 The south seas, Oceania.
2 "The courtship of the savages of New Holland consists of watching the
   lady's retirement, and then knocking her down with repeated blows of a
   club or wooden sword; after which the truly matrimonial victim is led
   streaming with blood to her future husband's party, where a scene
   ensues too shocking to relate." Collins's Hist. of the Colony in New
   Holland. [L.A.]

Whose sterile brink no buds of fragrance cheer   65
By love or pity nurtured with a tear.

What wonder then, the Western wilds among
Where the red Indian's hunter-bow is strung,
(Nature's tough son, whose adamantine frame
No pleasures soften and no tortures tame)   70
If, fiercely pondering in her gloomy mind
The desperate ills that scowl on womankind,
The maddening mother gripes the infant slave,
And forces back the worthless life she gave?[1]

"Swift, swift," she cries, "receive thy last release;   75
Die, little wretch; die once and be at peace!

---

1   "In all unpolished nations, it is true, the functions in domestic economy
    which fall naturally to the share of the women, are so many, that they
    are subjected to hard labour, and must bear more than their full portion
    of the common burden. But in America their condition is so peculiarly
    grievous, and their depression so complete, that servitude is a name too
    mild to describe their wretched state. A wife, amongst most tribes, is no
    better than a beast of burden, destined to every office of labour and
    fatigue. While the men loiter out the day in sloth or spend it in amuse-
    ment, the women are condemned to incessant toil. Tasks are imposed
    upon them without pity, and services are received without complacency
    or gratitude.
       "Every circumstance reminds the women of this mortifying inferiority.
    They must approach their lords with reverence, they must regard them
    as more exalted beings, and are not permitted to eat in their presence.
       "There are many districts in America where this dominion is so griev-
    ous, and so sensibly felt, that some women, in a wild emotion of mater-
    nal tenderness, have destroyed their female children in their infancy, in
    order to deliver them from that intolerable bondage to which they knew
    they were doomed." [William] Robertson's Hist. of America, vol. ii. p.
    105.
       Hearne describes the women of the Northern tribes which he visited,
    as wading through the snow encumbered with heavy burdens, while the
    men, themselves carrying nothing, urged them on with blows and
    threats. He mentions other particulars, also illustrative of the wretched
    condition of the American females, too numerous and too horrid for
    poetical narration.
       Certainly Rousseau did not consult the interests of the weaker sex in
    his preference of savage life to civilized. [L.A.] As Aikin's note demon-
    strates, Rousseau was associated with the concept of the noble savage
    and the idealization of mankind in a state of nature.

Why shouldst thou live, in toil, and pain, and strife,
To curse the names of mother and of wife?[1]
To see at large thy lordly master roam,
The beasts his portion and the woods his home,   80
Whilst thou, infirm, the sheltering hut must seek,
Poorly dependent, timorously weak,
There hush thy babe, with patient love carest,
And tearful clasp him to thy milkless breast
Hungry and faint, while feasting on his way   85
Thy reckless hunter wastes the jocund day?
Or, harder task, his rapid courses share,
With patient back the galling burden bear,
While he treads light, and smacks the knotted thong,
And goads with taunts his staggering troop along?   90
Enough;.... 'tis love, dear babe, that stops thy breath;
'Tis mercy lulls thee to the sleep of death:
Ah! would for me, by like indulgent doom,
A mother's hand had raised the early tomb!
O'er these poor bones the moons had rolled in vain,   95
And brought nor stripes nor famine, toil nor pain;
I had not sought in agony the wild,
Nor, wretched, frantic mother! killed my child."
Want hardens man; by fierce extremes the smart
Inflames and chills and indurates his heart,   100
Arms his relentless hand with brutal force,
And drives o'er female necks his furious course.

Not such his mind where Nature, partial queen,
With lavish plenty heaps the bounteous scene;
In laughing isles with broad bananas crowned,   105
Where tufted cocoas shade the flowery ground;
Here, here at least, where dancing seasons shed
Unfading garlands on his sleeping head,

---

1 Felicia Hemans's "Indian Woman's Death-Song," from *Records of Women*,
   features a similar act of infanticide by an Indian woman (though in
   Hemans's poem the mother commits suicide as well). In fact, infanticide
   appears to have been common in British culture, and was widely written
   about though, as these authors argue, it is extremely difficult to disen-
   tangle historical facts from press sensationalism. For detailed accounts,
   see *Writing British Infanticide: Child-Murder, Gender, and Print,*
   1722–1859. Ed. Jennifer Thorn. Newark: U of Delaware P, 2003, 18–20;
   and Josephine McDonagh, *Child Murder and British Culture 1720–1900.*
   Cambridge: Cambridge UP, 2003, 5–6.

Love melts to love, and man's ingenuous mind
Feels nature's kindness prompt him to be kind;   110
He acts no tyranny, he knows no strife,
One harmless holiday his easy life.
Ah cheated hopes!.... see Lawless Love invade
The withering scene, and poison every shade;
Embruted nations couch beneath his yoke,   115
And infant gore on his dire altars smoke!
Lost Otaheite!.... Breathe one parting sigh,
Then swift, my friend, we turn the bashful eye.[1]

Thrice holy Power, whose fostering, bland embrace
Shields the frail scions of each transient race,   120
To whom fair Nature trusts the teeming birth
That fills the air, that crowds the peopled earth,
Maternal Love! thy watchful glances roll
From zone to zone, from pole to distant pole;
Cheer the long patience of the brooding hen,   125
Soothe the she-fox that trembles in her den,
'Mid Greenland ice-caves warm the female bear,
And rouse the tigress from her sultry lair.
At thy command, what zeal, what ardour, fires
The softer sex! a mightier soul inspires:....   130
Lost to themselves, our melting eyes behold
Prudent, the simple, and the timid, bold.
All own thy sway, save where, on Simoom[2] wing
Triumphant sailing o'er the blasted spring,
(Whether in Otaheitan groves accurst,   135
Or Europe's polisht scenes the fiend be nurst)
Unhallowed Love bids Nature's self depart,
And makes a desert of the female heart.
But O! how oft, their tender bosoms torn
By countless shafts, thy noblest votaries mourn!   140
See the soft hind forsake the dewy lawns
To shroud in thicket-shades her tender fawns;

---

1   It is supposed that two thirds of the children born in Otaheite are
    immediately murdered. For the particulars of that dreadful licentious-
    ness which is the consequence of the complete indolence of these
    islanders, and the countless and nameless evils and enormities which are
    its consequence, see Transactions of the [Church] Missionary Society,
    vol. i. [L.A.] Otaheite is the eighteenth-century name given to Tahiti.
2   Windstorm in Asia Minor.

Fearless for them confront the growling foe,
And aim with hoof and head the desperate blow
Freely for them with new-born courage face   145
The howling horrors of the deathful chase:
Ah! fond in vain, see fired by furious heat
The jealous stag invade her soft retreat,
Wanton in rage her pleading anguish scorn,
And gore his offspring with relentless horn.   150

Hark to that shriek! from Afric's palmy shore
The yell rolls mingling with the billows' roar:
Grovelling in dust the frantic mother lies;....
"My son, my son, O spare my son!" she cries:
"Sell not thy child! Yon dreary ocean crost,   155
To thee, to me, to all forever lost,
The white man's slave, no swift-returning oar
Shall homeward urge the wretched captive more,
No tidings reach:.... Who then with kindly care
Shall tend our age, and leafy beds prepare?   160
Who climb for us the cocoa's scaly side,
Or drain the juicy palm?.... who skim the tide,
Or bold in woods with pointed javelin roam,
And bear to us the savoury booty home?
Save thine own flesh!.... we must not, will not part....   165
O save this bleeding, bursting, mother's heart!"

Ah fruitless agony! ah slighted prayer!
That bids the husband and the father, spare!
On to the mart the sable tyrant drives
His flocks of children and his herds of wives: 170
For toys, for drams, their kindred blood is sold,
And broken female hearts are paid with gold;
Exulting Avarice gripes his struggling prize,
The savage tenders, and the Christian.... *buys.*[1]

---

1 These lines were written before the late glorious abolition: but there are
   still Christian nations to whom they apply with full force. [L.A.] A refer-
   ence to the abolition of the slave trade by the British Parliament in
   1807. Slavery in most of Britain's colonial holdings wasn't abolished
   until 1833.

Shrinkst thou, my startled friend, with feeling tear,   175
From tints too lively, numbers too sincere?
Swift wouldst thou fly to some unspotted scene
Where love and nature rule the blue serene?
Hail, Pastoral Life; to thy calm scenes belong
The lore of sages and the poet's song;   180
Nurse of rude man, in whose soft lap reclined,
Art, science, dawn upon his wakening mind,
And passion's tender strains, and sentiment refined!

Where cloudless heavens o'erarch Chaldea's plain,
Stretched by his nightly flock, the vacant swain,   185
His upturned gaze as sportful fancy warmed,
With ready crook the sand-drawn monsters formed;
Thence learn'd, Astronomy, thy studious eye,
To track yon orbs, to sweep yon pathless sky.
While still young David roamed the pastoral wild,   190
The harp, the song, his ardent soul beguiled,
And now to heaven upsoared the ethereal flame,
Now blazed some humble charmer's rustic fame.
E'en now, by Freedom led, see gay Content
Stoop from above, to shepherd-wanderers sent;   195
See o'er the green expanse of pathless plain
The sunburnt Tartars urge the tented wain;
How gay the living prospect! far and wide
Spread flocks and herds, and shouting herdsmen ride;
And hark! from youths and maids, a mingled throng,   200
How full, how joyous, bursts the choral song!

Free are these tribes and blest; a churlish soil
They till not, bowed by tyranny and toil;
Nor troll the deep for life's precarious stay;
Nor, beastlike, roam the tangled woods for prey;   205
Their lot, with sober kindness, gives to share
Labour with plenty, and with freedom, care:
Yet seek not here the boon, all boons above,
The generous intercourse of equal love;
A homely drudge, the Tartar matron knows   210
No eye that kindles and no heart that glows;
For foreign charms the faithless husband burns,
And clasps in loathed embrace, which fear returns,

The captive wife or tributary maid
By conquest snatched, or lawless terror paid.[1]   215

No!.... vain the search,.... of warm poetic birth,
Arcadian blossoms scorn the fields of earth;
No lovelorn swains, to tender griefs a prey,
Sigh, sing, and languish through the livelong day;
No rapturous husband and enamoured wife,   220
To live and love their only care in life,
With crook and scrip on flowery banks reclined
Breathe the warm heart and share the answering mind:
The sprightly Caffre o'er the moonlight meads
In jovial dance his dusky partner leads,   225
And vacant Hottentots, short labour done,
Toy, pipe, and carol, in the evening sun;
But the high promptings of the conscious soul
The weak that elevate, the strong control,
Respect, decorum, friendship, ties that bind   230
To woman's form the homage of the mind,
Heaven's nobler gifts, to riper ages lent,
Disdain the hunter's cave, the shepherd's tent,
And *lawless* man, or cold, or fierce, or rude,
Proves every mode of female servitude.   235

EPISTLE III

ARGUMENT OF EPISTLE III

Dawn of civilization, freedom, and the virtues. Troy taken—captives—Andromache. Spartans—character of their women—remarks. Athens—Phryne—Aspasia—degradation of the married

---

1 An annual tribute of women was exacted by the Tartars, or Huns, from
   the Chinese; and even the daughters, genuine or adopted, of the eastern
   emperors were claimed in marriage by the Tanjous as a bond of union
   between the nations. "The situation of these unhappy victims is
   described," says Gibbon, "in the verses of a Chinese princess, who
   laments that she had been condemned by her parents to a distant exile,
   under a barbarian husband; who complains that sour milk was her only
   drink, raw flesh her only food, a tent her only palace; and who
   expresses, in a strain of pathetic simplicity, the natural wish that she
   were transformed into a bird, to fly back to her dear country, the object
   of her tender and perpetual regret." Decline and Fall, vol. iv. p. 363, 8
   vol. edition. [L.A.] Tanjous: Unidentified, possibly a tribe from Tanjore
   (now Thanjavur) in Tamil Nadu, India.

women. Rome—present degraded state of both sexes—women in a condition approaching freedom, follow and imitate the course of the men with whom they are connected, as his shadow, the traveller. Ancient Rome—its female deities—Sabine women—mother and wife of Coriolanus. Cornelia. Portia. Arria. Corruption of manners in Rome—its conquest by the barbarians. Another scene of virtue and glory unfolded by the promulgation of christianity—its favourable effect on the condition of women—their zeal in its defence equal to that of men—Female martyrs. Marriage rendered indissoluble—belief of a reunion in a future state. Rise of superstition—monastic institutions. Convent. Saints Theresa, Clara, and Catharine of Siena. Conclusion.

YE heaven-taught bards, who first for human woe
Bade human tears to melting numbers flow;
Ye godlike sages, who with plastic hand
Moulded rude man, and arts and cities planned;
Ye holy patriots, whose protecting name   5
Still lives, and issuing from the trump of fame
Fans sacred Freedom's everlasting flame,
All hail!.... by you sublimed, the expanding heart
First learned the bliss its blessings to impart;
The fierce barbarian checked his headlong course,   10
And bent to Wisdom's hand his yielded force;
Each loftier Virtue bowed to meet the brave,
And clasped, a freeman, whom she scorned, a slave;
And smiling round, the daughter, mother, wife,
Fed the dear charities of social life.   15

Bright as the welcome orb that wakes to chase
The polar Night from Earth's reviving face....
(Grim Power that shakes the meteor from his hair,
While shaggy prowlers in the fitful glare
Roam with rude yells along the mountains drear,   20
Ravening and yet undisciplined to fear)
Behold, my friend, with pleased and anxious gaze
Fair Reason's day-star light her gradual blaze;
Pant up the steepness of her high career,
And win by toil the empire of the sphere;   25
While with slow hand the ungenial shades withdrawn,
Vapours and tempests struggle with the dawn.

Mark the last hour of Ilium,[1].... work divine!
Sunk her proud towers, and sunk each holy shrine:
Slaughter has done his work: the manly brave   30
Sighed as they fell, despairing of a grave.
Yet, weep not them! behold yon captive train;
Houseless and bound they strew the smoking plain;
Matrons and maids, gray sires and babes are there,
Shrill wails and frantic screams, deep groans and dumb
   despair.   35
Hark! 'tis the lost Andromache that shrieks,[2]
Her loose locks rent, and bruised her bleeding cheeks:
Home the proud victor bears his beauteous prize;
For death, for death she sues with fruitless cries.
Ah! might she wait that kind, that last release,   40
And drain the dregs of bitterness in peace!
But no;.... she bears the vengeful brand of strife,
Fires the loose rover, stings the jealous wife
What scorn, what rage, the wretched captive waits,
Envied and hated for the love she hates!   45
The rest, a mingled, nameless, feeble throng,
The savage squadrons drive with taunts along,
Destined to whirl with pain the slavish mill;
Bear ponderous logs, and sparkling goblets fill
To hostile Gods; explore the distant spring,   50
And faint with heat the cooling burthen bring;
In housewife tasks the midnight hours employ,
And lave those feet that spurned the dust of Troy.[3]

---

1 Troy.
2 Andromache is the devoted wife of the Trojan hero Hector, taken as a
   spoil of war and bride by the Greek Neoptolemus, whose father Achilles
   had slain Hector. Her story is related by Homer in the *Iliad*.
3 One of the most pathetic passages of Homer thus paints the situation of
   a female captive:
     "As when a woman weeps
     Her husband fall'n in battle for her sake,
     And for his children's sake, before the gate
     Of his own city; sinking to his side
     She close infolds him with a last embrace,
     And gazing on him as he pants and dies,
     Shrieks at the sight; meantime the ruthless foe
     Smiting her shoulders with the spear, to toil
     Command her and to bondage far away,
     And her cheek fades with horror at the sound."
   Odyss. viii. 523.—[trans. William] Cowper. [L.A.]

These were the days, while yet the scourge and chain
Quivered and clanked in wild War's demon train,   55
When Honour first his calm firm phalanx ranged;
Fury to Valour, men to heroes changed:
And mark! emerging from the gulf of night,
What towering phantom strikes our wondering sight?
Fierce with strange joy she stands, the battle won,   60
Elate and tearless o'er her slaughtered son.
"He died for Sparta, died unknown to fear,
His wounds all honest, and his shield his bier;
And shall I weep?" Stern daughters of the brave,
Thus maids and matrons hailed the Spartan's grave;   65
By turns they caught, they lit, the hero-flame,
And scorned the Woman's for the Patriot's name;
Unmoved, unconquered, bowed to fate's decree,
And taught in chains the lesson.... to be free.[1]
Souls of gigantic mould, they fill our gaze   70
With pigmy wonder and despairing praise:....
Thus when, 'mid western wilds, the delver's toil
Reared the huge mammoth from the quaking soil,
Columbia's swains in mute amazement eyed
And heaved the monstrous frame from side to side;   75
Saw bones on bones in mouldering ruin lie,
And owned the relics of a world gone by:....
Yet self-same clay our limbs of frailty formed,
And hearts like ours those dreadless bosoms warmed;
But war, and blood, and Danger's gorgon face,   80
Froze into stone the unconquerable race.

Graced by the sword, the chisel, and the pen,
Athens! illustrious seat of far-famed men,
Receive my homage! Hark! what shouts arise
As Phryne[2] gilds the pomp of sacrifice!   85
To Beauty's Queen the graceful dance they twine,
Trill the warm hymn, and dress the flowery shrine;
Priestess of love she fills the eager gaze,
And fires and shares the worship that she pays.

---

1 A captive Lacedæmonian woman, being asked by her master what she
  understood? replied, "How to be free." And on his afterwards requiring
  of her something unworthy, she put herself to death. Valerius Maximus.
  [L.A.]

2 A golden statue of Phryne the courtesan was placed by the Athenians in
  one of their temples amongst the images of their deities. [L.A.]

Haste, sculptor, haste! that form, that heavenly face   90
Catch ere they fade, and fix the mortal grace;
Phryne in gold shall deck the sacred fane,
And Pallas'[1] virgin image frown in vain.
Rise, bright Aspasia,[2] too! thy tainted name
Sails down secure through infamy to fame;   95
Statesmen and bards and heroes bend the knee,
Nor blushes Socrates to learn of thee.
Thy wives, proud Athens! fettered and debased,
Listlessly duteous, negatively chaste,
O vapid summary of a slavish lot!   100
They sew and spin, they die and are forgot.
Cease, headlong Muse! resign the dangerous theme,
Perish the glory that defies esteem!
Inspire thy trump at Virtue's call alone,
And blush to blazon whom She scorns to own.   105

Mark where seven hills uprear yon stately scene,
And reedy Tiber lingering winds between:
Ah mournful view! ah check to human pride!
There Glory's ghost and Empire's phantom glide:
Shrunk art thou, mighty Rome; the ivy crawls,   110
The vineyard flaunts, within thy spacious walls;
Still, still, Destruction plies his iron mace,
And fanes and arches totter to their base:
Thy sons.... O traitors to their fathers' fame!
O last of men, and Romans but in name!   115
See where they creep with still and listless tread,
While cowls, not helmets, veil the inglorious head.
If then, sad partner of her country's shame,
To nobler promptings deaf, the Latian dame
Nor honour's law nor nuptial faith can bind,   120
Vagrant and light of eye, of air, of mind,....
Whom now a vile gallant's obsequious cares
Engage, now mass, processions, penance, prayers,....
Think not 'twas always thus:.... what generous view,
What noble aim that noble men pursue,   125
Has never woman shared? As o'er the plain
The sun-drawn shadow tracks the wandering swain,

---

1 Athena, the virgin goddess of wisdom.
2 Greek courtesan (c. 470–410 BCE) noted for her beauty, wit, and learn-
   ing; consort of Pericles.

Treads in his footsteps, counterfeits his gait,
Erect or stooping, eager or sedate;
Courses before, behind, in mimic race,   130
Turns as he turns, and hunts him pace by pace;....
Thus, to the sex when milder laws ordain
A lighter fetter and a longer chain,
Since freedom, fame, and lettered life began,
Has faithful woman tracked the course of man.   135
Strains his firm step for Glory's dazzling height,
Panting she follows with a proud delight;
Led by the sage, with pausing foot she roves
By classic fountains and religious groves;
In Pleasure's path if strays her treacherous guide,   140
By fate compelled, she deviates at his side,....
Yet seeks with tardier tread the downward way,
Averted eyes, and timorous, faint delay.
In mystic fable thus, together trod
The dire Bellona and the Warrior God;   145
The golden Archer and chaste Huntress' queen
With deaths alternate strewed the sickening scene;
And Jove-born Pallas shared the Thunderer's state,
The shield of horror and the nod of fate.[1]

The indignant Muse from yon polluted ground   150
Shall chase the vampire forms that flit around;
Restore the scene with one commanding glance;
Awake old Rome, and bid her shades advance:
A sad but glorious pageant!.... First are borne
Her sculptured deities, and seem to mourn;   155
Dian and Vesta, powers of awful mien,
And in her purer garb the Paphian Queen;[2]
Here smiles the Appeaser of the angry spouse,[3]

---

1 Bellona: Roman goddess of war, consort of Mars, the god of War.
   Golden Archer: Apollo, god of, among other things, light, the sun, and
   archery. Chaste Huntress: Diana, the virgin goddess of the moon. Pallas:
   Athena/Minerva, supposedly born from the brow of Jove or Jupiter, the
   Thunderer.
2 Vesta: the Roman goddess of the hearth, or domesticity. Paphian Queen:
   Venus, the goddess of love.
3 Whenever a disagreement arose between a husband and wife, they
   repaired to the shrine of the Goddess Viriplaca (the appeaser of hus-
   bands); and there, having alternately spoken what they thought proper,
   they laid aside their contention, and returned in peace. Val. Max. [L.A.]

There *distaffed* Pallas knits her thoughtful brows;
Imperial Juno rears her head on high,   160
Unspotted guardian of the nuptial tie.
See then advance with wild disordered charms
The matron Sabines[1].... prize of lawless arms....
Such as they rushed athwart the clanging fight,
Bold in their fears and strong in nature's right: 165
Each lifts her babe; the babe, 'mid vengeful strife,
Lisps to his grandsire for his father's life;
The vanquisht grandsire clasps the blooming boy;
Rage sinks in tears, in smiles, in shouting joy;
Peace joins their hands, Love mingles race with race,   170
And Woman triumphs in the wide embrace.
I see her rise, the chaste polluted fair,
And claim the death of honour in despair.
Rome's Saviour wakes....[2] "By that ennobled shade,
By this pure blood, and by this reeking blade,   175
Vengeance I swear!".... Heaven blessed the generous rage
That lit the splendours of a brightening age;
The patriot spark from dying honour springs,
And female virtue buys.... the flight of Kings.

And who are they that lead yon suppliant train?   180
Mother and wife, when Latium's fertile plain
Fierce Volscians trod, the rebel's armed hate
They soothed, and soothing saved the tottering state:

---

1   Ancient people of central Italy, frequently at war with the Romans.
    According to legend, the followers of Romulus raped (or seized) the
    Sabine women when they could not find wives among their own people.
    "The Rape of the Sabine Women" was a popular subject of painting in
    the eighteenth century, and is depicted in works by Poussin and
    Delacroix.

2   Aikin includes a lengthy quotation in Latin from Ovid's *Fasti*, What
    follows is a translation by Sir James George Frazer: "Brutus came, and
    then at last belied his name, for from the half-dead body he snatched
    the weapon stuck in it, and holding the knife, that dripped with noble
    blood, he fearless spoke these words of menace: 'By this brave blood and
    chaste, and by thy ghost, who shall be god to me I swear to be avenged
    on Tarquin and on his banished brood'" (Ovid, *Fasti* II: 837–43). Lucius
    Junius Brutus was the founder of the Roman Republic, and was one of
    the first consuls in 509 BCE. He is said to have discovered the body of
    his kinswoman, Lucretia, who had stabbed herself after having been
    raped by one of Tarquin's sons.

Rome crowned the sex.... a high and graceful meed....
And bade yon temple consecrate the deed.[1]   185
Hail! who thy sons to Glory's altar led,
And boldly called her lightnings on their head:
What though they fell? the pure ethereal flame
Touched but the life, and spared the nobler fame.
Lift thy proud head, and proudly tell their tale;   190
Cornelia, mother of the Gracchi, hail!

See there the ghost of noble Portia glide,
Cato to lead, and Brutus at her side![2]
Souls have no sex; sublimed by Virtue's lore
Alike they scorn the earth and try to soar;   195
Buoyant alike on daring wing they rise
As Emulation nerves them for the skies.
See Pætus' wife,[3] by strong affection manned,
Taste the sharp steel and give it to his hand:
But what avails? On Rome's exhausted soil   200
Nor patriots' fattening blood, nor heroes' toil,
One plant, one stem, of generous growth may rear
To grace the dark December of her year.
Whelmed in the flood of vice, one putrid heap,
Rank, sex, age, race, are hurried to the deep;   205

---

1   The Roman Senate caused a temple to *Female Fortune* to be erected on
    the spot where the wife and mother of Coriolanus met him, and pre-
    vailed upon him to return. Some new privileges were also granted to the
    women on that occasion. [L.A.] The narrative of the life of Coriolanus,
    believed to be a Roman soldier who lived in the 5th century BCE, is
    told by Livy and Plutarch, and forms the basis for Shakespeare's late
    play (1605–08). According to these accounts, Coriolanus' mother con-
    vinces her son not to invade Rome; women are then celebrated in Rome
    as instruments of public safety.
2   Cornelia was the mother of the Gracchi (Tiberius (168–133 BCE) and
    Gaius (190–100 BCE)). She devoted herself to raising her sons for
    heroic military careers and was a model of Roman motherhood. Portia
    (or Porcia) was the daughter of Cato Uticensis and the wife of Marcus
    Brutus (the murderer of Caesar). She was an ardent supporter of
    Republican liberties, and stabbed herself before Brutus to show him that
    it was not so hard to die for the cause of freedom.
3   Arria (d. 42 CE) was the wife of Caecina Paetus, who was condemned to
    death for his role in a conspiracy against the emperor Claudius. Deter-
    mined not to survive her husband, Arria stabbed herself and handed the
    dagger to her husband with the remark, "Paetus, it doesn't hurt."

Low-bending sycophant and upstart knave,
Athlete and mime, loose dame and minion slave.
Wild in the frighted rear the crowds recoil,
Urged by the barbarous brood of war and spoil;
Nearer and nearer yet, with harpy rush   210
They sweep; they pounce, they violate, they crush;
Flap their triumphant wings o'er grovelling Rome,
And roost in Glory's desolated home.
Scared at the portent, see the phantom train
Veil their wreathed brows; then, rising in disdain,   215
With thunders borne upon the howling wind,
Leave Rome and all her infamy behind.

Is frighted Virtue then for ever fled
To veil in heaven her scorned and houseless head,
While Vice and Misery lord it here below   220
O'er God's waste scene of bliss and beauty? No!
Virtue, pure essence mingled with the whole,
Its subtle, viewless, all-inspiring soul,....
Virtue, the mental world's pervading fire,
Unquenched remains, or nature must expire.   225
Now fresh and strong in renovated rays
She flings on eastern hills the glorious blaze;
Now, wrapt in richer lustre, slopes her beams
Tranquil and sweet along the western streams;
Now, with faint twinkling of a single star,   230
She greets the guideless pilgrim from afar;
And red with anger now, a dreadful form,
She glares in lightning through the howling storm.

From Juda's rocks[1] the sacred light expands,
And beams and broadens into distant lands;   235
Heaven's thunder speaks, the mighty bolt is hurled;
Pride, bite the dust! and quake, thou guilty world!
But, O ye weak, beneath a master's rod
Trembling and prostrate, own a helping God!
Ardent in faith, through bonds and toil and loss   240

---

1   Judah, the southernmost of two kingdoms remaining after the division
    of the kingdom of Jews that occurred under Rehoboam, was continually
    at war with the northern kingdom Israel. In the Bible, Judah (931–586
    BC), whose capital was Jerusalem and whose dynasty was the house of
    David, is portrayed as more loyal to God than Israel.

Bear the glad tidings, triumph in the cross!
Away with woman's fears! proud man shall own
As proud a mate on Virtue's loftiest throne;
On to the death in joy.... for Jesus' sake
Writhed on the rack, or blackening at the stake,   245
Scorn the vain splendours of the world below,
And soar to bliss that only martyrs know![1]

Now comrades, equals, in the toilsome strife,
Partners of glory and coheirs of life,
See sex to sex with port sublimer turn,   250
And steadier flames and holier ardours burn;
At God's pure altar pledged, the nuptial band
Turns to a lifelong vow, and dreads no severing hand;
E'en death, they deem, (once sped the second blow
That social lays the sad survivor low,   255
Shrouds the dissolving forms in kindred gloom,
Mingles in dust and marries in the tomb,)
With stronger, purer, closer ties shall bind
The blest communion of the immortal mind,
Free the winged soul to larger bliss above,   260
And ope the heaven of everlasting love.

O faith, O hope divine! ordained to flow
A stream of comfort through the vales of woe!
Rise, mystic dove! explore on venturous wing

---

1   "Viros cum Mucio, vel cum Aquilio, aut Regulo comparo? *Pueri et
     Mulierculæ* nostræ cruces et tormenta, feras, et omnes suppliciorum ter-
     riculas inspiratâ patientiâ doloris illudunt." Minucius Felix. Do I
     compare our men with Mucius or Aquilius, or Regulus? Even our *Boys
     and Women*, with an inspired patience of suffering, deride crosses and
     racks, wild beasts, and all the terrors of punishment. [L.A.]
         Minucius Felix, a native of the Roman province of Africa, lived
     between the mid-second and mid-third century CE and hailed the mar-
     tyrdoms of the Early Christians in his *Octavius*. Mucius: Gaius Mucius
     Scaevola was a heroic Roman warrior who held his hand in fire to
     demonstrate his imperviousness to pain. Aquilius: Manius Aquilius was
     a consul who crushed a slave revolt in Sicily (101 BCE), but was later
     tortured to death by Mithridates, who poured molten gold down his
     throat. Regulus: Marcus Atilius Regulus defeated the Carthaginians
     (256 BCE), but was tortured to death when he returned with a peace
     treaty. In her *Memoirs of the Court of King James*, Aikin engages in a
     lengthy diatribe against state-sponsored torture: II: 158–171.

The wastes of winter and the wilds of spring;   265
Bear back thine olive from the emerging strand,
Restore the virtues, and redeem the land:
Rebel no more, again repentant man
Shall own, shall bless, the mighty Maker's plan;
Heaven's warmest beam salute his second birth,   270
And one wide Eden round the peopled earth.
Vain hope! the wretch, or slave or tyrant born,
Who looked with terror up, or down with scorn,
Untaught to hope in that all-seeing mind
Unbounded love with boundless power combined,   275
Self-judged, self-doomed, a timorous outcast trod,
Nor dared to claim a father in his God:
Hence, Superstition, spleenful, doting, blind,
Thy mystic horrors shake his palsied mind;
Hence, as thy baleful spells in misty gloom   280
Wrap the fair earth and dim her orient bloom,
'Wildered, the maniac eyes a fancied waste,
And starves 'mid banquets that he dares not taste.
The yawning cloister shows its living grave,
Receives the trembler, and confirms him.... slave.   285
And thee, O woman, formed with smiling mien
To temper man, and gild the social scene,....
Bid home-born blessings, home-born virtues rise,
And light the sunbeam in a husband's eyes,....
Thy dearest bliss the sound of infant mirth,   290
His heart thy chief inheritance on earth,....
Thee too, as fades around heaven's blessed light,
And age to age rolls on a darker night,
With steely gripe the exulting hag invades,
And drags relentless to her sullen shades: 295
O hear the sighs that break the sluggish air
Mixt with the convent hymn, the convent prayer,
The languid lip-devotion of despair!

But ne'er could cloister rule or midnight bell,
Penance, or fast, in dank and lonesome cell,   300
Break the mind's spring, or stupefy to rest
The master-passion of an ardent breast.
In that dim cell the rapt Theresa lies
Ingulft and lost in speechless ecstasies;

All-powerful Love has lit the holy flame,   305
The fewel altered, but the fire the same.[1]

Her fearful nuns see dark-browed Clara school,
And tight and tighter strain her rigid rule:
Claims not the Thirst of Sway his lion's part
E'en in that pale ascetic's bloodless heart?[2]   310

Hail, lofty Catharine, visionary maid!
Carest by princes, by a pope obeyed;
Nor blush to own, though dead to all below,
A brave ambition and a patriot glow.[3]

---

1 Saint Theresa, born in Old Castile in 1515; a nun, and one of the most
   enthusiastic of devotees. She thus describes her feelings in a Life of
   herself: "In this representation which I made to place myself near to
   Christ, there would come suddenly upon me, without either expectation
   or preparation on my part, such an evident feeling of the presence of
   God, as that I could by no means doubt, but that either he was within
   me, or else I all engulfed in him. This was not in the manner of a vision,
   but I think they call it Mystical Theology; and it suspends the soul in
   such sort, that she seems to be wholly out of herself. The will is in the
   act of loving, the memory seems to be in a manner lost, the understand-
   ing in my opinion discourses not; and although it be not lost, yet it
   works not, as I was saying, but remains as it were amazed to consider
   how much it understands." [L.A.]
2 Saint Clara, a celebrated abbess, born at Assisi in 1193. She put herself
   under the direction of St. Francis d'Assisi, and by his assistance founded
   a convent of which she became abbess. Her whole life appears to have
   been employed in the work of enforcing cloister discipline; but rigid as
   was the *rule* she imposed upon her nuns, Clara went far beyond it in the
   austerities she practised upon herself. Pope Innocent IV visited this
   abbess in her last moments, and soothed her departing spirit by the
   assurance that her *rule* should never in after times be mitigated. [L.A.]
3 "Saint Catharine of Sienna was born in the city whence she takes her
   name in 1347. She vowed virginity at eight years of age, and soon after
   assumed the Dominican habit. She became famous for her revelations;
   and being ingenious, a good writer for her age, and distinguished for
   piety and charity, her influence was considerable. She went to Avignon
   to procure a reconciliation between the Florentines and Pope Gregory
   XI, who had excommunicated them; and by her eloquence she per-
   suaded that pontiff to restore the papal seat to Rome after it had been
   seventy years at Avignon. Gregory however lived to repent of the step,
   and on his deathbed exhorted all persons present not to (*continued*)

But cease! of amorous worship, bigot pride,   315
Distorted virtue, talent misapplied,
No more:.... with anxious heart and straining mind
Long have I scanned the annals of the kind;
Here let me pause, o'erwearied and opprest;
Thou, my calm friend, thou moralize the rest.   320

EPISTLE IV

ARGUMENT OF EPISTLE IV

Recurrence to the subject—many varieties of female condition
still unnoticed—ancient German women—inhabitants of the
Haram—Hindoo widow—fascinating French woman—English
mother. Survey of a Turkish haram—mean and childish charac-
ter of the women, haughty yet contemptible one of the men—
fatal effects of polygamy—Man cannot degrade the female sex
without degrading the whole race. Ancient Germans—their
women free and honoured—hence the valour of the men, the
virtue of both sexes, the success of their resistance to Rome.
Chivalry personified and depicted—his valour—his devotion to
the ladies, his pure and romantic love—his lady described as
endowed with all virtues and graces, but found to be a visionary
being, only existing in the Fairy land of Spenser—contrasted by
the giddy and unprincipled women introduced into the French
court by Francis I. Gallantry, the parasite and treacherous cor-
ruptor of the sex—Man always suffers by degrading woman—
public freedom dependent on domestic virtue. Switzerland virtu-
ous when first made free—virtuous still, though opprest by
France—Swiss women died fighting for their country. France not
pure enough for freedom, yet had some heroines—Cordé—
Roland. Transition to England—address to the author's female
companions—survey of its female characters from the earliest
times. Boadicea—Ethelfleda. Revival of letters gives consequence
to women—Sir Thomas More and his daughter—Lady Jane

---

credit visions of private persons, acknowledging that he himself had
been deceived by an enthusiast, and foresaw that it would produce evil
consequences to the church. In the schism that succeeded, Catharine
adhered to Urban VI. She died in 1380, and was canonized by Pope
Pius II in 1461. There is extant of hers a volume of 'Italian letters,'
written to popes, princes, cardinals, &c., besides several devotional
pieces." General Biography. [L.A.]

Grey—Queen Elizabeth—Mrs. Hutchinson—Lady R
meration concluded—Exhortation to Englishmen
favour on the mental improvement of females—to
women to improve and principle their minds, and by their me.
induce the men to treat them as friends. Valediction.

Fain would I greet my gentle friend again;
Yet how renew, or where conclude, the strain?
Still as I gaze what mingled throngs appear!
What varying accents rush upon my ear!
Stern, awful, chaste, in savage freedom bred,   5
Here, German matrons shout o'er Varus dead;[1]
There, languid beauties, 'mid a haram's gloom,
In jealous bickerings pine away their bloom;
Here, well-dissembling, with a decent pride,
The victim-widow laves in Ganges' tide,   10
Clasps the loathed corse, invites the dreaded flame,
And dies in anguish, not to live with shame.
I turn, and meet the animated glance
Shot by the dames of gay seductive France;
Then melting catch the gaze, so fond, so mild,   15
Some English mother bends upon her child.
A thought, a look, a line, the meanest ask
To swell my growing tale, and lengthen out my task.

A glorious task! were mine the godlike power,
By Genius snatched in some propitious hour,   20
To bid the fleeting airy forms be still,
Or move, or change, obedient to my will;
Then fix the groupe, and pour in living light
Its vivid picture on the enraptured sight,
And bid it speak, in forceful tones and clear,   25
To Truth and Feeling just, to Fancy dear.
It may not be:.... my fainter sketch shall glide
Like dim reflections on an evening tide;
My task like hers, the soft Corinthian maid,

---

1 Publius Quintilius Varus (d. 9 CE), a Roman general, was appointed
    governor of Germany by Augustus. He led three Roman legions against
    German uprisings where they were massacred by the troops of
    Arminius. Varus then committed suicide.

To trace a tintless shadow of a shade![1]　　　　　30
But to that shade fond fancy would supply
The bloom, the grace, the all-expressive eye;
Still would she gaze, till swam her cheated sight,
And the true lover blessed her wild delight.
Me such bright dreams delude not:.... thoughtful, cold,　　35
The fading lines I languidly behold;
But thou, my friend, assert the generous part,
O praise, O foster, with a partial heart!
So shall the power my happier pencil guide,
And Friendship grant me what the Muse denied.　　　40

Come, pierce with me the Haram's jealous walls:
I see, I see, the soul-degraded thralls!
With childlike smile, one glittering dame surveys
Her splendid *caftan* and her diamonds' blaze;
One spreads the *henna*; one with sable dye　　　45
Wakes the dim lustre of her languid eye;[2]
Some seek the bath:.... O life, are these thy joys?
These all thy cares? How the dull prospect cloys!
Yet turn not from the view; deign first to scan
That lordly thing, the Asiatic Man.　　　　　50
O speaking lesson! marked with grateful awe;
Self is his God, his wildest will is law;
Him Beauty serves, all emulous to bless;
Yet where his envied, dear-bought happiness?
'Tis his,.... each proud, each manly virtue wreckt,　　55
Truth, science, freedom lost in base neglect,....
A pampered slave, in lazy state to sit
Shut from the sun of reason and of wit,
By senses cloyed of sensual bliss bereft,
And a dull drug his only refuge left.　　　　60
One equal sole companion, skilled to blend
In one dear name the mistress and the friend,
Was Nature's boon; but when insatiate Man

1　In classical legend, the origin of painting is attributed to a young woman
　of Corinth who, seeing the shadow of her beloved on the wall, traced
　the outline of his head.
2　The caftan is an upper robe of rich materials worn by the Turkish ladies.
　Henna, or alkanet, is a drug employed by them to tinge red the ends of
　the fingers and the inside of the hand. They increase the apparent lustre
　of the eye by introducing, within the edge of the eyelid, crude antimony
　in powder. [L.A.]

Grasps wider joys, and scorns her sacred plan,
Farewell life's loveliest charm, farewell the glow   65
Affection casts upon the scene below;
Farewell each finer art, each softer grace,
All that adorns and all that lifts the race!
Woman no more, a deed-inspiring mate,
Shall fan the kindling glories of the state;   70
Suspicion's evil eye, with dire control,
Blights all the fairest blossoms of her soul,
And bids each rankling thorn, each poisonous weed,
A hostile crop, by righteous doom succeed.
Man, stamp the moral on thy haughty mind: 75
Degrade the sex, and thou degrad'st the kind!¹
Mark the bold contrast! hail, my friend, with me
The generous son of German liberty:
Barbarian? Yes: To spread the winged sail
Of venturous Commerce to the speeding gale,   80
To urge his ploughshare o'er the conquered soil,
And earn from Culture's hand the meed of toil,
As yet he knew not; nurst amid alarms,
His care was freedom, his rude trade was arms:
But this he knew; to woman's feeling heart   85

---

1 The following passage is cited in confirmation of the sentiments here
expressed, from Mr. Southey's noble and eloquent introduction to his
translation of The Chronicle of the Cid. "The continuance of polygamy
was his (Mahommed's) great and ruinous error: where this pernicious
custom is established, there will be neither connubial, nor paternal, nor
brotherly affection; and hence the unnatural murders with which Asiatic
history abounds. The Mahommedan imprisons his wives, and some-
times knows not the faces of his own children; he believes that despot-
ism must be necessary in the state, because he knows it to be necessary
at home: thus the domestic tyrant becomes the contented slave, and the
atrocity of the ruler and the patience of the people proceed from the
same cause. It is the inevitable tendency of polygamy to degrade both
sexes: wherever it prevails, the intercourse between them is merely
sexual. Women are only instructed in wantonness, sensuality becomes
the characteristic of whole nations, and humanity is disgraced by crimes
the most loathsome and detestable. This is the primary and general
cause of that despotism and degradation which are universal throughout
the East." &c. [L.A.] Rodrigo Díaz de Vivar (c. 1040–99), known as El
Cid Campeador, is considered the national hero of Spain. He is
renowned for his military conquest of Valencia, which he wrested from
Moorish control. Robert Southey was poet laureate from 1813 to his
death in 1843.

Its best its dearest tribute to impart;
Not the cheap falsehoods of a flattering strain,
Not idle gauds, vain incense to the vain;
But such high fellowship, such honoured life
As throws a glory round the exulting wife,   90
Seats her revered, sublime, on Virtue's throne,
Judge of his honour, guardian of her own.[1]
Dear was to him the birthright of the free;
More welcome death than her captivity;
And hence his valour's rude but vigorous stroke   95
Stunned Rome, and snapped her vainly-fitted yoke;[2]
(So swells Araxes[3] foaming in his pride,
So wrecks the insulting Spanner of his tide;)
And still he lives along the warning page
Of piercing Tacitus:[4] ... Prophetic Sage!   100
With awe, with envy, with a patriot dread,
He saw the Western Genius lift his head;
Marked his large limbs to bracing hardship bared,
His stubborn mind for worst extremes prepared;
Marked the chaste virtues of his frugal home,   105
And read the destinies of stooping Rome.[5]

---

1 "These too (the women) are the most respected witnesses, the most
   liberal applauders of every man's conduct. The warriors come and show
   their wounds to their mothers and wives, who are not shocked at count-
   ing, and even requiring them." Tacit. de Morib. vii. [Tacitus, *Germania*,
   7] Aikin's translation. [L.A.]
2 "Tradition relates, that armies beginning to give way have been brought
   again to the charge by the females, through the earnestness of their sup-
   plications, the interposition of their bodies, and the pictures they have
   drawn of impending slavery,.... a calamity which these people bear with
   more impatience for their women than for themselves; so that those
   states who have been obliged to give among their hostages the daughters
   of noble families, are most effectually bound to fidelity." Ibid. viii. [L.A.]
3 Aras is a river in Turkey. In Greco-Roman times it was the major trade
   route from the Caspian Sea to Asia Minor.
4 Cornelius Tacitus (c. 55–after 117 CE) was a great Roman historian, the
   author of *Germania, Annals* and *Histories* of the Roman emperors.
5 "May the nations retain and perpetuate, if not an affection for us, at
   least an animosity against each other! since, while the fate of the empire
   is thus urgent, fortune can bestow no higher benefit upon us than the
   discord of our enemies." Ibid. xxxiii. et pass. [L.A.]

From Elbe and Weser,[1] or some unknown North
Derived, what bold yet courteous form rides forth
To view? At all points armed, with lance in rest,
Gilded his spurs, and plumed his haughty crest;   110
One steel-clad arm uprears a silver shield,
"Such is my faith!" upon its burnisht field
The motto quaint; its fond device, a heart
That burns and bleeds with Cupid's fiery dart.
Claspt to his mailed breast he bears a glove,   115
Dear parting token of his lady-love:
At speed he comes; he 'lights, he bends the knee
Proud where she sits.... It is, 'tis Chivalry!....
Love's gallant martyr! Honour's generous child!
Thy bright extravagance, thy darings wild,   120
O who may think by pedant rules to try
That owns a woman's heart, a poet's eye;
An eye by Glory's dazzling glance controled,
A coward heart that dotes upon the bold?
How dear the contrast! he, whose haughty brow   125
Scowls on the pride of man, nor deigns to bow;
Stung by a look, who challenges the strife
Where angry comrades stake the bauble, life;
Humble and suppliant bows her scorn to meet,
And soothes himself to meekness at her feet: 130
Then, at a word, again her own true knight
Tilts for her fame, or combats in her right.

Courts, tourneys, camps, high dames, a dazzling train,
A masque of glory, danced before his brain;
He lived in trance, and so the enchantment wrought   135
That 'mid the high illusions of his thought
Passion grew worship, and his heart a shrine
Where Beauty reigned all awful and divine;
Where steadfast, pure, Love burned a sacred flame;
Long years it burned, unquenchably the same,   140
Fed but on looks, and fanned with suppliant breath,
To her whose smile was life, whose frown was death.
But she, his Goddess; how may fancy trace
Her bright perfections and amazing grace?
Methinks I see a sweet and holy band,   145
A wreath of hovering Virtues, hand in hand

---

1   Rivers flowing through northern and central Germany.

The new Pandora[1] bless, and on her head
In one rich dower their mingled treasury shed.
Majestic Honour, first, with matron care
Forms her high gait, and dignifies her air;   150
But chasing Pride, sweet Modesty the while
On her cheek blushes, Cheerfulness her smile
Blends with the blush, and innocently free
She learns the look, the tone, of Courtesy.
A thousand Graces in harmonious play   155
Throned in her eyes assert alternate sway;
With frank Benevolence they glance around,
Or dewed by Pity bend upon the ground,
Now seek the skies, by soaring Faith inspired,
Now beam with pure Serenity retired.   160

But say, this paragon, this matchless fair,
Trod she this care-crazed earth? No;.... born of air,
A flitting dream, a rainbow of the mind,
The tempting glory leaves my grasp behind;
Formed for no rugged clime, no barbarous age,   165
She blooms in Fairy land the grace of Spenser's page.[2]

---

1 In Greek mythology, Pandora was the first woman on earth, endowed
   with every "feminine" charm, including curiosity and deceit, which led
   her to open the forbidden box of human evils, thus releasing misery
   upon humanity. Only Hope remained in her box, to console suffering
   humans.

2 On the obscure and much controverted subject of chivalry, I find it nec-
   essary in this place to hazard a few observations. Several circumstances
   convince me, and especially some striking facts in the history of Alboin
   king of the Lombards, and in that of the northern pirates, that a truly
   chivalrous spirit of honour and generosity had been introduced into the
   commerce of warriors with each other, in all the relations of peace and
   war, long before the refinements of gallantry, or even a tolerable
   decency of behaviour towards the weaker sex, came to be considered as
   incumbent on the brave and the noble. I also find that even during
   those ages when the spirit of chivalry is supposed to have been at its
   height, and when a very romantic kind of gallantry did in fact prevail, in
   the times, for instance, commemorated by the narrative of Froissart,
   when, for their ladies' love, a party of young knights took a solemn vow
   to keep one of their eyes blinded with a silken patch till they should
   have achieved some signal deed of arms,.... manners were still gross, and
   morals extremely corrupt. In France, the nuptial tie, seldom cemented
   by mutual preference and inclination, has in no age been sufficient to

Not such the dames with revelry and sport
Who tripped the wanton maze of Gallia's court,
By love and Francis[1] lured in evil hour
From hearths domestic and the sheltering bower.   170
New to the discipline of good and ill,
Unformed of manners, impotent of will,
What thirst of empire seized the giddy train!
Man bowed obsequious, and deferred the rein;
(So Mars on Venus smiled in courts above,   175
So crouched in all the loyalty of love,)
Ah! feigned humility to scorn allied,
That stoops to conquer, flatters to deride!
Learn, thoughtless woman, learn his arts to scan,
And dread that fearful portent.... kneeling Man!   180
Dread the gay form whom now, her favourite birth,

---

restrain the wanderings of the imagination, or preserve the innocency of
domestic life. In Spain, an absurd spirit of jealous rigour long fostered
in both sexes the taste for clandestine amours; and the Spanish or Por-
tuguese author of Amadis de Gaul, accounted the most moral as well as
popular work of its kind, has represented his adorable and peerless
Oriana herself as more fortunate in the constancy of her lover, but not
more discreet in her loves, than the hapless Dido of ancient story. In
England and the northern parts of the continent, if morals were some-
what more pure during these ages than in the south, manners were still
more coarse. I am compelled to infer, that it was not till knight errantry,
ceasing to exist in reality, had become a frame for the poetic fictions of a
dignified and learned age, that it assumed the pure and lofty character
which delights us in the beautiful coinage of Spenser's brain, stamped
with the impress of all the Virtues, and superscribed with the titles of a
Maiden Queen. [see Edmund Spenser, *The Faerie Queene* (1956)] [L.A.]
Alboin (c. 530–72) was king of the Lombards, who settled his people
through conquest in northern Italy. Alboin forced his second wife,
Rosamund, to marry him after killing her father (also a king). Jean
Froissart (c. 1337–1405) is an important chronicler of medieval France.
The Amadis de Gaul is a Castilian tale of knight-errantry, written at the
beginning of the fourteenth century. Aikin compares the heroine of this
tale, Oriana, to Dido (who, according to ancient Greek and Roman
sources, is the founder and first queen of Carthage), as both were said
to have had sexual relations with their lovers outside marriage. Dido is
"hapless" as she is abandoned by her lover Aeneas; she is believed to
have committed suicide as a result.

1 Gallia is France. Francis I (1494–1547) was a King of France noted for
liberality, patronage of the arts, and submission to the political influence
of his numerous mistresses.

Some smiling mischief trusts upon the earth
Veiled in a scented cloud;.... it melts, and see
Come dancing forth the phantom Gallantry.
His are the lowly bow, the adoring air,   185
The attentive eye that dwells upon the fair;
His the soft tone to grace a tender tale,
And his the flattering sighs that more prevail;
His the whole art of love: ... but all is art,
For kindly Nature never warmed his heart;   190
No hardy knight with wrong-redressing brand
He roams on Honour's pilgrimage the land;
No awful champion vowed to Virtue's aid
He flings his buckler o'er the trembling maid;
No high enthusiast to his peerless love   195
He plights pure vows and registered above;....
Canker of Innocence! he lives at ease,
His only care his wanton self to please:
Hymen's dear tie, for him a sordid league
Knit by Ambition, Avarice, or Intrigue,   200
He scorns, he tramples, and insulting bears
To other shrines his incense and his prayers;
There, skilled in perfidy, he hangs to view
A hundred fopperies Passion never knew....
Liveries that love by telegraph convey,[1]   205
Lines traced in blood, and quaint acrostic lay....
Poor trifles all; ... but trifles poor as these
Cheat the cold heart, the vagrant fancy seize,
From sober love, from faithful duty wean,
And sell to fear and sin the fancied queen.   210

Thus woman sinks, withdrawn each thin pretence,
The dupe of Vanity, the slave of Sense:
The light seducer, with brief rapture fraught,
Smiles on her prostrate dignity of thought,
And boasts his deeper wiles, his keener art,   215
Lord of the fond, confiding, female heart.
Vain boast, as profligate! he too shall find,
The sex dishonoured, Honour scorns the kind;
For never yet with cap and oaken crown,
Symbol of joy and charter of renown,   220

---

1   The emblematical meaning given to different colours, once so familiar
    to the gallant and the fair, is here alluded to. [L.A.]

Has man-exalting Freedom deigned to grace
A spurious rabble and adulterous race,
Steept in corruption, destined to be base.

Pure was the heart of Switzerland, when Tell[1]
Aimed the avenging shaft, and cried "Rebel!"   225
Pure was the self-devoted blood that dyed
The mangled breast of her bold Winkelreid;
Pure were the mountain homes whence foaming out
The patriot-torrent rushed, and gave the rout,
Where rose the pile of bones to tell mankind[2]   230
"This monument the Spoiler left behind."
Nor Virtue yet had fled her rock-built bower
When Gaul's intruding Demon, drunk with power,
Burst on that paradise: appalled he found
A Spartan fortitude embattled round;   235
Rapt by a fine despair, the maid, the wife,
Charged by their heroes' side and fired the strife....
The strife victorious;.... but opprest, betrayed,
Fell the brave patriot few.... no friend to aid.
Then, spotless victims of a doom severe,   240
They died upon their murdered country's bier;
Died not in vain,.... to stamp on that proud name
The weight of vengeance and the curse of shame.[3]

---

1 William Tell was a legendary Swiss patriot who inspired rebellion
   against an Austrian bailiff who, in 1307, gave Tell the choice of shooting
   an apple off the head of his son with an arrow or imprisonment.
2 The pile of bones was at Morat, where the duke of Burgundy was
   defeated by the Swiss. It was at the battle of Sempach that Arnold
   Winkelreid, recommending his family to that country for which he
   devoted himself, rushed upon a wedge of Austrian spears, and, burying
   as many of them as he could grasp, in his own body, thereby made a
   passage for the Swiss, who could not before bring their shorter weapons
   to bear upon the enemy; through which they advanced and slaughtered
   the invaders. [L.A.] Arnold Winkelreid is a legendary Swiss hero,
   famous for his act of self-sacrifice. There is, however, no historical
   record to substantiate his existence or that of his deed.
3 After the last struggle of the democratic Cantons against the hordes of
   France, many females were found among the slain. [L.A.] Until the
   invasion of Napoleon in 1798, Switzerland was a loose federation of
   largely independent small states called cantons that had existed from the
   late thirteenth century until 1798.

Plant thy bright eagles o'er each prostrate realm,
Audacious France! and headlong from his helm   245
Each dozing steersman dash,.... but hope not thou,
Amid the plundered baubles of thy brow,
To twine a wreath from Freedom's sacred tree:
It blooms with virtue, but it dies with thee.

Once we had hope. When Tyranny and Wrong   250
Had stung thy patient bosom deep and long,
To vengeance roused, a generous short-lived red
Flushed o'er thy cheek, and all the wanton fled:
And failed thy daughters then? No, by thy hand,
Devoted brave Cordé![1] No, pure Roland!   255
No, by thy high "Appeal," thy parting breath,
Thy sage's fortitude, thy patriot's death![2]

But blest the land where ages glide away,
And not a single heroine starts today:
'Tis angry skies must nurse that daring form,   260
As billows rock the Petrel[3] of the Storm:
Domestic virtue, femininely frail,
Courts the pure azure and the summer gale,
A brooding Halcyon,[4] on her island-nest
Lulled on old Neptune's[5] pleased pacific[6] breast.   265

---

1   Charlotte Corday (1768–93), who supported the Girondists (a moder-
    ate republican party during the French Revolution), assassinated Marat,
    leader of the much more radical Jacobins, on 13 July 1793, because of
    his role in the Reign of Terror. She was herself guillotined on 17 July
    1793.
2   Madame Roland's "Appeal to impartial Posterity," containing memoirs
    of her own life, is here alluded to; and her apostrophe to the statue of
    Liberty, on passing it in her way to the guillotine, "O Liberty, how many
    horrors are perpetrated in thy name!" Her noble fortitude during her
    imprisonment was also conspicuous. [L.A.] Madame Roland (1754–93)
    was, together with her husband, an influential member of the Girondist
    faction. Roland fell out of favor during the reign of terror and died on
    the guillotine on 8 November 1793.
3   Small seabird.
4   Kingfisher, anciently fabled to breed in a nest floating at sea.
5   Classical god of the sea.
6   Peaceful, calm.

Such lot is ours, so rests our rock-bound isle,
A soft asylum reared in ocean's smile.
Thither fond Fancy flies, with busy care
Decks forth the scene, and paints it fresh and fair;
Soft Memory comes, adds every touching grace,   270
The form familiar, and the well-known face;
Quick beats my heart, mine eyes with rapture stream,
And truth and daylight burst upon my dream.

Rapt while I stand, my weary wanderings past,
Like some poor exile, welcomed home at last,   275
You, you I hail, dear playmates, who with me
Led the blind game, or wove the dance of glee;
(Fond mothers now, who watch with tenderer joy
Your tottering girl, or prompt your lisping boy;)
And rapt, inspired, beyond the trick of art,   280
Trace English manners with an English heart.
But not alone one fleeting speck of time
Shall flash in my contemporary rhyme;
Our sex's honour, and our country's weal,
Past or to come, this patriot breast must feel;   285
O'er the long lapse of years these eyes must roll,
And all its mazes agitate my soul:
For who that marks along the valley gleam
The silver waves of some majestic stream,
Served by a hundred rills, that winds along   290
Pride of the land and theme of poet's song,
Burns not, enamoured of the scene, to climb
Some airy mount, contemplative, sublime,
Whence all its sweeps, its whole expanding course;
Trackt from its small and weed-entangled source   295
To that wide rush of waves that spreads the plain
Where mists o'erhang its marriage with the main,
With eagle-ken in fleet succession caught,
May fill at once the hunger of his thought?

Like Ceres maddening on her car-borne way,   300
Her virgin daughter snatcht in face of day,
The fierce Bonduca, brave and injured queen,
In fire and carnage wraps the blasted scene,
And bids her barbarous wrongs, her vengeful rage,

Tell the dark story of the Roman age.[1]   305
Roused at her call, yon rude and frantic band
Yell round their Mona's violated strand,
Dire with funereal weeds and streaming hair,
And lurid torches tost with angry glare:
The chilled invader bows his pallid face,   310
And deprecates the Furies of the place.[2]
Hail, Ethelfleda! On his Alfred's child
The parting Genius gazed, and fondly smiled;
Wise in the council, dauntless in the fight,
She streaks the gloom and sheds a troubled light,   315
A beacon fire, whose fitful gleams display
The raging Dane, and England's evil day.[3]

But few our Amazons. While Egypt bleeds,
And Syrian echoes ring of Richard's deeds,

---

1   The outrages and insults inflicted upon Boadica and her daughters by
    the Romans, and the sanguinary vengeance taken by her upon the
    Roman colonies, are sufficiently known to every reader of early British
    history. [L.A.] Ceres was the Roman goddess of grain and fertility.
    Bonduca (also Boadica, Boudicca, or Boudicea) was queen of the Iceni
    (ancient Britons) and took poison in 62 CE after being defeated by the
    Romans.
2   When Suetonius Paulinus landed his army on the island of Mona,
    "there stood along the beach," says Tacitus, "a thick and mingled crowd
    of men and arms; the women running up and down like Furies with
    funereal garb, dishevelled hair, uplifted torches; whilst the Druids
    around, hurling forth dire imprecations, their hands raised to heaven, so
    affrighted the soldiers with the strangeness of their appearance, that they
    stood as if stupefied, affording a motionless body to the weapons of the
    enemy." Annal. xiv. 30. [L.A.] In 61 Suetonius made an assault on
    Mona (the Welsh Isle of Anglesey), a refuge for British fugitives and
    druids. The revolt was led by Boadica.
3   "In all these noble toils for the defence and security of his dominions,
    Edward (the elder) was greatly assisted by his sister Ethelfleda, widow of
    Ethered governor of Mercia. This heroic princess (who inherited more
    of the spirit of the great Alfred than any of his children), despising the
    humble cares and trifling amusements of her own sex, commanded
    armies, gained victories, built cities, and performed exploits which
    would have done honour to the greatest princes. Having governed
    Mercia eight years after the death of her husband, she died AD 920, and
    Edward took the government of that country into his own hand."
    [Robert] Henry's Hist. of Britain [1788], vol. iii. p. 93. [L.A.]

Edwards and Henries with victorious lance   320
Bear down the lily in the field of France,
And York and Lancaster with rival hate
Shake at the deep foundations of the state,
(Bred of intestine fires, the earthquake's shock
So strews the forest, splits the solid rock,)   325
Our timorous mothers, from invading strife
Wrapt in a meek monotony of life,
Humbly content to pace with duteous round
Their little world,.... the dear domestic ground,....
Wards of protecting Man, nor dared to claim,   330
Nor dared to wish, the dangerous meed of fame,
Till, snatcht in triumph from his ancient tomb,
The lamp of Learning blazed upon the gloom,
And wide around to kindling hope revealed
The bloodless contests of a nobler field,   335
And courteous Wisdom to the bashful throng
Waved his pure hand, and beckoned them along.

Thou gav'st the call, O England's martyred sage!
O More! the grief and glory of thy age!
Bounteous as Nature's self, thy heart assigned   340
Its own large charter to a daughter's mind;
Spread with adventurous hand its swelling sails
Free to the breath of Greek and Roman gales,
And heaped its freight with riches, dug or wrought
In mines of science and in looms of thought.   345
Splendid example! fame that shall not fade!
Large debt, in gratitude how fondly paid!
She, she it was, when that stern tyrant's breath
Doomed thy firm virtue to the axe of death,
Burst the mute throng to snatch a last farewell,   350
And pale and shrieking on thy bosom fell;
Weeping who clasped thy knees, and felt it sweet
To kiss in dust thy consecrated feet;
Called thy soul back, that winged her flight above,
And drew thy latest looks of sorrowing love.[1]   355

---

1 Sir Thomas More [1478-1535] is highly commended by Erasmus for
   making his daughters partakers in all the benefits of a learned educa-
   tion. His favourite daughter, Margaret, wife of William Roper, esq.
   "became a mistress of the Greek and Latin languages, of arithmetic, and
   the sciences then generally taught, and of various musical   (*continued*)

Rise, gentle Grey! forth from the sainted dead
Lift the meek honours of thy victim-head!
Mockt with no pageant-rule, no vain renown,
Take thy due homage, take thy lasting crown!
O ripe in suffering, fair in spotless truth!   360
The fruits of Virtue with the flowers of Youth
Shall wreath thy brow, and Learning to thy hand
Yield his large scroll, thy sceptre of command,
While Wisdom hears thy parting accents mild,
And cries, "Behold me honoured in my child!"[1]   365

The dread Eliza bids. Wake, O my strain!
Wake the long triumph of the Maiden Reign:[2]

---

instruments. She wrote with elegance both in English and Latin. In the latter her style was so pure, that cardinal Pole could scarcely be brought to believe that her compositions were the work of a female. Her reverence and affection for her father were unbounded. After his head had been exposed during fourteen days upon London bridge, she found means to procure it, and, preserving it carefully in a leaden box, gave directions that it should be placed in her arms when she was buried; which was accordingly done." The scene particularly referred to is thus related. After receiving sentence Sir Thomas More was conveyed to the Tower. "At the Tower-wharf, his favourite daughter, Mrs. Roper, was waiting to take her last farewell of him. At his approach, she burst through the throng, fell on her knees before her father, and, closely embracing him, could only utter, 'My father, oh my father!' He tenderly returned her embrace, and, exhorting her to patience, parted from her. She soon in a passion of grief again burst through the crowd, and clung round his neck in speechless anguish. His firmness was now overcome; tears flowed plentifully down his cheeks, till with a final kiss she left him." General Biography. [ed. Richmond Mangnall], 1805. [L.A.]

1 A more illustrious instance than that afforded by lady Jane Grey, of the power of learning and philosophy to fortify and tranquillize a youthful and feminine mind under the severest trials, is nowhere to be found. Her dying confession of her fault in not refusing with sufficient steadiness the crown that had been forced upon her, and the willingness she expressed to expiate that fault by death, sufficiently evince her just and magnanimous way of thinking. [L.A.] Lady Jane Grey (1536/7–54) ruled England for just over a week; she was succeeded, and subsequently executed, by Mary I. She came to be regarded as a Protestant martyr.

2 Elizabeth I (1533–1603), Queen of England and Ireland (1558–1603), never married, hence she was known as the Virgin Queen. Elizabeth I

Here Faction, vanquisht terror of the land,
Suppliant to kiss the chastenings of her hand;
(The fiend of Rome with imprecating eye   370
Fang-drawn and chained, and idly muttering by,)
Reviving France with fixt and awful air
Watching her glance, and grateful Henry there:
Here refuged Belgia from the tyrant's frown
Creeps to her knees, and lifts the proffered crown;   375
There gloomy Philip eyes a hostile main,
And o'er his foiled Armada mourns in vain.
High o'er her head the golden censer swings
That wafts all sweetness to the sense of kings;
Her dulcet voice each hymning Muse applies,   380
And the graced mortal half assumes the skies.
But mark pale Mary's vengeful spectre gleam
Clouding the pomp, and dash her glorious dream,
Brand her base envy, blaze each treacherous art,
And bare the meanness of her selfish heart;   385
Stung to the soul, her gallant Essex chide
Her captious favour and exacting pride,
Then bow his neck to death,.... and seem to cry,
"Relentless Mistress, see, despair, and die!"
Yet, O Britannia! on thy glory's car   390
The brightest gem shall flame that Maiden Star,
Queen of th' ascendant, whose propitious ray
Wisdom and wit, and arts and arms obey;
Blest orb, that flashed on Spenser's dazzling sight
Long meteor-streams and trails of fairy-light;   395
Twinkled on Shakespeare's lowly lot, and shed
A smile of love on Bacon's boyish head:

---

was the subject of Aikin's first history, *Memoirs of the Court of Queen Elizabeth* (1818). This stanza alludes to the following events during her reign: her success in sustaining the Protestant claim to the English throne and in foiling Roman Catholic efforts to crown Mary Queen of Scots; her keeping the peace with Henry III of France; her aid to Protestants in the Netherlands (Belgia); her defeat of the Spanish Armada of Philip II in 1588; her execution of rival Mary Queen of Scots in 1587 and her favorite, Robert Devereux, third Earl of Essex, in 1601, after he conspired against her. Elizabeth reigned during the English Renaissance of literature and humanistic learning, led by Edmund Spenser, William Shakespeare, and Francis Bacon. Excerpts from Aikin's *Memoirs*, which allude to some of these events, are included below, see pp. 100-22.

Now gleams the lode-star of our northern skies,
And points our galaxy to distant eyes.

But thou, pure partner of man's noblest cause,   400
Take, generous Hutchinson, this heart's applause:
'Twas thine to stem a foul and angry tide,
A high-souled helpmate at the patriot's side;
Then cast, sad relict! on an angry shore,
All wreckt, all lost, the gallant struggle o'er,   405
Yet, greatly constant to a husband's trust,
True to the joyful memory of the just,
Chide back thy tears, uplift thy mourning head,
And live, the high historian of the dead;
Knock at thy children's breasts, and cry with pride,   410
"Thus lived our patriot, thus our martyr died!"[1]
So virtuous Russell burst the shades of life,
And shone a heroine, for she loved, a wife.
"Grant me but her!" the noble culprit cried,
"No friend, no advocate, I ask beside."   415
Secure in conscious fortitude she rose,
A present aid,.... and checked her gushing woes

---

[1] The admirable Memoirs of Colonel Hutchinson, by his widow, ought to
be known to every reader capable of being warmed to a noble emula-
tion. The work is inscribed to her children, and is introduced by a kind
of dirge, in which after mentioning that some mourners, who have doted
on "mortal excellencies," are only to be consoled by removing every
thing that may "with their remembrance renew their grief," she pro-
ceeds: "But I that am under a command (of her husband at his death)
not to grieve at the common rate of desolate women, while I am study-
ing which way to moderate my woe, and if it were possible to augment
my love, can for the present find out none more iust to your deare father
nor consolatory to myselfe then the preservation of his memory, which I
need not guild with such flattering commendations as the higher
preachers doe equally give to the truly and titulary honourable; a naked
undrest narrative, speaking the simple truth of him, will deck him with
more substantiall glorie, than all the panegyricks the best pens could
ever consecrate to the best men." [L.A.] Lucy Hutchinson (1620–81)
was married to John Hutchinson, one of the signatories to Charles I's
death warrant. Though he escaped punishment for this when the monar-
chy was restored, in part because of his wife's interventions, he was
arrested in 1663 for his alleged involvement in an armed rising. After his
death in captivity the following year, his wife Lucy composed memoirs
of his life to vindicate his reputation. The *Memoirs* were first printed in
1806, and were frequently republished thereafter.

And ruled her trembling hand,.... while all around
A thrill of anguish ran, and mingling cries resound.
Vain every hope; the murderous doom is sped,   420
And Charles and vengeance claim his forfeit head.
But not from life, from only life to part,
Could wring a murmur from that patriot heart;
One dear companion of the darksome way
His eyes require, and mourn her lonely stay: 425
"Farewell, farewell!" he cries, "I look my last,
And now 'tis o'er;.... death's bitterness is past!"[1]
Such were the dames who grace our storied page:
Life's guiding lamp they hand from age to age[2]
Assert their sex beyond the loftiest pen,   430
And live on tongues and reign in hearts of men.
Enough, indulgent Muse! evoke no more
The blissful phantoms from their silent shore,
Nor give again my curious eye to range
O'er times, o'er realms, remote and rude and strange;   435
Yet O be present still! but meek, subdued,
In sober, wistful, contemplative mood:
Her trusted stores while faithful Memory brings,
And Judgement ponders o'er the sum of things,
Aid my full heart, obtest[3] the mingled throng,   440
And point the varied moral of my song.

Sons of fair Albion, tender, brave, sincere,
(Be this the strain) an earnest suppliant hear!
Feel that when heaven, evolved its perfect plan,
Crowned with its last best gift transported Man,   445
It formed no creature of ignoble strain,
Of heart unteachable, obtuse of brain;

---

1 The history of lord William Russell and his lady,—her attendance upon
   him at his trials—his expression after parting with her,—and the other
   traits illustrative of their heroic affection and excelling virtues, are too
   familiarly known to need repetition. [L.A.] Lord William Russell
   (1639–83), known as "the Patriot," was executed in 1683 by King
   Charles II for his supposed participation in the Rye House Plot; William
   III later vindicated his innocence. His wife Rachel Wriothesley
   (1636–1723), Lady Russell, was tireless in her efforts to save his life and
   restore his good name.
2 Life's guiding lamp ...: "Vitai lampada tradunt" [they pass on the lamps
   of life]. Lucretius. [L.A.]
3 Adjure, beg earnestly, supplicate.

(Such had not filled the solitary void,
Nor such his soul's new sympathies employed,)
But one all eloquent of eye, of mien;   450
Intensely human; exquisitely keen
To feel, to know. Be generous then, unbind
Your barbarous shackles, loose the female mind;
Aid its new flights, instruct its wavering wing,
And guide its thirst to Wisdom's purest spring: 455
Sincere as generous, with fraternal heart
Spurn the dark satirist's unmanly part;
Scorn too the flatterer's, in the medium wise,
Nor feed those follies that yourselves despise.

For you, bright daughters of a land renowned,   460
By Genius blest, by glorious Freedom crowned;
Safe in a polisht privacy, content
To grace, not shun, the lot that Nature lent,
Be yours the joys of home, affection's charms,
And infants clinging with caressing arms: 465
Yours too the boon, of Taste's whole garden free,
To pluck at will her bright Hesperian[1] tree,
Uncheckt the wreath of each fair Muse assume,
And fill your lap with amaranthine[2] bloom.
Press eager on; of this great art possest,   470
To seize the good, to follow still the best,
Ply the pale lamp, explore the breathing page,
And catch the soul of each immortal age.
Strikes the pure bard his old romantic lyre?
Let high Belphoebe warm, let Amoret sweet inspire:[3]   475
Does History speak? drink in her loftiest tone,
And be Cornelia's[4] virtues all your own.
Thus self-endowed, thus armed for every state,

---

1 Western or pertaining to the land of the west.

2 Purple flower, in classical mythology, a fadeless, immortal flower.

3 It ought always to be remembered for the honour of Spenser, that no
poet has given such pure and perfect, such noble, lovely, and at the
same time various drafts of female characters. His Belphoebe, his
Amoret, his Canace, his Britomart and his Pastora, are a gallery of por-
traits, all beautiful, but each in a different style from all the rest. [L.A.]
These female characters appear in Edmund Spenser's *The Faerie Queene*
(1596).

4 Mother of the Gracchi, model of Roman motherhood. (See note 2,
p. 75).

Improve, excel, surmount, subdue, your fate!
So shall at length enlightened Man efface   480
That slavish stigma seared on half the race,
His rude forefathers' shame; and pleased confess,
'Tis yours to elevate, 'tis yours to bless;
Your interest one with his; your hopes the same;
Fair peace in life, in death undying fame,   485
And bliss in worlds beyond, the species' general aim.
"Rise," shall he cry, "O Woman, rise! be free!
My life's associate, now partake with me:
Rouse thy keen energies, expand thy soul,
And see, and feel, and comprehend the whole;   490
My deepest thoughts, intelligent, divide;
When right confirm me, and when erring guide;
Soothe all my cares, in all my virtues blend,
And be, my sister, be at length my friend."

Anna, farewell! O spirit richly fraught   495
With all that feeds the noble growth of thought!
(For not the Roman, not the Attic store,
Nor poets' song, nor reverend sages' lore,
To thee a Wakefield's[1] liberal love denied,
His child and friend, his pupil and his pride,)   500
Whose life of female loveliness shall teach
The finisht charm that precept fails to reach;....
Born to delight, instructed to excel,
My judge, my sister, take this heart's farewell!

---

1 Gilbert Wakefield (1756–1801), a biblical scholar and religious contro-
versialist, was the father of Anne Wakefield Aikin, the poem's dedicatee.
A classical scholar, Wakefield taught at Warrington Academy from 1779
to 1783 with Lucy Aikin's aunt and uncle, Anna and Rochemont Bar-
bauld. He was known for his translations of the New Testament, critical
commentaries on the scriptures, *Silva Critica* (1789), as well as editions
of various classical writers. Throughout the 1790s, Wakefield penned
several pamphlets attacking the Pitt government; one of these publica-
tions resulted in his prosecution and conviction for seditious libel. Wake-
field was imprisoned in Dorchester jail for two years. He died just a few
months after his release in May 1801.

II. Histories

1. From *Memoirs of the Court of Queen Elizabeth*. 2 vols. London: Longman, Hurst, Rees, Orme, and Brown, 1818

[Throughout her lifetime, Lucy Aikin was known, first and foremost, for her histories. For her first court memoir, Aikin chose the formidable subject of Elizabeth I, England's first true Queen regnant (Queen reigning in her own right), and certainly her most revered Queen. Though many records and histories of Elizabeth's reign had been written, as Aikin points out in her preface, none had been offered in the particular form of the court memoir. The court memoir is a genre that had thrived in France, and had only recently been imported into Britain. The *OED* defines memoir as "Records of events or history written from the personal knowledge or experience of the writer, or based on special sources of information," and, in order to write a history of the private lives of the monarchs, as Aikin does, she relied not only on published writing but manuscript sources owned by private individuals. Her aim was to write a species of "lighter literature"; though she claims to avoid "as much as possible all encroachments on the peculiar province of history," her work inevitably combines domestic and political history. Thus Aikin touches upon a wide range of subjects in her *Memoirs*: the domestic life and manners of the court; the institutions of power; the rituals and ceremonies of the monarchy; the religious controversies of the day; and the cultural history of the period.

Memoirs of the Court of Queen Elizabeth was immediately successful, reaching its fourth edition in 1819. It was first published in America in 1821, and was translated into German in 1819, Dutch in 1821, and French in 1827. Demand for the book continued throughout the century; it was in its eighth printing by 1869, and four US editions were printed by 1807. It was also a critical success. The following account, from *The North British Review*. No. 84, June 1865, describes the book's reception and influence:

> The decided bent of [Aikin's] mind, however, was towards history; and her first publication of any consequence was the Memoirs of the Court of Queen Elizabeth, which appeared in 1819, and drew on her no small degree of attention. It may indeed be fairly considered a noteworthy book of its time. It

had merits of its own, in a lively, intelligent, impartial style of narrative, and was, we believe, the first of those works of historical gossip which Miss Strickland's indefatigable labours have since made so familiar to the public, and to which Walter Scott's novels no doubt contributed a powerful impulse. But it should be remembered, and Miss Aikin must have the credit due from the fact, that she began to contemplate her work in 1814, before even the first of the Waverly Novels had appeared; years before Kenilworth had set the world mad about Queen Bess and the Earl of Leicester. "I intend," she says, writing at that date to her brother, "to collect all the notices I can of the manners of the age, the state of literature, arts, etc., which I shall interweave, as well as I am able, with the biographies of the Queen, and the other eminent characters of her time, binding all together with as slender a thread of political history as will serve to keep other matters in their places." So that the plagiarism of the topic, if any, was the other way. Miss Aikin could not have set on the track of Elizabethan gossip by any historical fiction of Walter Scott's, but Scott may have been induced by Miss Aikin's book to think of Kenilworth as a subject. (From "Review of *Memoirs, Miscellanies, and Letters of the Late Lucy Aikin,*" 166–67.)

In its review of Walter Scott's *The Fortunes of Nigel*, the *Edinburgh Review* similarly praised Aikin's *Memoirs of the Court of James I* as "a work as entertaining as a novel, and far more instructive than most histories. It is not only full of interest and curiosity, but is written throughout with the temperance, impartiality, and dispassionate judgment of a true historian, in a style always lucid and succinct, and frequently both animated and elegant": *Edinburgh Review*, 37:73 (June 1822): 212–23.

In the preface that follows, Aikin delivers her fullest articulation of her ambitions for the genre of the court memoir. *Memoirs of the Court of Elizabeth the First*, I: iii–viii.]

PREFACE

In the literature of our country, however copious, the eye of the curious student may still detect important deficiencies.

We possess, for example, many and excellent histories, embracing every period of our domestic annals;—biographies, general and particular, which appear to have placed on record the name of every private individual justly entitled to such commemoration;—and numerous and extensive collections of original letters, state-papers and other historical and antiquarian documents;—whilst our comparative penury is remarkable in royal lives, in court histories, and especially in that class which forms the glory of French literature,—memoir.

To supply in some degree this want, as it affects the person and reign of one of the most illustrious of female and of European sovereigns, is the intention of the work now offered with much diffidence to the public.

Its plan comprehends a detailed view of the private life of Elizabeth from the period of her birth; a view of the domestic history of her reign; memoirs of the principal families of the nobility and biographical anecdotes of the celebrated characters who composed her court; besides notices of the manners, opinions and literature of the reign.

Such persons as may have made it their business or their entertainment to study very much in detail the history of the age of Elizabeth, will doubtless be aware that in the voluminous collections of Strype, in the edited Burleigh, Sidney, and Talbot papers, in the Memoirs of Birch, in various collections of letters, in the chronicles of the times,—so valuable for those vivid pictures of manners which the pen of a contemporary unconsciously traces,—in the Annals of Camden, the Progresses of Nichols, and other large and laborious works which it would be tedious here to enumerate, a vast repertory existed of curious and interesting facts seldom recurred to for the composition of books of lighter literature, and possessing with respect to a great majority of readers the grace of novelty. Of these and similar works of reference, as well as of a variety of others, treating directly or indirectly on the biography, the literature, and the manners of the period, a large collection has been placed under the eyes of the author, partly by the liberality of her publishers, partly by the kindness of friends.

In availing herself of their contents, she has had to encounter in full force the difficulties attendant on such a task; those of weighing and comparing authorities, of reconciling discordant statements, of bringing insulated facts to bear upon each other, and of forming out of materials irregular in their nature and abundant almost to excess, a compact and well-proportioned structure.

How far her abilities and her diligence may have proved themselves adequate to the undertaking, it remains with a candid public to decide. Respecting the selection of topics it seems necessary however to remark, that it has been the constant endeavour of the writer to preserve to her work the genuine character of Memoirs, by avoiding as much as possible all encroachments on the peculiar province of history;—that amusement, of a not illiberal kind, has been consulted at least equally with instruction;—and that on subjects of graver moment, a correct sketch has alone been attempted.

By a still more extensive course of reading and research, an additional store of anecdotes and observations might unquestionably have been amassed; but it is hoped that of those assembled in the following pages, few will be found to rest on dubious or inadequate authority; and that a copious choice of materials, relatively to the intended compass of the work, will appear to have superseded the temptation to useless digression, or to prolix and trivial detail.

The orthography of all extracts from the elder writers has been modernized, and their punctuation rendered more distinct; in other respects reliance may be placed on their entire fidelity.

[The following excerpt, taken from the beginning of the first chapter and covering the years 1533 to 1536, illustrates Aikin's general chronological approach, as well as her considerable dramatic skill in setting the scene and synthesizing a great deal of historical information in an accessible and lively form (I: 1–24).]

On the 7th of September 1533, at the royal palace of Greenwich in Kent, was born, under circumstances as peculiar as her afterlife proved eventful and illustrious, ELIZABETH daughter of king Henry VIII. and his queen Anne Boleyn.[1]

Delays and difficulties equally grievous to the impetuous temper of the man and the despotic habits of the prince, had for years obstructed Henry in the execution of his favourite project of repudiating, on the plea of their too near alliance, a wife who had ceased to find favour in his sight, and substituting on her throne the youthful beauty who had captivated his imagination. At length his passion and his impatience had arrived at a pitch capable of bearing down every obstacle. With that contempt of decorum which he displayed so remarkably in some former, and many later transactions of his life, he caused his private marriage

---

1 Second wife of Henry VIII (c. 1500–36) and mother of Elizabeth I, Anne Boleyn was executed on charges of adultery, incest and treason, after she failed to produce a male heir to the throne.

with Anne Boleyn to precede the sentence of divorce which he had resolved that his clergy should pronounce against Catherine of Arragon;[1] and no sooner had this judicial ceremony taken place, than the new queen was openly exhibited as such in the face of the court and the nation.

An unusual ostentation of magnificence appears to have attended the celebration of these august nuptials. The fondness of the king for pomp and pageantry was at all times excessive, and on this occasion his love and his pride would equally conspire to prompt an extraordinary display. Anne, too, a vain, ambitious, and light-minded woman, was probably greedy of this kind of homage from her princely lover; and the very consciousness of the dubious, inauspicious, or disgraceful circumstances attending their union, might secretly augment the anxiety of the royal pair to dazzle and impose by the magnificence of their public appearance. Only once before, since the Norman conquest, had a king of England stooped from his dignity to elevate a private gentlewoman and a subject to a partnership of his bed and throne; and the bitter animosities between the queen's relations on one side, and the princes of the blood and great nobles on the other, which had agitated the reign of Edward IV., and contributed to bring destruction on the heads of his helpless orphans, stood as a strong warning against a repetition of the experiment.[2]

The unblemished reputation and amiable character of Henry's "some-time wife," had long procured for her the love and respect of the people; her late misfortunes had engaged their sympathy, and it might be feared that several unfavorable points of comparison would suggest themselves between the high-born and high-

---

1 First wife of Henry VIII (1485–1536). Henry's attempt to have their 24-year marriage annulled—because all their sons had died in childhood, leaving only one of their six children, Princess Mary (later Queen Mary I) as heiress presumptive, at a time when there was no established precedent for a woman on the throne—set in motion a chain of events that led to England's break with the Roman Catholic Church. When Pope Clement VII refused to annul the marriage, Henry defied him by creating the Anglican Church so that he could marry Anne Boleyn.

2 Edward IV (1442–83) married Elizabeth Woodville, a commoner. After Edward IV's death, Edward V (Edward IV's eldest son) reigned for two months before being deposed by his uncle, Richard III. Edward IV's legitimate sons, Edward V and Richard, Duke of York, were sent to the Tower of London and not seen publicly afterwards. Their fate is a mystery, though it is widely believed they were murdered, possibly by their uncle, who would become Richard III.

minded Catherine and her present rival—once her humble attendant—whose long-known favour with the king, whose open association with him at Calais, whither she had attended him, whose private marriage of uncertain date, and already advanced pregnancy, afforded so much ground for whispered censures.

On the other hand, the personal qualities of the king gave him great power over popular opinion. The manly beauty of his countenance, the strength and agility which in the chivalrous exercises of the time rendered him victorious over all competitors; the splendour with which he surrounded himself; his bounty; the popular frankness of his manners, all conspired to render him, at this period of his life, an object of admiration rather than of dread to his subjects; while the respect entertained for his talents and learning, and for the conscientious scruples respecting his first marriage which he felt or feigned, mingled so much of deference in their feelings towards him, as to check all hasty censures of his conduct. The protestant party, now considerable by zeal and numbers, foresaw too many happy results to their cause from the circumstances of his present union, to scrutinize with severity the motives which had produced it. The nation at large, justly dreading a disputed succession, with all its long-experienced evils, in the event of Henry's leaving behind him no offspring but a daughter whom he had lately set aside on the ground of illegitimacy, rejoiced in the prospect of a male heir to the crown.[1] The populace of London, captivated, as usual, by the splendors of a coronation, were also delighted with the youth, beauty, and affability of the new queen.

...

The personal history of Elizabeth may truly be said to begin with her birth; for she had scarcely entered her second year when her marriage—that never-accomplished project, which for half a century afterwards inspired so many vain hopes and was the subject of so many fruitless negotiations, was already proposed as an article of a treaty between France and England.

Henry had caused an act of succession to be passed, by which his divorce was confirmed, the authority of the pope disclaimed,

---

1   Until Queen Mary (b. 1516, r. 1553–58), daughter of Henry VIII and Catherine of Aragon, no women had ruled as Queen Regnant. Mary restored England to Roman Catholicism, and had almost 300 religious dissenters burned at the stake in the Marian Persecutions, earning her the sobriquet of Bloody Mary. Her re-establishment of Roman Catholicism was reversed by her successor and half-sister, Elizabeth I.

and the crown settled on his issue by Anne Boleyn. But, as if half-repenting the boldness of his measures, he opened a negotiation almost immediately with Francis I.,[1] for the purpose of obtaining a declaration by that king and his nobility in favor of his present marriage, and the intercession of Francis for the revocation of the papal censures fulminated against him. And in consideration of these acts of friendship, he offered to engage the hand of Elizabeth to the duke d'Angoulême, third son of the French king. But Francis was unable to prevail upon the new pope to annul the acts of his predecessor; and probably not wishing to connect himself more closely with a prince already regarded as a heretic, he suffered the proposal of marriage to fall to the ground.

The doctrines of Zwingle and of Luther[2] had at this time made considerable progress among Henry's subjects, and the great work of reformation was begun in England. Several smaller monasteries had been suppressed; the pope's supremacy was preached against by public authority; and the parliament, desirous of widening the breach between the king and the pontiff, declared the former, head of the English church. After some hesitation, Henry accepted the office, and wrote a book in defence of his conduct. The queen was attached, possibly by principle, and certainly by interest, to the antipapal party, which alone admitted the validity of the royal divorce, and consequently of her marriage; and she had already engaged her chaplain Dr. Parker, a learned and zealous reformist, to keep a watchful eye over the childhood of her daughter, and early to imbue her mind with the true principles of religious knowledge.

But Henry, whose passions and interests alone, not his theological convictions, had set him in opposition to the old church establishment, to the ceremonies and doctrines of which he was even zealously attached, began to be apprehensive that the whole fabric would be swept away by the strong tide of popular opinion which was now turned against it, and he hastened to interpose in its defence. He brought to the stake several persons who denied the real presence, as a terror to the reformers; whilst at the same time he showed his resolution to quell the adherents of popery,

---

1   Francis I of France (1494–1547, reigned 1515–47).
2   Ulrich Zwingle (1484–1531) and Martin Luther (1483–1546), leaders, respectively, of the Swiss and German Protestant Reformations. In 1812, Aikin published a translation from the French of *The Life of Ulrich Zwingle.*

by causing bishop Fisher and sir Thomas More[1] to be attainted of treason, for refusing such part of the oath of succession as implied the invalidity of the king's first marriage, and thus, in effect, disallowed the authority of the papal dispensation in virtue of which it had been celebrated.

Thus were opened those dismal scenes of religious persecution and political cruelty from which the mind of Elizabeth was to receive its early and indelible impressions.

The year 1536, which proved even more fertile than its predecessor in melancholy incidents and tragical catastrophes, opened with the death of Catherine of Arragon; an event equally welcome, in all probability, both to the sufferer herself, whom tedious years of trouble and mortification must have rendered weary of a world which had no longer a hope to flatter her; and to the ungenerous woman who still beheld her, discarded as she was, with the sentiments of an enemy and a rival. It is impossible to contemplate the life and character of this royal lady, without feelings of the deepest commiseration. As a wife, the bitter humiliations which she was doomed to undergo were entirely unmerited; for not only was her modesty unquestioned, but her whole conduct towards the king was a perfect model of conjugal love and duty. As a queen and a mother, her firmness, her dignity, and her tenderness, deserved a far other recompense than to see herself degraded, on the infamous plea of incest,[2] from the rank of royalty, and her daughter, so long heiress to the English throne, branded with illegitimacy, and cast out alike from the inheritance and the affections of her father. But the memory of this unhappy princess has been embalmed by the genius of Shakespeare, in the noble drama of which he has made her the touching and majestic heroine;[3] and let not the praise of magnanimity be denied to the daughter of Anne Boleyn, in permitting

---

1 Sir Thomas More (1478–1535) was a lawyer, author, and statesman, who in his lifetime gained a reputation as a leading humanist scholar, and occupied many public offices, including Lord Chancellor (1529–32). Both he and John Fisher (c. 1469–1535), a Catholic bishop, were beheaded in 1535 when they refused to sign the Act of Succession that would make Henry VIII Supreme Head of the Church in England.
2 Henry sought to have his marriage to Catherine annulled on the grounds that their marriage was incestuous, since she had formerly, and briefly, been married to his elder brother, Arthur.
3 *Henry VIII*, now widely believed to be a collaboration between Shakespeare and John Fletcher.

those wrongs and those sufferings which were the price of her glory, nay of her very existence, to be thus impressively offered to the compassion of her people.

...

[The following excerpt, covers the accession and coronation of Queen Elizabeth following Mary I's death in 1558 (I: 228–51).]

Never perhaps was the accession of any prince the subject of such keen and lively interest to a whole people as that of Elizabeth.

Both in the religious establishments and political relations of the country, the most important changes were anticipated; changes in which the humblest individual found himself concerned, and to which a vast majority of the nation looked forward with hope and joy.

With the courtiers and great nobles, whose mutability of faith had so happily corresponded with every ecclesiastical vicissitude of the last three reigns, political and personal considerations may well be supposed to have held the first place; and though the old religion might still be endeared to them by many cherished associations and by early prejudice, there were few among them who did not regard the liberation of the country from Spanish influence as ample compensation for the probable restoration of the religious establishment of Henry or of Edward. Besides, there was scarcely an individual belonging to these classes who had not in some manner partaken of the plunder of the church, and whom the avowed principles of Mary had not disquieted with apprehensions that some plan of compulsory restitution would sooner or later be attempted by an union of royal and papal authority.

With the middling and lower classes religious views and feelings were predominant. The doctrines of the new and better system of faith and worship had now become more precious and important than ever in the eyes of its adherents from the hardships which many of them had encountered for its sake, and from the interest which each disciple vindicated to himself in the glory and merit of the holy martyrs whose triumphant exit they had witnessed. With all the fervor of pious gratitude they offered up their thanksgivings for the signal deliverance by which their prayers had been answered. The bloody tyranny of Mary was at an end; and though the known conformity of Elizabeth to Romish rites might apparently give room for doubts and suspicions, it should seem that neither catholics nor protestants were willing to believe that the daughter of Anne Boleyn could in her heart be a papist. Under this impression the citizens of London, who spoke the sense of their own class throughout the kingdom, welcomed the new queen as a protectress sent by Heaven itself: but even in the first transports of their joy, and amid the pompous pageantries by which their loyal congratulations were expressed, they took care to intimate, in a manner not to be misunderstood, their hopes and expectations on the great concern now nearest to their hearts.

Prudence confined within their own bosoms the regrets and murmurs of the popish clergy; submission and a simulated loyalty were at present obviously their only policy: thus not a whisper breathed abroad but of joy and gratulation and happy presage of the days to come.

The sex, the youth, the accomplishments, the graces, the past misfortunes of the princess,[1] all served to heighten the interest with which she was beheld: the age of chivalry had not yet expired; and in spite of the late unfortunate experience of a female reign, the romantic image of a maiden queen dazzled all eyes, subdued all hearts, inflamed the imaginations of the brave and courtly youth with visions of love and glory, exalted into a passionate homage the principle of loyalty, and urged adulation to the very brink of idolatry.

The fulsome compliments on her beauty which Elizabeth, almost to the latest period of her life, not only permitted but required and delighted in, have been adverted to by all the writers who have made her reign and character their theme: and those of the number whom admiration and pity of the fair queen of Scots have rendered hostile to her memory, have taken a malicious pleasure in exaggerating the extravagance of this weakness, by denying her, even in her freshest years, all pretensions to those personal charms by which her rival was so eminently distinguished. Others however have been more favorable, and probably more just, to her on this point; and it would be an injury to her memory to withhold from the reader the following portraitures which authorize us to form a pleasing as well as majestic image of this illustrious female at the period of her accession and at the age of five-and-twenty....

On November 23d the queen set forward for her capital, attended by a train of about a thousand nobles, knights, gentlemen, and ladies, and took up her abode for the present at the dis-

---

1   A reference to Elizabeth's imprisonment, first in the Tower and then at Woodstock, during 1554 and 1555.

solved monastery of the Chartreux, or Charterhouse, then the residence of lord North; a splendid pile which offered ample accommodation for a royal retinue. Her next remove, in compliance with ancient custom, was to the Tower. On this occasion all the streets from the Charterhouse were spread with fine gravel; singers and musicians were stationed by the way, and a vast concourse of people freely lent their joyful and admiring acclamations, as preceded by her heralds and great officers, and richly attired in purple velvet, she passed along mounted on her palfrey, and returning the salutations of the humblest of her subjects with graceful and winning affability.

With what vivid and what affecting impressions of the vicissitudes attending on the great must she have passed again within the antique walls of that fortress once her dungeon, now her palace! She had entered it by the Traitor's gate, a terrified and defenceless prisoner, smarting under many wrongs, hopeless of deliverance, and apprehending nothing less than an ignominious death. She had quitted it, still a captive, under the guard of armed men, to be conducted she knew not whither. She returned to it in all the pomp of royalty, surrounded by the ministers of her power, ushered by the applauses of her people; the cherished object of every eye, the idol of every heart.

Devotion alone could supply becoming language to the emotions which swelled her bosom; and no sooner had she reached the royal apartments, than falling on her knees she returned humble and fervent thanks to that Providence which had brought her in safety, like Daniel from the den of lions, to behold this day of exaltation....

...

It was a very different spirit, however, from that of romance or of knight-errantry which inspired the bosoms of the citizens whose acclamations now rent the air on her approach. They beheld in the princess whom they welcomed the daughter of that Henry who had redeemed the land from papal tyranny and extortion; the sister of that young and godly Edward,—the Josiah of English story,—whose pious hand had reared again the altars of pure and primitive religion; and they had bodied forth for her instruction and admonition, in a series of solemn pageants, the maxims by which they hoped to see her equal or surpass these deep-felt merits of her predecessors.

These pageants were erections placed across the principal streets in the manner of triumphal arches: illustrative sentences in English and Latin were inscribed upon them; and a child was stationed in each, who explained to the queen in English verse the meaning of the whole. The first was of three stories, and represented by living figures: first, Henry VII. and his royal spouse Elizabeth of York, from whom her majesty derived her name; secondly, Henry VIII. and Anne Boleyn; and lastly, her majesty in person; all in royal robes. The verses described the felicity of that union of the houses to which she owed her existence, and of Concord in general. The second pageant was styled "The seat of worthy governance," on the summit of which sat another representative of the queen; beneath were the cardinal virtues trampling under their feet the opposite vices, among whom Ignorance and Superstition were not forgotten. The third exhibited the eight Beatitudes all ascribed with some ingenuity of application to her majesty. The fourth ventured upon a more trying topic: its opposite sides represented in lively contrast the images of a decayed and of a flourishing commonwealth; and from a cave below issued Time leading forth his daughter Truth, who held in her hand an English bible, which she offered to the queen's acceptance. Elizabeth received the volume, and reverently pressing it with both hands to her heart and to her lips, declared aloud, amid the tears and grateful benedictions of her people, that she thanked the city more for that gift than for all the cost they had bestowed upon her, and that she would often read over that book. The last pageant exhibited "a seemly and mete personage, richly apparelled in parliament robes, with a sceptre in her hand, over whose head was written 'Deborah, the judge and restorer of the house of Israel.'"

To render more palatable these grave moralities, the recorder of London, approaching her majesty's chariot near the further end of Cheapside, where ended the long array of the city companies, which had lined the streets all the way from Fenchurch, presented her with a splendid and ample purse, containing one thousand marks in gold. The queen graciously received it with both hands, and answered his harangue "marvellous pithily." ...

The reader may here be reminded, that five-and-twenty years before, when the mother of this queen passed through London to her coronation, the pageants exhibited derived their personages and allusions chiefly from pagan mythology or classical fiction. But all was now changed; the earnestness of religious controversy in Edward's time, and the fury of persecution since, had put to flight Apollo, the Muses, and the Graces: Learning indeed had kept her station and her honors, but she had lent her lamp to other studies; and whether in the tongue of ancient Rome or modern England, Elizabeth was hailed in Christian strains, and as the sovereign of a Christian country. A people filled with earnest zeal in the best of causes implored her to free them once again from popery; to overthrow the tyranny of error and of superstition; to establish gospel truth; and to accept at their hands, as the standard of her faith and the rule of her conduct, that holy book of which they regarded the free and undisturbed possession as their brightest privilege.

[In the next excerpt, covering the years 1582-87, Aikin considers Elizabeth's character. The passage demonstrates Aikin's interest in psychologizing her subjects, as well as her willingness to be critical of them. The passage also includes an account of the origins of the Dissenting sects, demonstrating how Aikin seamlessly wove together different topics in her narrative (II: 104–10).]

The disposition of Elizabeth was originally deficient in benevolence and sympathy, and prone to suspicion, pride and anger; and we observe with pain in the progress of her history, how much the influences to which her high station and the peculiar circumstances of her reign inevitably exposed her, tended in various modes to exasperate these radical evils of her nature.

The extravagant flattery administered to her daily and hourly, was of most pernicious effect; it not only fostered in her an absurd excess of personal vanity, but, what was worse, by filling her with exaggerated notions both of her own wisdom and of her sovereign power and prerogative, it contributed to render her rule more stern and despotic, and her mind on many points incapable of sober counsel. This effect was remarked by one of her clergy, who, in a sermon preached in her presence, had the boldness to tell her, that she who had been meek as lamb was become an untameable heifer; for which reproof he was in his turn reprehended by her majesty on his quitting the pulpit, as "an over confident man who dishonored his sovereign."

The decay of her beauty was an unwelcome truth which all the artifices of adulation were unable to hide from her secret consciousness; since she could never behold her image in a mirror, during the latter years of her life, without transports of impotent anger; and this circumstance contributed not a little to sour her temper, while it rendered the young and lovely the chosen objects of her malignity....

The perils of many kinds, from open and secret enemies, by which Elizabeth had found herself environed since her unwise and unauthorized detention of the queen of Scots, aggravated the mis-trustfulness of her nature; and the severities[1] which fear and anger led her to exercise against that portion of her subjects who still adhered to the ancient faith, increased its harshness. It is true that, since the fulmination of the papal anathema, the zealots of this church had kept no measures with respect to her either in their words, their writings, or their actions. Plans of insurrection and even of assassination were frequently revolved in their councils, but as often disappointed by the extraordinary vigilance and sagacity of her ministers; while the courage evinced by herself under these circumstances of severe probation was truly admirable. Bacon relates that "the council once represented to her the danger in which she stood by the continual conspiracies against her life, and acquainted her that a man was lately taken who stood ready in a very dangerous and suspicious manner to do the deed; and they showed her the weapon wherewith he thought to have acted it. And therefore they advised her that she should go less abroad to take the air, weakly attended, as she used. But the queen answered 'that she had rather be dead than put in custody.'" ...

When angry, she observed little moderation in the expression of her feelings. In the private letters even of Cecil, whom she treated on the whole with more consideration than any other person, we find not unfrequent mention of the harsh words which he had to endure from her, sometimes, as he says, on occasions when he appeared to himself deserving rather of thanks than of censure. The earl of Shrewsbury often complains to his correspondents of her captious and irascible temper; and we find Walsingham taking pains to console sir Henry Sidney under some manifestations of her dis-pleasure, by the assurance that they had proceeded only from one of those transient gusts of passion for which she was accustomed to make sudden amends to her faithful servants by new and extraor-dinary tokens of her favor.

There was no branch of prerogative of which Elizabeth was more tenacious than that which invested her with the sole and supreme direction of ecclesiastical affairs. The persevering efforts therefore of the puritans, to obtain various relaxations or alterations of the laws which she in her wisdom had laid down for the government of the church,—on failure of which they scrupled not to recall to her memory the strong denunciations of the Jewish prophets against

---

1   Mary was imprisoned for 19 years, from 1568, when she fled Scotland
     for England, until her execution in 1587. For Aikin's account of their
     relationship, and Elizabeth's role in her cousin's death, see pages 114-
     20, below

wicked and irreligious princes,—at once exasperated and alarmed her, and led her to assume continually more and more of the incongruous and odious character of a protestant persecutor of protestants. But the puritans themselves must have seemed guiltless in her eyes compared with a new sect, the principles of which, tending directly to the abrogation of all authority of the civil magistrate in spiritual concerns, called forth about this time her indignation manifested by the utmost severity of penal infliction.

It was in the year 1530 that Robert Brown, having completed his studies in divinity at Cambridge, began to preach at Norwich against the discipline and ceremonies of the church of England, and to promulgate a scheme which he affirmed to be more conformable to the apostolic model. According to his system, each congregation of believers was to be regarded as a separate church, possessing in itself full jurisdiction over its own concerns; the *liberty of prophesying* was to be indulged to all the brethren equally, and pastors were to be elected and dismissed at the pleasure of the majority, in whom he held that all power ought of right to reside. On account of these opinions Brown was called before certain ecclesiastical commissioners, who imprisoned him for contumacy; but the interference of his relation lord Burleigh procured his release, after which he repaired to Holland, where he founded several churches and published a book in defence of his system, in which he strongly inculcated upon his disciples the duty of separating themselves from what he stated antichristian churches. For the sole offence of distributing this work, two men were hanged in Suffolk in 1583; to which extremity of punishment they were subjected as having impugned the queen's supremacy, which was declared felony by a late statute now for the first time put in force against protestants. Brown himself, after his return from Holland, was repeatedly imprisoned and, but for the protection of his powerful kinsman might probably have shared the fate of his two disciples. At length, the terror of a sentence of excommunication drove him to recant, and joining the established church he soon obtained preferment. But the Brownist sect suffered little by the desertion of its founder, whose private character was far from exemplary: in spite of penal laws, of persecution, and even of ridicule and contempt, it survived, increased, and eventually became the model on which the churches not only of the sect of Independents but also of the two other denominations of English protestant dissenters remain at the present day constituted.

[This excerpt covers the years 1586–87, during which Mary, Queen of Scots was arrested, tried and executed, after she was held for a period of nineteen years in close custody (II: 171–87). This was one of the greatest crises of Elizabeth's reign, and of particular interest to a feminist historian. Aikin demonstrates sympathy for Elizabeth's predicament at the same time that she holds the monarch accountable for the execution of her cousin and heir to the English throne.]

Soon after the arrival of Mary at Fotheringay,[1] Elizabeth, according to the provisions of the late act, issued out a commission to forty noblemen and privy-councillors, empowering them to try and pass sentence upon Mary daughter and heir of king James V. and late queen of Scots; for it was thus that she was designated, with a view of intimating to her that she was no longer to be regarded as possessing the rights of a sovereign princess. Thirty-six of the commissioners repaired immediately to Fotheringay, where they arrived on October 9th 1586.... None of her papers were restored, no counsel was assigned her; and her request that her two secretaries, whose evidence was principally relied on by the prosecutors, might be confronted with her, was denied. But all these were hardships customarily inflicted on prisoners accused of high treason; and it does not appear that, with respect to its forms and modes of proceedings, Mary had cause to complain that her trial was other than a regular and legal one....

Intercepted letters, authenticated by the testimony of her secretaries, formed the chief evidence against Mary. From these the crown lawyers showed, and she did not attempt to deny, that she had suffered her correspondents to address her as queen of England; that she had endeavoured by means of English fugitives to incite the Spaniards to invade the country; and that she had been negotiating at Rome the terms of a transfer of all her claims, present and future, to the king of Spain, disinheriting by this unnatural act her own schismatic son. The further charge of having concurred in the late plot for the assassination of Elizabeth, she strongly denied and attempted to disprove; but it stood on equally good evidence with all the rest; and in spite of some suggestions of which her modern partisans have endeavoured to give her the benefit, there appears no solid foundation on which an impartial inquirer can rest any doubt of the fact....

After her sentence had been ratified by both houses of parliament, it was thought expedient, probably by way of feeling the

---

1   Mary I of Scotland (known as Mary, Queen of Scots) (1542–87), was
    Queen of Scotland from 1542 to 1567.

pulse of the people, that solemn proclamation of it should be made in London by the lord-mayor and city officers, and by the magistrates of the county in Westminster. The multitude, untouched by the long misfortunes of an unhappy princess born of the blood-royal of England and heiress to its throne,—insensible too of every thing arbitrary, unprecedented, or unjust, in the treatment to which she had been subjected, received the notification of her doom with expressions of triumph and exultation truly shocking. Bonfires were lighted, church bells were rung, and every street and lane throughout the city resounded with psalms of thanksgiving.[1]

It is manifest, therefore, that no deference for the opinions or feelings of her subjects compelled Elizabeth to hesitate or to dissemble in this matter.

Had she permitted the execution of the sentence simply, and without delay, all orders of men attached to the protestant establishment would have approved it as an act fully justified by state expediency and the law of self-defence; and though misgivings might have arisen in the minds of some on cooler reflection, when alarm had subsided and the bitterness of satiated revenge had begun to make itself felt,—these "compunctious visitings" could have led to no consequences capable of alarming her. It must have been felt as highly inequitable to reproach the queen, when all was past and irrevocable, for the consent which she had afforded to a deed sanctioned by a law, ratified by the legislature and applauded by the people, and from which both church and state had reaped the fruits of security and peace. Foreign princes also would have respected the vigor of this proceeding; they would not have been displeased to see themselves spared by a decisive act the pain of making disregarded representations on such a subject, and a secret consciousness that few of their number would have scrupled under all the circumstances to take like vengeance on a deadly foe and rival, might further have contributed to reconcile them to the fact. Even as it was, pope Sixtus V himself could scarcely restrain his expressions of admiration at the completion of so strong a measure as the final execution of the sentence: his holiness had indeed a strange passion for capital punishments, and he is said to have envied the queen of England the glorious satisfaction of cutting off a royal head:—a sentiment not much more extraordinary from such a personage, than the ardent desire which he is reported to have expressed, that it were

---

1 Hollinshed's Castrations. [L.A.]

possible for him to have a son by this heretic princess; because the offspring of such parents could not fail, he said, to make himself king of the world.

But it was the weakness of Elizabeth to imagine, that an extraordinary parade of reluctance, and the interposition of some affected delays, would change in public opinion the whole character of the deed which she contemplated, and preserve to her the reputation of feminine mildness and sensibility, without the sacrifice of that great revenge on which she was secretly bent. The world, however, when it has no interest in deceiving itself, is too wise to accept of words instead of deeds, or in opposition to them; and the sole result of her artifices was to aggravate in the eyes of all mankind the criminality of the act, by giving it rather the air of a treacherous and cold-blooded murder, than of solemn execution done upon a formidable culprit by the sentence of offended laws. The parliament which Elizabeth had summoned to partake the odium of Mary's death, met four days after the judges had pronounced her doom, and was opened by commission. An unanimous ratification of the sentence by both houses was immediately carried, and followed by an earnest address to her majesty for its publication and execution; to which she returned a long and labored answer.

She began with the expression of her fervent gratitude to Providence for the affections of her people; adding protestations of her love towards them, and of her perfect willingness to have suffered her own life still to remain exposed as a mark to the aim of enemies and traitors, had she not perceived how intimately the safety and well-being of the nation was connected with her own. With regard to the queen of Scots, she said, so severe had been the grief which she had sustained from her recent conduct, that the fear of renewing this sentiment had been the cause, and the sole cause, of her withholding her personal appearance at the opening of that assembly, where she knew that the subject must of necessity become matter of discussion; and not, as had been suggested, the apprehension of any violence to be attempted against her person;—yet she might mention, that she had actually seen a bond by which the subscribers bound themselves to procure her death within a month.

So far was she from indulging any ill will against one of the same sex, the same rank, the same race as herself,—in fact her nearest kinswoman,—that after having received full information of certain of her machinations, she had secretly written with her own hand to the queen of Scots, promising that, on a simple confession of her guilt in a private letter to herself, all should be buried in oblivion. She doubted not that the ancient laws of the land would have been sufficient to reach the guilt of her who had been the great artificer of the recent treasons; and she had consented to the passing of the late statute, not for the purpose of ensnaring her, but rather to give her warning of the danger in which she stood. Her lawyers, from their strict attachment to ancient forms, would have brought this princess to trial within the county of Stafford, have compelled her to hold up her hand at the bar, and have caused twelve jurymen to pass judgement upon her. But to her it had appeared more suitable to the dignity of the prisoner and the importance of the cause to refer the examination to the judges, nobles, and counsellors of the realm;—happy if even thus she could escape that ready censure to which the conspicuous station of sovereigns on all occasions exposed them.

The statute, by requiring her to pronounce judgement upon her kinswoman, had involved her in anxiety and difficulties. Amid all her perils, however, she must remember with gratitude and affection the voluntary association into which her subjects had entered for her defence. It was never her practice to decide hastily on any matter; in a case so rare and important some interval of deliberation must be allowed her; and she would pray Heaven to enlighten her mind, and guide it to the decision most beneficial to the church, to the state, and to the people.

Twelve days after the delivery of this speech, her majesty sent a message to both houses, entreating that her parliament would carefully reconsider the matter, and endeavour to hit upon some device by which the life of the queen of Scots might be rendered consistent with her own safety and that of the country....

... It appears unquestionable that to affected delays a real hesitation succeeded. When her pride was no longer irritated by opposition, she had leisure to survey the meditated deed in every light; and as it rose upon her view in all its native deformity, anxious fears for her own fame and credit, yet untainted by any crime, and perhaps genuine scruples of conscience, forcibly assailed her resolution. But her ministers, deeply sensible that both she and they had already gone too far to recede with reputation or with safety, encountered her growing reluctance with a proportional increase in the vehemence of their clamors for what they called, and perhaps thought, justice. All the hazards to which her excess of clemency might be imagined to expose her were conjured up in the most alarming forms to repel her scruples. A plot for her assassination was disclosed, to which the French ambassador was ascertained to have been privy;—rumors were raised of invasions and insurrections; and it may be suspected that the queen, really alarmed in the first instance by the representations of her council, voluntarily contributed afterwards to keep up these delusions for the sake of terrifying the minds of men into an approval of the deed of blood.

At length, on February 1st 1587, her majesty ordered secretary Davison to bring her the warrant, which had remained ready drawn in his hands for some weeks; and having signed it, she told him to get it sealed with the great seal ... in obedience to which Mary underwent the fatal stroke on February 8th.

The news of this event was received by Elizabeth with the most extraordinary demonstrations of astonishment, grief, and anger. Her countenance changed, her voice faltered, and she remained for some moments fixed and motionless; a violent burst of tears and lamentations succeeded, with which she mingled expressions of rage against her whole council. They had committed, she said, a crime never to be forgiven; they had put to death without her knowledge her dear kinswoman and sister, against whom they well knew that it was her fixed resolution never to proceed to this fatal extremity. She put on deep mourning, kept herself retired among her ladies abandoned to sighs and tears, and drove from her presence with the most furious reproaches such of her ministers as ventured to approach her. She caused several of the councillors to be examined as to the share which they had taken in this transaction. Burleigh was of the number; and against him she expressed herself with such peculiar bitterness that he gave himself up for lost, and begged permission to retire with the loss of all his employments. This resignation was not accepted; and after a considerable interval, during which this great minister deprecated the wrath of his sovereign in letters of penitence and submission worthy only of an Oriental slave, she condescended to be reconciled to a man whose services she felt to be indispensable.

But the manes of Mary, or the indignation of her son, could not be appeased, it seems, without a sacrifice; and a fit victim was at hand. From some words dropped by lord Burleigh on his examination, it had appeared that it was the declaration of Davison respecting the sentiments of the queen, as expressed to himself, which had finally decided the council to send down the warrant; and on this ground proceedings were instituted against the unfortunate secretary. He was stripped of his office, sent to the Tower ... [Davison was subsequently tried and sentenced to a fine of 10,000 marks and imprisonment during the Queen's pleasure.]

[In a later chapter examining the years 1591to 1593, Aikin examines the progress of the drama. Immediately before the following excerpt she examines the dramatic poets before Shakespeare, including Thomas Kyd and Christopher Marlowe. In her discussion of Shakespeare, Aikin demonstrates the wide cultural breadth of her "court memoirs" (II: 325–30).]

Of the works of these and other contemporary poets, the fathers of the English theatre, some are extant in print, others have come down to us in manuscript, and of no inconsiderable portion the titles alone survive. A few have acquired an incidental value in the eyes of the curious, as having furnished the groundwork of some of the dramas of our great poet; but not one of the number can justly be said to make a part of the living literature of the country.

It was reserved for the transcendent genius of Shakespeare alone, in that infancy of our theatre when nothing proceeded from the crowd of rival dramatists but rude and abortive efforts, ridiculed by the learned and judicious of their own age and forgotten by posterity, to astonish and enchant the nation with those inimitable works which form the perpetual boast and immortal heritage of Englishmen.

By a strange kind of fatality, which excites at once our surprise and our unavailing regrets, the domestic and the literary history of this great luminary of his age are almost equally enveloped in doubt and obscurity. Even of the few particulars of his origin and early adventures which have reached us through various channels, the greater number are either imperfectly attested, or exposed to objections of different kinds which render them of little value; and respecting his theatrical life the most important circumstances still remain matter of conjecture, or at best of remote inference.

When Shakespeare first became a writer for the stage;—what was his earliest production;—whether all the pieces usually ascribed to him be really his, and whether there be any others of which he was in whole or in part the author;—what degree of assistance he either received from other dramatic writers or lent to them;—in what chronological order his acknowledged pieces ought to be arranged, and what dates should be assigned to their first representation;—are all questions on which the ingenuity and indefatigable diligence of a crowd of editors, critics and biographers have long been exerted, without producing any considerable approximation to certainty or to general agreement.[1]

On a subject so intricate, it will suffice for the purposes of the present work to state a few of the leading facts which appear to rest on the most satisfactory authorities. William Shakespeare, who was born in 1564, settled in London about 1586 or 1587, and seems to have almost immediately adopted the profession of an actor. Yet his earliest effort in composition was not of the dramatic kind; for in 1593 he dedicated to his great patron the earl of Southampton, as "the first heir of his invention," his Venus and Adonis, a narrative poem of considerable length in the six-line stanza then popular. In the subsequent year he also inscribed to the same noble friend his Rape of Lucrece, a still longer poem of similar form in the stanza of seven lines, and containing passages of vivid description, of exquisite imagery, and of sentimental excellence, which, had he written nothing more, would have entitled him to rank on a level with the author of the Faery Queen, and far above all other contemporary poets. He likewise employed his pen occasionally in the composition of sonnets, principally devoted to love and friendship, and written perhaps in emulation of those of Spenser, who, as one of these sonnets testifies, was at this period the object of his ardent admiration.

Before the publication however of any one of these poems he must already have attained considerable note as a dramatic writer, since Robert Green, in a satirical piece printed in 1592, speaking of theatrical concerns, stigmatizes this "player" as "an absolute Joannes Factotum,"[2] and one who was "in his own conceit the only Shake-scene in a country."

The tragedy of Pericles, which was published in 1609 with the name of Shakespeare in the title-page, and of which Dryden says in one of his prologues to a first play, "Shakespeare's own muse his Pericles first bore," was probably acted in 1590, and appears to have been long popular. Romeo and Juliet was certainly an early production of his muse, and one which excited much interest, as may well be imagined, amongst the younger portion of theatrical spectators.

---

1   While most Shakespeare scholars have reached a general consensus on many of these issues, Aikin's comments about the uncertainties that surround the life, and to some extent of the works, of Shakespeare still hold true.

2   "A Jack of all trades, a would-be universal genius" (*OED*).

There is high satisfaction in observing, that the age showed itself worthy of the immortal genius whom it had produced and fostered. It is agreed on all hands that Shakespeare was beloved as a man, and admired and patronized as a poet. In the profession of an actor, indeed, his success does not appear to have been conspicuous; but the never-failing attraction of his pieces brought overflowing audiences to the Globe theatre in Southwark, of which he was enabled to become a joint proprietor. Lord Southampton is said to have once bestowed on him a munificent donation of a thousand pounds to enable him to complete a purchase; and it is probable that this nobleman might also introduce him to the notice of his beloved friend the earl of Essex. Of any particular gratuities bestowed on him by her majesty we are not informed: but there is every reason to suppose that he must have received from her on various occasions both praises and remuneration; for we are told that she caused several of his pieces to be represented before her, and that the Merry Wives of Windsor in particular owed its origin to her desire of seeing Falstaff exhibited in love.

It remains to notice the principal legal enactments of Elizabeth respecting the conduct of the theatre, some of which are remarkable. During the early part of her reign, Sunday being still regarded principally in the light of a holiday, her majesty not only selected that day, more frequently than any other, for the representation of plays at court for her own amusement, but by her license granted to Burbage in 1574 authorized the performance of them at the public theatre, *on Sundays only* out of the hours of prayer. Five years after, however, Gosson in his School of Abuse complains that the players, "because they are allowed to play every Sunday, make four or five Sundays at least every week." To limit this abuse, an order was issued by the privy-council in July 1591, purporting that no plays should be publicly exhibited on Thursdays, because on that day bear-baiting[1] and similar pastimes had usually been practised; and in an injunction to the lord mayor four days after, the representation of plays on Sunday (or the Sabbath as it now began to be called among the stricter sort of people) was utterly condemned; and it was further complained

---

1 Bear-baiting was a very popular sport during the Elizabethan era, and was conducted in purpose-built auditoriums. It was a contest in which the bear was chained to a stake by one hind leg or by the neck and set upon by dogs. The whipping of a blinded bear was another variation of bear-baiting.

that on "all other days of the week in divers places the players do use to recite their plays, to the great hurt and destruction of the game of bear-baiting, and like pastimes, which are maintained for her majesty's pleasure."

In the year 1589 her majesty thought proper to appoint commissioners to inspect all performances of writers for the stage, with full powers to reject and obliterate whatever they might esteem unmannerly, licentious, or irreverent:—a regulation which might seem to claim the applause of every friend to public decency, were not the state in which the dramas of this age have come down to posterity sufficient evidence, that to render these impressive appeals to the passions of assembled multitudes politically and not morally inoffensive, was the genuine or principal motive of this act of power....

III. Fiction

1. From *Lorimer: A Tale*. London: Henry Colburn, 1814

[In 1814, Aikin published her only work of fiction, *Lorimer: A Tale*. The work enjoyed moderate success; an American edition was published in 1816, and a second English edition was issued in 1818. It tells the story of a young man, Eustace Lorimer, who, contrary to the well-intentioned advice of his father, is seduced by a bigamous prostitute into marriage. Ashamed and tortured by this action, Lorimer removes himself from society and retires to the Continent. There he meets and falls in love with Bertha Fermor, the daughter of his father's best friend and executor. He avoids declaring himself to her, and even makes a proposal to her on behalf of another man (which Bertha rejects), and departs suddenly. However, when Fermor is imprisoned in Italy, Lorimer determines to marry Bertha in order to protect her. Lorimer remains tormented by his bigamy. While married, he refuses to divulge his secret to his wife, causing both of them great mental distress. In the excerpt, Lorimer's moody temperament is revealed when Bertha innocently asks him to explain why, loving her, he delivered the proposal of another man. His secret soon begins to destroy their trust in one another, and their marriage. The novel ends after Lorimer, separated from Bertha, returns to Edinburgh, where he discovers that his first marriage was invalid (since his first wife had been previously married); realizing that his marriage to Bertha is in fact lawful, the two resume their life together.

Lorimer's characterization is of considerable interest, insofar as it both borrows and anticipates the central features of the Byronic hero; like Byron's Child Harold, the hero of *Childe Harold's Pilgrimage* (1812–18), Lorimer casts himself apart from human society, in self-imposed exile abroad; like Byron's *Manfred* (1817), he has a dark, sinful secret that he refuses to reveal; and like all incarnations of the Byronic hero, he is by turns sullen, irritable and violent. *Lorimer* is also notable for its form, the tale, popularized and theorized by Maria Edgeworth in the first decade of the nineteenth century. Tales were often shorter than novels, and were often explicitly moralistic (to set themselves apart from novels). *Lorimer* is shorter than most novels, but it lacks the explicit didacticism of many of Edgeworth's tales. Indeed, it is arguably more aligned with the novel of sensibility; importantly, however, it is a man instead of a woman who falls prey to seduction and all the unhappiness it occasions (*Lorimer* 99–106).]

"But why," exclaimed Bertha, pursuing the train of her recollections, "why did you propose to me that Count Bononi? Had you no thoughts of me then for yourself?—or was it only to prove my heart? A little more and you would have broken it. Indeed it was a barbarous sport. Your leaving us, too, so abruptly; why was that? I wonder I never inquired before. But for that dear consoling little circumstance of the ribbon, I should have been quite in despair."
"What circumstance? what ribbon?" asked Eustace eagerly. Bertha seated herself on the bank, and invited her husband to place himself by her side: then, resting a hand upon his shoulder and smiling in his face, she began to relate to him all the circumstances of that behaviour of his in the garden, of which she had been a most attentive though unsuspected witness;[1] and she set off her little narrative with such a delicate and tender playfulness, such witchery of looks and tones at once arch and simple, that the delighted Lorimer considered her with a sort of astonishment, and thought that till this moment he had felt but half her fascinations.

"Now," said she, when his raptures had a little subsided, "it remains for you to fill up the tale: remember that, with regard to your motives for quitting us, I am as much in the dark as ever; and, unless you let me into this secret, how can I be certain that

---

1 Bertha had observed Lorimer caressing a ribbon belonging to her, giving her hope that in fact he did love her.

you will not one day desert me again?" "I desert you, my dearest love!" cried he with an earnestness which surprised her, "what could ever put such a thought into your mind?" "Nay," returned she, "you may be certain I was but in jest. I really am not afraid of being forsaken." "No, no; I hope not," answered he: "death only shall divide us now. As to the past—I have loved you from the hour I first beheld you, though I did not immediately own it to myself. But I have been a strange wayward being, and there are feelings, there have been moments in my life, that it is painful to look back upon, even from felicity. My Bertha, do not ask me of the past: are we not happy now?" "Happy, my love! Yes, surely:— if we are not, who is? Forgive my questions; I will never repeat them."

As Bertha spoke these words she pressed her husband's hand, and looked up at him with an air of mingled sorrow and affection. He turned away his head without reply, and, springing from the ground, walked to some distance; then again approaching his wife, he seized her hand, and drawing her towards him, began to hurry her down the steep path with wild impetuosity, as if unable to bear the spot which had called forth such painful recollections, and prompted questions so embarrassing.

The sharp rocks bruised the feet of Bertha as she was borne along, her dress was torn by the bushes, and she was soon breathless with fatigue: yet she would not ask of her husband to slacken his speed, lest she should seem to remark upon the perturbation of mind which it indicated; and she had the fortitude to reach their home without having uttered a single murmur. Then, retiring immediately to her own apartment, she threw herself into a chair; and, mind and body both completely exhausted, burst into a flood of tears. But ashamed of this involuntary weakness, and fearful of Lorimer's observing its effects upon her features, she struggled to repress it, and to rejoin him before her absence could have awakened his attention. It was in vain: she saw by the first glance he cast upon her, that he was aware how her solitary moments had been occupied; he sighed, and with even more than his usual zeal began to busy himself in filling her a glass of wine, picking out for her the finest of the fruit that was set before them, and assembling around her all the little indulgences that affection could invent.

Touching to her were these silent tokens of self-reproach, which thus solicited forgiveness;—precious to him the looks of kindness which told him it was granted! But the incidents of this day had shaken, more than either party was yet aware, the foundation of their mutual happiness....

IV. Family Memoirs

1. From *Memoir of John Aikin, M.D. With a Selection of His Miscellaneous Pieces, Biographical, Moral, and Critical.* 2 vols. London: Baldwin, Cradock, and Joy, 1823

[Aikin was devoted to her father, largely having the care of him after he suffered a stroke in 1796 (he lived for another two and a half decades). It had become common for the survivors of an author or public figure to write a memoir of his life after his death, as a way to honor his memory, and remind the public of their contributions to society. In her memoir of her father, Aikin situates his life within the larger political movements of his time, as we find in the following excerpt (I: 130–32).]

It was in this state of his feelings, that the French revolution broke upon the world; and it will not appear wonderful that he should have been found in the number of its warm admirers, when it is recollected that its commencements were universally hailed by the friends of popular rights, in this and other countries, as the auspicious dawn of a new era of light and happiness.

But, it is well known that, even from the beginning, long before its progress was stained with blood and horrors, this great event was viewed with extreme jealousy by a majority of the higher classes in England, and especially by the established clergy; and that in most of our commercial towns, which have always been the strongholds of the protestant dissenters, and in corporate towns especially, the aristocratic and democratic parties, as they were then called, nearly coincided with the distinction of churchmen and dissenters. This division was rendered more exact, and the feelings which attended it doubly acrimonious, by the proceedings relative to the repeal of the corporation and test acts,[1] which happened to coincide in time with the promulgation of the new constitution of France. When, in

---

1 A series of acts, first promulgated in the 1660s and 1670s, which imposed tests and exclusions on those who refused to take the sacrament and oaths according to the rites of the Church of England, thus effectively excluding from public office Roman Catholics, Protestant Dissenters and Jews. Religious groups including Unitarians, Methodists, and Quakers campaigned for a change in the law in the late eighteenth century, though it was not until 1828 that both the Corporation Acts and Test Acts were repealed by Parliament.

March 1790, the dissenters found the abolition of this invidious law, which had nearly been carried in a former session, finally rejected by the votes of an overwhelming majority of the house of Commons, they were stung with a keen sense of the injustice of their country; and the best pens among them were sharpened for an appeal to public opinion,—the only resource which was left them. Bound to the dissenters by the ties of birth, connections, and personal obligations, Dr. Aikin did not hesitate on this occasion to stand forth as their champion; and two strongly written pamphlets attested his zeal in the cause. These pieces were published anonymously, but without any precautions for the concealment of the writer from the inquiries of either friends or foes.[1]

In those days of party violence, no one whose situation was in any respect a dependent one, was permitted to take the weaker side with impunity; nor was it long before Dr. Aikin was made to bear the penalty of his conscientious and disinterested efforts. Of the clergy resident in and near Yarmouth, whose literary acquirements and polished manners had hitherto rendered them his most congenial and agreeable associates, one alone had the courage and the liberality to stand by him without wavering in this season of trial. The members of the corporation and the high party generally, though not without some honorable exceptions, were pleased to consider themselves as absolved, *by circumstances*, from the engagement to support him, into which they had voluntarily entered on his coming to Yarmouth; and after studying to make him feel in various modes the weight of their displeasure, they entered into secret machinations for inviting another physician to take up his abode among them.

Meanwhile he continued to bear his head erect, as a man conscious of none but worthy motives, and prepared to stand to the consequences of his actions without shrinking;—but his natural disposition was so averse to turbulence and strife, that he could not see himself engaged, however innocently, in a conflict of this nature, without experiencing the most uneasy emotions; and he privately resolved, if the storm did not soon blow over, to yield to its fury and fly to the shelter of some friendly port....

[Also a literary biography, Aikin's *Memoir* recounts all of her father's many printed works. The following descriptions of his monumental, ten-volume *General Biography: Or, Lives, Critical*

---

1 An Address to the Opposers of the Repeal of the Corporation and Test Acts, 1790. Also attributed to Anna Barbauld.

and Historical, of the Most Eminent Persons of all Ages, Countries, Conditions, and Professions (1799–1815), is exemplary of the tribute she paid to her father in the memoir, and demonstrate the influence he had on her writing. She also provides a fascinating account of her father's writing practices (I: 156–59, 190–202).]

Towards the conclusion of the year [1796], Dr. Aikin, having secured as his coadjutor his beloved friend Dr. Enfield, engaged in the composition of his great work, the *General Biography;* which employed the larger portion of his time during a period of nineteen years, and extended to ten volumes quarto.

The design was not originally his own; but none could have coincided more happily with his talents, his acquirements, or the habits of his mind.

An author will seldom find cause to regret the time and labour which he may have bestowed upon an abortive or unsuccessful work, provided he has applied to it, during its progress, the full force of his mind. Such essays serve to root deeply in the mind ideas which afterwards spring up with renewed vigour and beauty, and in a more propitious season mature their fruits. Thus it proved in the instance before us.—The efforts which my father had bestowed upon the composition of his *Biographical Memoirs of Medicine,* had obliged him to meditate long and deeply on the subject of biographical writing in general;—to measure the positive and relative merits of the characters who came before him by a scale in his own mind; and to learn the art of conveying, by a few spirited strokes, a clear and lively image of the distinctive features of every individual. What he had thus practised with respect to the professors of a single art in one country alone, he now undertook to exercise on the eminent of many classes in all ages and countries.

In the preface to the work, which was composed with uncommon care and attention, he has given a distinct summary of his own views of the subject; which he will be found unswervingly to have followed; in fact, the principles upon which it is founded are so analogous to his settled habits of judging and feeling, that to those who knew him intimately this piece will appear not so much a prospectus of a book as an ingenuous exposition of his own standard of human greatness; and as such I shall extract some passages from it.[1] After observing that *selection, compass* and

---

1 Rudiments of the same ideas appear in a dialogue contained in *Evenings at Home,* entitled "*Great Men.*" Brindley is made an example in both pieces. [L.A.]

arrangement, are the three points chiefly to be considered in a biographical dictionary, and briefly stating, under the last head, the advantages of an alphabetical order, he thus proceeds:

> *Selection* is the most important point, and at the same time the most difficult to adjust, in a design of this nature..........
> In the long lapse of ages, from the first records of history, the names of those who have left behind them some memorials of their existence have become so numerous, that to give an account, however slight, of every person who has obtained temporary distinction in every walk of life, would foil the industry of any writer, as well as the patience of any reader. *Fame*, or *celebrity*, is the grand principle upon which the choice of subjects for a general biography must be founded; for this, on the whole, will be found to coincide with the two chief reasons that make us desirous of information concerning an individual,—curiosity, and the desire of enlarging our knowledge of mankind....

With respect to the *compass* of the work, he admits that biography will bear to be written much at large, and in judicious hands is often the more entertaining and instructive the more it is minute; and that in a plan so extensive as this characteristic sketches can alone be given; but he expresses a hope that they will be found to have dismissed few characters of *real eminence* "without fully answering the leading biographical questions, What was he? What did he? His moral and intellectual qualities, the principal events of his life, his relative merit in the department he occupied, and especially the manner in which he was first formed to his art or profession, with the gradations by which he rose to excellence, have engaged our attentive inquiries, and we have attempted to develop them with all the accuracy that conciseness would allow."

"If," he adds, "we have faithfully observed the rules of composition above suggested, it is evident we cannot have been mere copyists or translators; since we may venture to assert, that no model exists of a work of this species, executed with any degree of uniformity, upon such principles. For our materials, it is true, we must in general have been indebted to the researches of former historians and biographers.... But, in melting down the substance of different narrations into one, in proportioning the several parts, in marking out the characteristic features of the portrait, and in deducing suitable lessons and examples of human life, we have freely exercised our own judgements, and have aspired, at least, to the rank of original writers." ...

The copious extracts just given from a preface, all the promises of which were, on my father's part at least, so punctually fulfilled, may suffice as a general account of the nature of a work on which the opinions both of critics and readers have long since been pronounced; but a few particulars respecting the modes of study adopted by him during the course of his twenty years' task, and the effects upon his own mind of this application of his powers, may be thought no uninteresting or uninstructive part of his personal history.

It had been my father's previous practice to write over twice, and sometimes oftener, whatever he destined for the press; and with regard to his works in general, that *respect for the public*, which he always considered as one of the most indispensable of literary duties, led him to observe this custom to the end; but, with respect to his biographical articles, he soon discovered this laborious process to be unnecessary, and in fact scarcely practicable. Such, however, was his dread of suffering any marks of haste, either in style or matter, to escape him, that through the whole course of so long a work he persevered in the constant observance of another of his literary habits, which indicated the modest no less than the diligent composer. This was, never to commit a single page to the printer without causing it to be previously read aloud by one of his family in his own presence, and in that of any other members of the domestic circle who could be conveniently assembled. During these readings he listened with close attention, often mentioned the alterations which then suggested themselves to his mind, or the new ideas which struck him; and not only permitted, but invited and encouraged, the freest strictures even from the youngest and most unskilful of those whom he was pleased to call his *household critics*; good humouredly citing the story of Moliere's submitting all his pieces to the judgement of his old woman, as a proof that the honest impressions of *any* hearer or reader, were worth some attention. His principal object, however, in following this method was, to preserve his style from the fault which most of all offended him in every kind of writing,—*obscurity*; a fault which many instances prove that men of the most sagacious minds are frequently unable to detect in their own compositions except by experiment of their effect upon others. The statement of Gibbon, that he had never communicated to a single person any part of the manuscript of his history, was, I remember, particularly noted by my father on reading it, as a fact which went far in accounting for the perseverance of so able a writer in that enigmatical mode of expression which became the characteristic blemish of his manner.

How far the clearness of his own style, which is so perfect that I believe no one ever found it necessary to read a sentence of his a second time to find the meaning, is to be attributed to the occasional suggestions of others, I find it difficult to decide; as the distinctness of his ideas, and his entire freedom from affectation, were very likely of themselves to have ensured to him this advantage; but I can speak with all the certainty of personal experience to the pleasures and benefits derived to his family from his social and communicative habits of study. From witnessing so closely the progress of his various works, they insensibly acquired a lively interest in the subjects of them; these again became favorite topics of domestic discussion, and often led on to references to books and facts which from these associations were impressed indelibly on the memory. Nor could the reasoning powers fail of being strengthened and matured by these inquiries, carried on under the indulgent guidance of one who did not desire even from his own children a blind and prejudiced adherence to his opinions; but, on the contrary, never ceased to impress upon them as the most important of all maxims, that their reason was given them for the discovery of truth, and that there were no subjects on which it was not allowable, and even laudable, to exercise it independently, within the limits of modesty and candour. For myself,—if I may be pardoned the egotism,—I must ever regard it as the most important of many intellectual privileges for which I am grateful, to have grown up to maturity under the eye of my father during the time that he was engaged upon so many "fair designs," and especially on this; by virtue of which the illustrious of all ages were made to pass as it were before us in a long and leisurely procession, while we questioned each of his title to a pedestal in the Temple of Immortality. This was indeed philosophy teaching by example; and to the lessons then received, to the principles thus imbibed, I am bound, not in duty and affection alone, but in the strictest justice, to ascribe whatever favour any biographical attempts of my own may since have found with an indulgent public. But for my father they never would have had an existence,—to him is to be attributed whatever merit they possess; all that I can justly claim is that of having treasured up his precepts and followed to the best of my abilities his example.

2. From "Memoir of Anna Lætitia Barbauld," from *The Works of Anna Lætitia Barbauld, with a Memoir by Lucy Aikin*. 2 vols. Ed. Lucy Aikin. London: Longman, Hurst, Rees, Orme, Brown, and Green, 1825

[Aikin's work in collecting and editing her aunt's writing has been invaluable to modern scholars, as she printed many of the poems and shorter prose pieces that had not been published during her aunt's lifetime. In addition to the two-volume *Works*, in 1826 she also collected and edited *A Legacy for Young Ladies, Consisting of Miscellaneous Pieces, in Prose and Verse*, a series of short essays by Barbauld designed for young women. Aikin also, in the *Works*, included a brief memoir of Barbauld's life, which has proven to be influential in discussions about her aunt's legacy. In the first excerpt from Aikin's "Memoir," included below, she describes her aunt's refusal to open a women's school. In Aikin's account, Barbauld's refusal represents her good sense and her awareness that, because women and men were destined to fulfill different roles, their educational prospects should differ as well. Yet, as William McCarthy writes, these remarks of Barbauld have often been taken critically, especially by contemporary scholars, insofar as they "appear to rebuke a project cherished by feminists from Mary Astell to Virginal Woolf, the dream of equal schooling for men and women" ("Why Anna Letitia Barbauld Refused to Head a Women's College: New Facts, New Story." *Nineteenth-Century Contexts*, 2001; 23 (3): 250, 349–79. McCarthy has shown, however, that Aikin misrepresents Barbauld's letter, first, by suggesting that it was written to Mrs. Montagu when in fact it was written to her husband, and second, by omitting those portions of her letter in which she explains that her central objection was that operating such a school would impose undue demands on her time (and thus would interfere with her own literary pursuits). It seems, therefore, that Aikin may have been strategic in her editing of this letter, as she strove to represent her aunt's views as entirely innocuous. As was the case with her *Epistles*, it appears she succeeded in this object: the *Works* were "read approvingly by male reviewers" (McCarthy 350). "Memoir of Anna Barbauld," I: xvi–xxiv.]

... Whilst the prospects of the young couple were still full of uncertainty, some distinguished persons, amongst whom was Mrs. Montagu,—at once admirers of the genius of Miss Aikin and patrons of a more enlarged system of female education than was then prevalent,—were induced to propose to her to establish under their auspices what might almost have been called a College for young ladies. On a distant view, the idea had something noble and striking, but it was not calculated to bear a close examination; and it called forth from her the following remarks, well worthy of preservation, as a monument of her acuteness and good sense, and of the just and comprehensive ideas which, at a rather early age, and with slender opportunities of acquainting herself with the great world, she had been enabled to form of the habits and acquirements most important to females, and particularly to those of rank and fashion. It is also interesting as an instance of the humility with which she estimated her own accomplishments.

"A kind of Literary Academy for ladies (for that is what you seem to propose), where they are to be taught in a regular systematic manner the various branches of science, appears to me better calculated to form such characters as the '*Precieuses*' or the '*Femmes sçavantes*' of Moliere, than good wives or agreeable companions. Young gentlemen, who are to display their knowledge to the world, should have every motive of emulation, should be formed into regular classes, should read and dispute together, should have all the honours and, if one may so say, the pomp of learning set before them, to call up their ardour:—it is their business, and they should apply to it as such. But young ladies, who ought only to have such a general tincture of knowledge as to make them agreeable companions to a man of sense, and to enable them to find rational entertainment for a solitary hour, should gain these accomplishments in a more quiet and unobserved manner:—subject to a regulation like that of the ancient Spartans, the thefts of knowledge in our sex are only connived at while carefully concealed, and if displayed, punished with disgrace. The best way for women to acquire knowledge is from conversation with a father, a brother or friend, in the way of family intercourse and easy conversation, and by such a course of reading as they may recommend. If you add to these an attendance upon those masters which are usually provided in schools, and perhaps such a set of lectures as Mr. Ferguson's, which it is not uncommon for ladies to attend, I think a woman will be in a way to acquire all the learning that can be of use to those who are not to teach or engage in any learned profession. Perhaps you may think, that having myself stepped out of the bounds of female reserve in becoming an author, it is with an ill grace I offer these sentiments: but though this circumstance may destroy the grace, it does not the justice of the remark; and I am full well convinced that to have a too great fondness for books is little favourable to the happiness of a woman, especially one not in affluent circumstances. My situation has been peculiar, and would be no rule for others." ...

[Barbauld proceeds to object to the age proposed, saying that girls of fifteen are too old to cultivate a love of learning; and to plead her own lack of qualification, having only experience in teaching boys.]

The arguments thus forcibly urged, appear to have convinced all parties concerned, that she was right in declining the proposal. Mr. Barbauld soon after accepted the charge of a dissenting congregation at Palgrave near Diss, and immediately before his marriage announced his intention of opening a boarding-school at the neighbouring village of Palgrave in Suffolk.

[The following excerpt treats the reception of Barbauld's *Eighteen Hundred and Eleven*. In it, Aikin expresses her outrage—shared by many of her aunt's friends—at the cruel treatment she received from many reviewers of the poem, above all John Wilson Croker in the *Quarterly Review*.]

... Having thus braced her mind, as it were, to the tone of original composition [with the publication of her Introductory Essay in the *British Novelists* and with her collection of prose and verse, *The Female Speaker*], she produced that beautiful offspring of her genius, Eighteen Hundred and Eleven,—the longest, and perhaps the most highly finished, of all her poems. The crisis at which this piece was produced, and concerning which it treats, was confessedly one of the most distressful within the memory of the present generation, and the author's own state of spirits deepened the gloom. She, like Cassandra, was the prophetess of woe: at the time, she was heard perhaps with less incredulity, but the event has happily discredited her vaticination in every point. That the solemn warning which she here attempted to hold forth to national pride and confidence, should cause her lines to be received by the public with less applause than their intrinsic merit might well have claimed, was perhaps in some degree to be expected; that it would expose its author—its venerable and female author—to contumely and insult, could only have been anticipated by those thoroughly acquainted with the instincts of the hired assassin of reputation shooting from his coward ambush. Can any one read the touching apostrophe,

Yet O my country, name beloved, revered!—

the proud and affectionate enumeration of the names which encircle the brow of Britain with the halo of immortal glory; of the spots consecrated by the footsteps of genius and virtue, where the future pilgrim from the West would kneel with beating heart; the splendid description of London with all its "pomp and circumstance" of greatness,—the complacent allusion to "angel charities," and "the book of life" held out "to distant lands,"— and doubt for a moment that this strain was dictated by the heart of a true patriot, a heart which feared because it fondly loved?

This was the last of Mrs. Barbauld's separate publications. Who indeed, that knew and loved her, could have wished her to expose again that honoured head to the scorns of the unmanly, the malignant, and the base? Her fancy was still in all its brightness; her spirits might have been cheered and her energy revived, by the cordial and respectful greetings, the thanks and plaudits, with which it was once the generous and graceful practice of contemporary criticism to welcome the re-appearance of a well-deserving veteran in the field of letters. As it was, though still visited by

.... the thoughts that voluntary move
Harmonious numbers,

she for the most part confined to a few friends all participation in the strains which they inspired. She even laid aside the intention which she had entertained of preparing a new edition of her Poems, long out of print and often inquired for in vain;—well knowing that a day must come when the sting of Envy would be blunted, and her *memory* would have its fame.

No incident worthy of mention henceforth occurred to break the uniformity of her existence. She gave up all distant journeys; and confined at home to a narrow circle of connexions and acquaintance, she suffered life to slide away, as it were, at its own pace ...

V. Literary Criticism and Biography

1. Review of William Wordsworth, *Poems in Two Volumes*. *Annual Review*, vol. 6 (1807), 521–29

[The *Annual Review*, published between 1802 and 1808 by Longman, was edited by Aikin's brother, Arthur. As an annual, it sought to take notice of every publication printed during a given year in all genres, from literature to topography, architecture to mineralogy. Arthur Aikin prided himself on the independence of the review; once he briefly resigned from the editorship when it appeared that the owner of the journal (Thomas Longman) had tampered with a few of his reviews. (Longman himself claimed that he had no knowledge of the interventions.) As was the practice at the time, all reviews were unsigned. The authorship of the reviews of Wordsworth's and Byron's 1807 volumes of poetry have been attributed to Aikin by Donald Reiman in *The Romantics Reviewed*.[1] (Aikin acknowledged the Byron review in her letters, *Memoirs*, 164).

William Wordsworth (1770–1850) is now considered one the leading poets of the Romantic period. However, with the exception of *Lyrical Ballads* (1798), an anonymous, collaborative work with poems by Wordsworth and Samuel Taylor Coleridge, most of Wordsworth's early volumes of poetry, including *Poems in two Volumes*, were poorly received by critics and did not sell well. Like many critics, Aikin assesses Wordsworth's poetry by reference to the poetical system he established in the preface to *Lyrical Ballads*.]

Mr. Wordsworth is a writer whose system and practice of poetry are both so entirely his own, that in order to appreciate as fairly as we wish to do, the value of these volumes, it will be necessary for us to enter somewhat at length into a discussion of the theory of the art. His own theory of it the author has given in the preface to a former work, published before this review existed; and as we do not perceive that his style of writing has since undergone any material alteration, we shall refer to it without scruple, as containing the principles upon which the poems immediately before us have been composed.

On glancing the eye over Mr. Wordsworth's poems, the first

---

1 *The Romantics Reviewed: Contemporary Reviews of British Romantic Writers* (New York: Garland, 1972), Part A, I: 13-21; Part B, I: 1-3.

thing that strikes the reader is, the extreme simplicity of their language: he may peruse page after page without meeting with any of those figures of speech which distinguish we do not say verse from prose, but a plain style from one that may be called cultured, or ornate. Should we however attribute this peculiarity to indolence or deficiency of skill, Mr. W. would complain of injustice, for he has anticipated the charge, and in the preface to "Lyrical Ballads" has endeavoured to repel it. The highly metaphysical language employed in this preface, and the spirit of mysticism by which it is pervaded, render it somewhat difficult of comprehension, but this, as well as we can collect, is the substance of that portion of it which is to our present purpose.

It was his intention, he says, in his poems to take incidents and situations from humble life, and describe them in the real language of men in that class, only freed from its grosser vulgarisms. He has preferred such incidents and situations, because the feelings of persons in low life are stronger, less complex, and therefore more easy to be developed, than those of persons who move in a wider circle—their language he has preferred for similar reasons, and also because he thought that any departure from nature in this respect must weaken the interest of his poems, both as being a departure from nature, and because the language which the imagination of even the greatest poet suggests to him, must, in liveliness and truth, fall far short of that which is uttered by men in real life, and under the pressure of actual passions. All that is called poetic diction, he therefore despises, and has shunned with the same care that others seek it, convinced that a poet may give all the pleasure he wishes to do without its assistance. At the same time he has "endeavoured to throw over his draughts a certain colouring of the imagination, whereby ordinary things should be presented to the mind in an unusual way, and further, and above all, to make these incidents and situations interesting by tracing in them, truly though not ostentatiously, the primary laws of our nature chiefly as far as regards the manner in which we associate ideas in a state of excitement." This last expression savours to us of a jargon with which the public has long been surfeited, and it is evident that not a position is here advanced which might not easily be combated; but as the practical success of a poet is the true test of the justness of his principles, we shall reserve our remarks on this head till we come to extracts. Anticipating an obvious question, why with his sentiments did he write in rhyme and measure? Mr. W. now proceeds sensibly enough to defend his practice in this respect on the ground of the pleasure which the experience of ages has proved these devices to be capable of affording—he adds, that "from the tendency of metre to divest language in a certain degree of its reality, and throw a kind of half consciousness of unsubstantial existence over the whole composition, there is little doubt that more painfully pathetic incidents and situations may be endured in verse, especially in rhymed verse, than in prose"—He brings in proof, "the reluctance with which we recur to the more distressing parts of the Gamester and Clarissa Harlowe,[1] while Shakespeare's writings in the most pathetic scenes never act upon us as pathetic beyond the bounds of pleasure." Is not Mr. W. aware that these very arguments might equally be urged in favour of that poetic diction which he is so anxious to banish from his pages, and that the same instances might be adduced in its support that he here brings in favour of metre? It is not poetical diction, much more than mere verse, which produces the difference here pointed out between the writings of Shakespeare, and those of More and Richardson? But Mr. W. is persuaded that he has absolutely established it as a principle that in the dramatic parts of his compositions a poet should employ no other language than such as nature would suggest to his characters, (which after all is a very vague direction, since nature is by no means uniform in her promptings of this kind, and education and local circumstances produce endless diversities of style and expression,) and he endeavours to show that even where the poet speaks in his own character, he should employ no other diction than that of good and select prose. He begins by defining a poet as a man "endued with more lively sensibilities, more enthusiasm and tenderness, who has a greater knowledge of human nature, and a more comprehensive soul, than are supposed to be common among mankind," and in fine, as one chiefly distinguished from others, "by a greater promptness to think and feel without immediate external excitement, and a greater power in expressing such

---

1   *The Gamester*, adapted by Edward Moore in 1753 from an earlier stage play, is a popular domestic or middle-class tragedy in which a wife strives to save her husband who is a good man but addicted to gambling; he commits suicide at the end of the play. *Clarissa* (1748) is Samuel Richardson's tragic novel in which the eponymous heroine struggles to assert her virtuous independence; she is abducted and raped by the man to whom her parents had planned to forcibly marry her. She ultimately becomes ill as a result of the trauma she has suffered and dies.

thoughts and feelings as are thus excited in him." These "passions and thoughts, and feelings," he affirms to be the same as those of other men; but even if they were not, he proceeds to insist, that as a poet does not write for poets, but for men in general, in order to excite rational sympathy, he must still express himself as other men do. Now it appears to us in the first place, that this definition of a poet is both imperfect and incorrect. It is only that of a person of strong sympathies, who possesses in an unusual degree the power of imagining and describing the feelings of other human beings. A good novel writer must be all this—a descriptive or lyric poet, though perfect in his kind, need not. But one who really deserves the name of a poet, must certainly add another faculty which is not even hinted at in this definition—we scarcely know how to name it, but it is that kind of fancy, akin to wit, which "glancing from heaven to earth, from earth to heaven," pervading, as it were, the whole world of nature and of art, snatches from each its beauteous images combines, adapts, arranges them by a magic of its own, peoples with them its new creations, and at length pours forth in one striking, brilliant, yet harmonious whole.

This faculty, which Mr. W. overlooks, is doubtless the true parent of that diction which he despises; nor will either the frigid reasonings of metaphysicians, or the still more·frigid caricatures and miserable apings of mere versifiers, ever deter the genuine poet from employing it; it is his native tongue, and he must speak it, or be dumb. It is idle and sophistical to contend that because he does not write to poets he must not write like a poet. Many there are who are capable of being moved to rapture by a picture of Raphael or Titian, though they themselves could never guide a pencil—many there are who can follow with their eye the boldest soarings of the Theban eagle, though nature has not lent to them even the rudiments of a wing. If men in general are to be supposed incapable of understanding any expressions but what they would themselves have used in similar circumstances, rich and figurative diction must indeed, on most occasions be proscribed, but let it be remembered that such an interdiction would curtail the eloquence of Burke no less than the poetry of Shakespeare; so sweeping a clause is this, so fatal to the scintillations of wit, and the sports of fancy. Our author afterwards speaks of poetry as a thing too high and sacred to be profaned by the addition of trifling ornaments of style: we cannot understand what his notion of poetry is, after all, for he here plunges into the very depths of mysticism, but we suppose Virgil and

Milton must have had some idea of its power and dignity, and it does appear to us somewhat ridiculous, not to say arrogant, in Mr. Wordsworth, to imagine that he has discovered any thing, either in the trivial incidents which he usually makes the subjects of his narrations, or in the moral feelings and deductions which he endeavours to associate with them, too sublime for the admission of such decorations as these masters have not deemed derogatory from the highest themes they ever touched. But we believe one great source of what we consider as the errors of this writer to be his failing to observe the distinction between rhetorical and poetical diction; the former it is that offends; but in his blind zeal he confounds both under the same note of reprobation. He quotes Dr. Johnson's paraphrase of, "Go to the ant thou sluggard," and justly stigmatizes it as "a hubbub of words"; but is this a specimen of poetical diction? Surely not. It contains not one of those figures of speech,—similes, metaphors, allusions, and the like—which take their birth from that inventive, or combining, faculty which we mentioned above, but is tediously lengthened out by that accumulation of idle epithets, frivolous circumstances, and pompous and abstract terms, with which the rhetorician never fails, in prose or verse, to load his feeble and high sounding pages. It is this, this spirit of paraphrase and periphrasis, this idle parade of fine words, that is the bane of modern verse writing; let it be once thoroughly weeded of this, and it will be easy for the pruning hand of taste to lop away any redundancy of metaphor, personification, &c. which may still remain. Thus much for the system of Mr. Wordsworth, which appears to us a frigid and at the same time an extravagant one; we now proceed to examine what its practical application has produced; and whether our author has succeeded according to his intention, by giving us in plain rhymed and in measured prose, matter so valuable and interesting as to be capable of affording pleasure equal, or superior, to that usually produced by poems of a similar class composed in a more ornate and polished style. We shall also examine how far the principle of association, on which many of the pieces are composed, appears to have been productive of beauties or defects. ...

The Sonnets, a portion of which are dedicated to liberty, are formed on the model of Milton's and have a certain stiffness— but they hold a severe and manly tone which cannot be in times like these too much listened to—they bear strong traces of feeling and of thought, and convince us that on worthy subjects this man can write worthily....

One of the Odes to Duty, is a meanly written piece, with some good thoughts, the other is a highly mystical effusion, in which the doctrine of pre-existence[1] is maintained. The pieces entitled Moods of my own Mind, are some of them very happy, some quite the reverse. When a man endeavours to make his reader enter into an association that exists in his own mind between daffodils waving in the wind, and laughter—or to teach him to see something very fine in the fancy of crowning a little rock with snow-drops; he fails, and is sure to fail, for it would be strange indeed if any one besides himself ever formed associations so capricious and entirely arbitrary.[2] But when he takes for his theme the youthful feelings connected with the sight of a butterfly, and the song of the cuckoo, he has struck a right key, and will wake an answering note in the bosoms of all who have mimicked the bird or chaced the insect.[3] There is an exquisiteness of feeling in some of these little poems that disarms criticism....

There are likewise some "Elegiac Stanzas" of great pathos, and a perfectly original turn, which increase our regret at the quantity of mere gossip that this author has allowed to escape him.

We have now bestowed upon these volumes a survey more detailed and laborious than our usual practice, or, in some respects, their importance, might seem to require; but we were anxious to combat a system which appears to us so injurious to its author, and so dangerous to public taste.

Mr. W. doubtless possesses a reflecting mind, and a feeling heart; but nature seems to have bestowed on him little of the fancy of a poet, and a foolish theory deters him from displaying even that little. In addition to this, he appears to us to starve his mind in solitude.—Hence the undue importance he attaches to trivial incidents—hence the mysterious kind of view that he takes of human nature and human life—and hence, finally, the unfortunate habit he has acquired of attaching exquisite emotions to objects which excite none in any other human breast. He says himself in the concluding verse of his volumes,

"Thanks to the human heart by which we live,
"Thanks to its tenderness, its joys, its fears.

---

1   The belief that each individual possesses a pre-existent soul that enters (or is placed by God) inside the body once it is formed.
2   "I wandered lonely as a cloud" and "Who fancied what a pretty sight."
3   "To the Cuckoo" and "To the Butterfly."

"To me the meanest flower that blows doth give,
"Thoughts that do often lie too deep for tears."

This is all very well; these are pleasures that we cannot esti-
mate, and of which we should be sorry to deprive a humble
recluse; we only wish to hint, that a lasting poetical reputation is
not to be built on foundations so shadowy.

2. Review of Lord Byron's *Hours of Idleness*, *Annual Review*, vol. 6 (1807), 529–31

[One of Lord Byron's earliest collections of verse, *Hours of Idle-
ness, a Series of Poems, Original and Translated* was savaged in *The
Edinburgh Review* by Henry Brougham. Byron was scolded, not
so much for writing the verse and translations in the first place,
but for printing these manuscript poems and school exercises. In
her review, Aikin takes a much more favorable view of the poems,
and of amateur writing more generally. She also takes notice of
the melancholic, confessional nature of Byron's poetry, as well as
its tendencies towards "libertinism," all features that would
become central to his fame.]

The very modest preface which introduces these poems con-
cludes, after expressing the hopes and fears of a young author, as
follows.

"The opinion of DR. JOHNSON on the Poems of a noble relation
of mine,[1] 'That when a man of rank appeared in the character of
an author, his merit should be handsomely acknowledged,' can
have little weight with verbal, and still less with periodical cen-
sors, but were it otherwise, I should be loth to avail myself of the
privilege, and would rather incur the bitterest censure of anony-
mous criticisms than triumph in honours granted solely to a
title."

The spirit of this sentence pleases us, it shows a sensible and
manly pride unsubdued as yet by vulgar adulation. With regard
to the sentiment of Dr. Johnson, we are inclined to make this dis-
tinction. The merit of *the work itself* ought certainly to be appre-

---

1 The Earl of Carlisle, whose works have long received the meed of public
applause; to which, by their intrinsic worth, they were well entitled.
[Byron]

ciated (and always will be by us) without the slightest reference to the rank of its author but in cases like that before us, the merit of *the man* ought indeed to be "handsomely acknowledged." Between the amateur, even the feeblest, of literature, and the amateur of boxing and horse-racing, the merest stringer of rhymes, and the mere lounger and layer of wagers, the distance is so incalculably great, the advantage on the side of the former, both to himself and to society at large, so clear, and so important, that whenever a young nobleman shows himself disposed to employ his "Hours of Idleness" in paying his humble devoirs to any of the Nine,[1] whether within or without success, we shall certainly be disposed to yield him all praise and honour. The poems before us give proof of very promising talents, the age of the author at the time of writing them considered. Though somewhat incorrect, they are not tame, though juvenile, they are neither extravagant, nor altogether trite. The translations and imitations are usually elegant, but paraphrastic and deficient in vigour. The original pieces are better, especially those which may be supposed to express the real sentiments of the writer....

But the best poem in the volume is one which fills us with melancholy. Whether or not it is the real history of the author, is not for us to pronounce; but certain we are that it is that of many a man.

We would not be thought to encourage confessions of libertinism, for certain it is that unreluctant avowal of criminality is the token of incorrigibleness, rather than the herald of reformation. But whatever may be the effect of stanzas like these on the mind of the author, supposing them prompted by real circumstances, we deem them capable of producing in the minds of the young and innocent, reflections humbling indeed, but salutary.

VI. Essays

1. From "Words upon Words." *Memoirs, Miscellanies and Letters of the Late Lucy Aikin.* Ed. Philip Hemery Le Breton. London: Longman, Green, Longman, Roberts, & Green, 1864. 61–62; 70; 76–78

[Aikin does not appear to have been interested in the genre of the essay; this is the only essay of hers that survives. In it, she considers the origin and cultural significance of words, endorsing a

---

1 The nine muses of Greek mythology.

thoroughly modern view of language as a living entity, and "as a running commentary on the history of the manners and pursuits of every passing age" (79). At the same time, Aikin critiques current linguistic habits and trends, including the absorption of Scottish idioms and slang.]

"What is it you read, my lord?" "Words, words, words!" replies Hamlet, as who should say air, breath, sound, and emptiness. This always offended me. From my youth upwards, I have been a lover of words, a chooser of words, in a slender and superficial manner, a student of words, and instead of acquiescing in such disparagement, reducing them almost to "air nothing," I proclaim myself ready to maintain against all comers that words are things; nay, and things of pith and moment, life and passion. Have we not the right word, the very word, the word of advice, the word in season, the word of comfort, the warning word, the cruel word, and the kind one? And what are these but things? How they fasten themselves on our memory, with a grasp never to be shaken off while life endures! How our associations cling and swarm, and cluster round them! How our hearts beat at the sound with recollected joy, grief, pity, hope, indignation, or gratitude! Things! Nay, I am more inclined to call them persons, in such vivid individuality of feature do they rise before "the eye of mind." Have they not also—at least the more distinguished of their race—their pedigrees, their biographies, their private, sometimes their scandalous, histories and anecdotes? Are there not among them ranks and degrees, nobles and commoners, decent people and rabble, natives and aliens, legitimates and illegitimates, pure breeds and mongrels?

A full and true history of words, including only those of our own country, might be made as long, perhaps, too, as full of instruction and entertainment, as a history of England itself. But what Hercules in literature would prove equal to the task? The labour of a life would be lost in it, considering the multitude of collateral branches which it would shoot out, this way and that, upward and downward, into depths, into darkness, out of sight, and beyond all computation of distance.

Hearken to the pregnant hint thrown out as he passes, by the philosophical historian of the "Decline and Fall."[1] After observing that "so sensible were the Romans of the imperfection of

---

1 A reference to Edward Gibbon's influential *The History of the Decline and Fall of the Roman Empire*, published between 1776 and 1789.

valour without skill and practice, that in their language the name of an army was borrowed from the word which signifies exercise," (*exercitus ab exercitando*); he adds in a note, "There is room for a very interesting work, which should lay open the connection between the languages and manners of nations." No doubt, for the field remains as open at the present day as fourscore years ago, when this suggestion was first offered....

The farther research is carried, into whatever language, the more unfathomable become those gulfs of antiquity into which its origins are seen to open. The roots both of the Greek and the German have been traced to the Sanscrit—Sanscrit, of which it cannot even be conjectured how many ages have revolved since it was a living tongue. And had the Sanscrit no parent? Who can answer? What we know certainly in this matter is, that for centuries upon centuries, words have been suffering so much of transformation, disguise and corruption, by accident, error and caprice, learned and unlearned,—by the licences of poets, the figures of orators, the affectations of pedants and coxcombs, the blunders of travellers, and the innovations of colonists—that in numberless instances their radical idea is lost beyond hope of retrieval, and all that can be done is to make use of them like technical terms, standing for some single definite notion to be learned by practice alone....

... The written language of Scotland, that of her early literature, her court and her aristocracy, has long since merged in that of Great Britain; and the vulgar idioms of Ayrshire or Lothian have assuredly no inherent right to a toleration, in books or in conversation, refused to those of Lancashire or Devon. But the privilege accorded to Scotland in this respect stands on higher ground. It has been won for her by the excellence—not indeed of her graver prose writers, nor yet of her more polished versifiers, from Drummond to Thomson and Beattie,[1] all of whom came as near to the English tongue as they were able—but by her truly national poets, and her novelist of world-wide fame. Possessed from early times of a national music, the country was rich in ancient ballads and in popular songs, which embodied in the racy idioms of a mother-tongue the traditions of the past, and the fresher inspirations of passion, of fancy, and of humour. In this

---

1 All well-known Scottish poets. William Drummond (1585–1649) was also a historian; James Thomson (1700–48) was best known for his immensely popular poetical series, *The Seasons* (1726–30); James Beattie (1735–1803) was also a philosopher.

rustic dialect, imperfectly spelled out, there was found, or fancied, a character of mingled simplicity, tenderness and archness, which happily corresponded with the pastoral style, so long the delight, or pretended delight, of the whole of lettered and polished Europe....

Percy's "Reliques,"[1] the most popular of poetical collections, and one which effected a signal revolution in literary taste, owed the larger and more interesting portion of its ditties to the bards of the "North countrie," on which ever side of the border. The repulsiveness of consulting a glossary was surmounted for their sake; and thus the Northumbrian English, and the lowland Scotch, idioms which most nearly approached each other, while their respective speakers continued hereditary foes, became alike familiar to the numerous admirers and the swarm of affected imitators of the ancient ballad.

Burns[2] next arose—a poet always, but twice a poet when he trusted himself with his native Doric, which found favour for his sake, even in Attic ears. The "Minstrelsy of the Scottish Border" followed; then "The Lay of the Last Minstrel," and the rest of that brilliant group of metrical romances struck off with such dazzling rapidity on the same glowing anvil—finally the "Waverly novels."[3]

During the Scott mania to which the English public was wrought up by these powerful and repeated efforts, which survived for many years the last and mightiest "master of the spell," it was not perceived that we were negligently losing sight of the ancient land-marks of the neighbour tongues; nay, that we were suffering our very bulwarks and fortresses to become Scottish colonies and dependencies, through a process of settlement and occupation not unlike that by which we have seen Texas and other portions of Mexico transmuted into a territory of the United States.[4] Our own people were turning Scotch without

---

1 Thomas Percy (1729–1811), writer and Church of Ireland bishop of Dromore, collected a three-volume anthology, *Reliques of Ancient English Poetry: Consisting of Old Heroic Ballads, Songs, and Other Pieces of Our Earlier Poets* in 1765.
2 Robert Burns (1759–96), popular Scottish poet.
3 Poems, and novels, by Sir Walter Scott (1771–1832), hugely popular Scottish author of the period.
4 The Mexican–American War was an armed military conflict between the United States and Mexico from 1846 to 1848 in the wake of the 1845 US annexation of Texas.

knowing it. We began to allow the macaronic[1] of the Edinburgh Review for actual *English*! Instead of acting on behalf of another it was for his *behoof*. Staircases, or pairs of stairs, were totally disused and we were left to ascend by *a stair* as *fully more* convenient. Friends looked *over* the window, and joined each other *on* the street. Forgetful of our honest old idiom "*this here*" and "*that there*" we ceased to perceive any clear difference, however the confusion might perplex us, between this and that, these and those. Inroads and incursions, eruptions and invasions, were all metamorphosed into *raids* and *forays*, and transplanted by writers, too, of no inconsiderable pretensions, into historical narratives of distant times and other countries. A species of anachronism and absurdity scarcely less gross than that committed by Cowper in his translation of Homer, where he repeatedly mentions tapestry by the name of *arras*![2] In fine, our very instinct of shall and will, should and would, began to waver, and we were left to get out of this sad scrape not as well as we could, but as *we best might*. At length there are encouraging tokens of the decline of this insidious epidemic. No recent cases have been observed, and we might now be beginning to congratulate ourselves on a happy return to vernacular soundness, but for the alarming visitations of another and a far worse contagion—not a brogue, not a dialect; a contraband importation from some province, respectable though obscure, from innocent cottages, or simple rustic farms, where genuine Anglo-Saxon lingers still—but a pestilence drawn forth, reeking and flagrant, from the metropolitan dens of all abomination and corruption, moral and physical, and philological. It is, in short, *slang*, which has dared to intrude itself into common speech, and the literature of *the million*. *Slang*, a term unknown as yet to dictionary or glossary, but which a very high authority has taken the laudable precaution to interpret to the ignorant and the innocent. It is derived, he informs us, from the verb to *sling*, and designates the idiom of those whose career is likely to terminate in *suspension*. What more is to be said!

---

1 Composed of or characterized by a mixture of languages.
2 Aikin is objecting to the use of an old-fashioned word (arras), imported from France (deriving from the name of a town in Artois famed for its manufacture of the fabric) in an English translation of a Greek text.

VII. Children's Literature

1. From *Poetry for Children: Consisting of Short Pieces, to Be Committed to Memory. Selected by Lucy Aikin.* Seventh Edition. London: Longman, Hurst, Rees, Orme, and Brown: 1818. (First Edition 1801), iii–vii, 1–3

[In *Poetry for Children,* Aikin includes short selections from a wide range of poets, including Shakespeare, Milton, Dryden, Pope, Gay, Addison, Crabbe, Gray, Cowper, and Barbauld. Like her father and aunt, Aikin believed that political topics such as slavery, poverty, war, and cruelty to animals were suitable for children, and many of the poems attempt to teach proper ethical behavior and progressive political views. Aikin's selections also include eleven "original" poems; there are two poems devoted to birds, poems that describe other geographical regions (Constantinople, Arabia, Canada, and others). Two examples are included below.]

Preface.
To Parents.

Since dragons and fairies, giants and witches, have vanished from our nurseries before the wand of reason, it has been a prevailing maxim, that the young mind should be fed on mere prose and simple matter of fact.[1] A fear, rational in its origin, of adding, by superstitious and idle terrors, to the natural weakness of child-hood, or contaminating, by anything false or impure, its truth and innocence,—has, by some writers, and some parents, been carried to so great an excess, that probably no work would be considered by them as unexceptionable for the use of children, in which any scope was allowed to the fanciful or marvellous. It may well be questioned, however, whether the novel-like tales now

---

1   During the late eighteenth and early nineteenth century, many (espe-cially male) authors perceived that there was a threat to fairytales and other fantasy literature for children. It was typically authors like Anna Barbauld, Maria Edgeworth, and Sarah Trimmer who were blamed with such an assault; Barbauld herself was famously "damned" by Charles Lamb as one of "those *Blights & Blasts* of all that is *Human* in man & child." These attacks were, however, largely unfair, and as Aikin's com-mentary suggests, the issue was a complex one.

written for the amusement of youth, may not be productive of more injury to the mind, by giving a false picture of the real world, than the fairy fictions of the last generation, which only wandered over the region of shadows;—whether a romantic sensibility be not an evil, more formidable in magnitude, and protracted in duration, than a wild and exalted fancy.

Poetry has many advantages for children over both these classes of writing. The magic of rhyme is felt in the very cradle—the mother and the nurse employ it as a spell of soothing power. The taste for harmony, the poetical ear, if ever acquired, is so almost during infancy. The flow of numbers easily impresses itself on the memory, and is with difficulty erased. By the aid of verse, a store of beautiful imagery and glowing sentiment may be gathered up as the amusement of childhood, which, in riper years, may soothe the heavy hours of languor, solitude, and sorrow; may strengthen feelings of piety, humanity, and tenderness; may soothe the soul to calmness, rouse it to honourable exertion, or fire it with virtuous indignation.

But when we consider how many of the subjects of verse are unintelligible to children, or improper for them;—how few poems have been written, or how few poets could be trusted to write, to them;—we shall not be surprised to find it a frequent complaint with judicious instructors, that so few pieces proper for children to commit to memory are to be found either in the entire works of poets, or in the selections made for them purposely for the use of young people. To meet the wishes of parents and teachers is the object of the following selection. It was thought that all the pieces ought to be short enough to be learned at one or two lessons, and good enough to be worth remembering; that their style should have nothing in it that a well-educated child might not, their matter nothing that he should not, understand as soon as he should be at all able to feel the beauties of *real poetry*.

Natural history, that popular and delightful study, justly claimed a considerable part of the work, as being at once pleasing and useful to children.

Description of different times and seasons, of objects of nature and art, of various occupations and modes of life, opened another copious source. Moral sentiment furnished a third portion. Miscellaneous *scraps*, laboriously gleaned from a vast number of poets, formed the remainder of the little volume.

No arrangement appeared necessary;—the only point of this nature which has been studied was,—to mingle the pieces as much as possible. Some valuable poems were passed over on account of their occurrence in almost all other selections;—the brevity required in the pieces precluded the insertion of others;— but it is hoped that the smallness of the work will exculpate the compiler from the imputation of any sins of omission. Some liberties have unavoidably been taken, in order to make *wholes* of fragments.

Such is the plan of the work;—of its execution the compiler can only say that it has cost much time, and much thought.

It is now trusted to a candid public, with the hope, that a performance, aspiring, from its very nature, to little applause, will not incur the hazard of much censure....

2. From "On the Spirit of Aristocracy. A Dialogue. Albert, Sophia." *Memoirs, Miscellanies and Letters of the Late Lucy Aikin*. Ed. Philip Hemery Le Breton. London: Longman, Green, Longman, Roberts, & Green, 1864. 29–33

[Both John Aikin and Anna Barbauld wrote numerous "dialogues" for young persons (included in *Evenings at Home* and collected by Aikin in *Works of Anna Lætitia Barbauld*. Typically, these dialogues were between a young person and an adult, and touched upon some moral or political theme. Aikin also wrote several of them, which were collected and published by her niece and nephew after her death. The following is a short excerpt from her dialogue "On the Spirit of Aristocracy," which demonstrates her interest in teaching the young the absurdities of England's class system.]

Sophia. ... this morning [Frank and Harry] got upon rather an interesting subject, as I thought, and I should be glad, my dear uncle, to hear your opinion upon it. Frank says there is more of the spirit of aristocracy in England than in any other country in Europe. This Harry denies, but what say you? ...

A[lbert]. That this is not the country in which there is the broadest line of demarcation between patrician and plebian, *noble* and *roturier*, is evident from our possessing no native words to express exactly this distinction. We have, indeed, lords and commoners, but as the younger children of peers have always been included in the latter class, the nobility have never with us, as in France or Germany, formed a race, or *caste*, who could insult the rest of the nation by the boast of better blood than theirs. In one sense, therefore, the assertion is plainly incorrect.

S. This was Harry's argument....

A. But in spite of this, if it is meant to assert that this is the country in which people are most uniformly deferential in their manners towards those whom they regard as their superiors, and contemptuous to their inferiors, I am afraid it may be true. We are certainly very great respecters of persons.

S. What can be the reason of it?

A. Several reasons, or rather several causes, may be assigned. In the first place, although we have never, correctly speaking, had patrician families, or a privileged order like the French noblesse, the distinction of ranks has always been very strongly marked among us. You may have read that in old times there was a difference made in gentlemen's houses between those who sat above and those who sat below the salt;[1] and in every baronial hall there were distinct tables for guests of different degrees, who were thus in presence without ever being in company with one another. There were also sumptuary laws by which the use of rich furs, velvet, gold lace, and other expensive materials and fashions of dress, and even of some luxuries of the table, was restricted to persons of a certain rank or fortune. Down to the overthrow of monarchy at the death of Charles I., the ceremonial of the English court had been almost oriental in its servility, and was viewed with surprise by foreign ambassadors. No one presumed to speak to Queen Elizabeth, but on his knees, and in her days a private gentleman or a knight was expected to stand 'cap in hand' even to a peer. Now, although these appendages of barbarism and the feudal system have long been swept away, I think you will perceive that it may well require ages to wear out the marks left by them on the manners and customs of a people. Down to the present day does not an insignificant young gentlewoman like yourself expect her shoemaker or her milliner to stand in her awful presence while receiving her orders?

S. Why, that is what those kind of people do of course; one never tells them to do it, or thinks about it.

---

1 Referring to the custom whereby, in the houses of people of rank, a large saltcellar was placed near the middle of a long table, with the places above assigned to guests of distinction, and those below to dependents, inferiors, and poor relations.

A. Precisely, because there *is* so much in England of the spirit of aristocracy. In America, or in the France of the present day, you would find that such observances are by no means matters of course. There, a common workman would make no scruple of seating himself beside you.

S. How horrid!

A. Yes, "how horrid!" With English young ladies that silly exclamation, too, is quite of course. You cannot bear the notion of your inferiors forgetting their distance towards you, and yet if you were to call upon a duchess, and she should motion you to a stool at the lower end of the room, you would scarcely be able to find the terms strong enough to express your indignation at the arrogance of her behaviour. Is there not a greater distance between you, the daughter of a private gentleman of small fortune, and a duchess, than between you and a respectable milliner?

S. I do not well know what to say to that. In fortune there is, no doubt, and in what one may call consequence, but in another way there seems not to be. It is said, I believe, that a gentleman or gentlewoman is company for anybody; now I—that is to say, papa is a gentleman, and he sometimes visits noblemen, but a milliner is not a gentlewoman.

A. Speak out at once, child, without affectation, the thing that is in your head, which is this: that when your great neighbours at the castle invite what are called the country families once in the season, you go there with your sister and are received by the duchess as a person of her society; whilst the milliner is never received by you or your sister on that footing.

S. That was what I meant, my dear uncle, but I did not know exactly how to express it.

A. Your claim, then, to a kind of social equality with a duchess is that of a gentlewoman born? But what if the milliner should turn out to be better gentlewoman of the two? With respect to the one you employ, I happen to know this to be the case. She is the granddaughter of a lord, a poor one indeed, but still a lord.

S. Is it possible?

A. Stranger things are very possible in this world of mutability. Her mother married ill, in every sense of the term, was cast off by her noble father and family, and sank into indigence. She herself married a man of very respectable character, an artist, but he was carried off at an early age and left her with the charge of a young family with whom she creditably maintains by the profits of her business. Yet this lady you keep standing at your audience!

S. Oh! but indeed, my dear uncle, I had no idea that she was such a real gentlewoman. I will always make her sit down in future.

A. So far, well. But the disciples of Pythagoras abstained from crushing even a worm, for fear of dispossessing some kindred soul,[1] and I would conjure you by your own gentility to forbear to keep standing *any* milliner or dressmaker you may in future employ, lest you should again be guilty of the horror of failing in respect to the granddaughter of a lord. It is very difficult to know the negative in these cases.

S. You are laughing at me.

A. Oh! by no means. I only suggest the motive most likely to be effectual in persuading you to treat what you call "those kind of people" like fellow-creatures....

---

1 A reference to the philosopher's belief in transmigration, or the reincarnation of the soul again and again into the bodies of humans, animals, or vegetables.

Appendix A: Selected Letters

[Aikin was an avid letter writer. A selection of her correspondence was published by her niece and nephew in their 1864 *Memoirs, Miscellanies and Letters of the Late Lucy Aikin,* and a small collection of her letters is held by the Department of Rare Books & Special Collections, University of Rochester Library. It is likely, however, that these represent only a small proportion of her total output. The letters in *Memoirs* include the two decades–long correspondence she had with the Reverend Dr. William Ellery Channing (1780–1842), a collection that was republished with Channing's letters in 1874. Channing was the foremost Unitarian preacher in the United States in the early nineteenth century and a leading Unitarian theologian. Aikin was strongly influenced by his spiritual views, though, as the following excerpts demonstrate, she held ongoing conversations with him on a wide range of subjects, from politics to women's rights, and from literature to history. The following selections from her letters are those most relevant to her writing on women and to her historiography. All her letters, both to Channing as well as to friends and family members, demonstrate how she directed her considerable observational and analytical powers to her own historical moment. Her letters also reflect her intellectual curiosity, her enduring commitment to political and social justice, and her affability and sociability.]

1. Lucy Aikin to Mrs. Taylor,[1] July 1806, Stoke Newington (*Memoirs*, 134–35)

As I was determined to "exert my energies," I readily accompanied my friends on board Mr. W. Carr's ship, whence we saw Nelson's body[2] carried in procession up the river. The ships with their lowered flags, the dark boats of the river fencibles, the magnificent barges of His Majesty and the city companies, and above all, the mournful notes of distant music, and the deep sound of the single minute-gun, the smoke of which floated heavily along the surface of the river, conspired to form a solemn, sober, and appropriate pomp, which I found awfully

---

1 Mrs. Susanna Taylor (1755–1823) and her husband, hymn writer John Taylor (1750–1826), were members of a prominent Unitarian family from Norwich.

2 Horatio Nelson, Viscount and Vice-Admiral (1758–1805), was the most famous military hero of his day, renowned for his participation in the Napoleonic Wars. He was killed in the Battle of Trafalgar. Aikin's letter relates events that took place in early January, 1806.

affecting. It did but increase my eagerness to witness the closing scene of this great pageant exhibited the next day at St. Paul's. Richard, who was our active and attentive squire, will probably have given you an account of our adventures on this occasion, and the order of procession you would see in the papers; but perhaps you might not particularly attend to a circumstance which struck me most forcibly—the union of all ranks, from the heir-apparent to the common sailor, in doing honour to the departed hero. In fact, the royal band of brothers, with their stately figures, splendid uniforms, and sober majestic deportment, roused, even in me, a transient emotion of loyalty; but when the noble Highlanders and other regiments marched in who vanquished Buona-parte's Invincibles in Egypt, and, reversing their arms, stood hiding their faces with every mark of heartfelt sorrow, and especially when the victorious captains of Trafalgar showed their weather-beaten and undaunted fronts, the bier in silent mournful state, and when, at length, the gallant tars appeared bearing in their hands the tattered and blood-stained colours of the "Victory"—and I saw one of the poor fellows wiping his eyes by stealth on the end of the flag he was holding up—I cannot express to you all the proud, heroic, and patriotic feelings that took possession of my heart, and made tears a privilege and luxury. No, on that day an Englishman could not despair of his country!

2. Lucy Aikin to Mrs. Taylor, August 1816, Stoke Newington (*Memoirs* 142–43)

... Elizabeth [i.e., Aikin's *Memoirs of the Court of Elizabeth I*] goes on with increasing facility and satisfaction. Your opinion on the advantages of this mode of history writing, is peculiarly gratifying to me. It appears to me that a historian who undertakes to narrate the events of centuries must necessarily neglect the illustration of their literature, their biography, the manners, and domestic morals; but are not these, to the great body of readers, at once the most instructive, and the most amusing branches of knowledge of past ages? On the other hand, the mere antiquarian presents all the minuter parts of this knowledge in a detail which is often dry and disgusting; he is frequently destitute of all powers of writing, and almost always void of that philosophical spirit which combines, which generalises, and infers. Yet the writer of essays on the progress of civilisation, on manners, &c. is still worse; he is generally a Scotch or French metaphysician, who sets out with a system; if the former, he gives you facts so exaggerated, so embellished, or so distorted, that you would give the world to get clear out of your head all the error that he has put into it. All these things I see and feel, and of course I promise myself that my work shall be of a kind free from all the objections of all the others; yet thus it will not be, or if it is, it will have faults of its own as great, perhaps, as theirs. In short, perfection and man! To do our best, and estimate our efforts with humility, is all that remains, and both shall be my study....

3. Lucy Aikin to Anna [Letitia] (Aikin) Le Breton, 5 July 1824 (Aikin Family Papers, Department of Rare Books & Special Collections, University of Rochester Library)

... I am glad to learn that you are to visit before your return both Mrs. Piper & Mrs. Ward; these successive domestications in different families appear to me an important supplement to female education, & unless I have overrated more than even affection justifies, your powers of observation & reflection, you will reap from them important benefits. I think I observed to you when we parted, that in thus making a part now of one circle, now of another, by turns, we insensibly learn to be glad of all our knowledge & sorry for all our ignorance. One accomplishment or qualification is valued in one house, another in another, & while we converse only with those whose pursuits are innocent & laudable & by whom we are ourselves treated with kindness & hospitality we naturally desire to conform ourselves, if possible, to all their tastes, & to make ourselves useful or agreeable in some point to every member of each family in which we are entertained. This cheerful compliance with the habits & pursuits of others, this eagerness to oblige all in their turns, is the true secret of being an agreeable visitor ...

One thing, my love, I am particularly desirous of pointing out to you at present;—it is this. You will, in all probability, be very early called upon to take the station of mistress of a family;[1] it is one which cannot be well filled without a good deal of knowledge of a kind to which you have as yet never turned your attention; I earnestly recommend it to you to begin, & improve the opportunities which you now enjoy. I understand that your aunt has every thing very nice & in good order about her;—observe the details of her management; how her table is set out; what means are employed to give a good air to family dinners; get a notion if you can, what quantities of various articles are used in the house; do not think it too much trouble to ask for receipts for any dish which pleases or is new to you (which is always a compliment) & copy them out. If you show yourself desirous of information on these heads your aunt, I doubt not, will be willing to give it you. You may afterwards make your comparisons between her conduct of a family & that of the other friends whom you visit, &

---

1   Anna Le Breton became engaged in 1833; during the courtship, Aikin wrote a series of letters encouraging her in this relationship.

learn something from all. This kind of knowledge is by no means difficult to acquire; it asks no more than common attention, common capacity; but one thing is absolutely necessary towards obtaining it, & that is, not to despise it. Of this capital error, should you be disposed to entertain it, a very few reflections, with your own *very* good sense will suffice to cure you. "Whatever is worth doing at all," my wise & excellent father used to say, "is worth doing well." How important then is it to do well what must be done constantly? Do not think the occupations of a good housewife mean or insignificant. Nothing can be insignificant on which so much of daily comfort depends, nothing can be mean which so high a principle as the sense of duty can be made to bear upon. I might add the remark, that in your situation your praise or dispraise, your real consequence & credit in society, will assuredly depend more upon your conduct of your father's family than upon any other acquirement or accomplishment whatever, & justly; because, though as I before observed, to gain the necessary knowledge requires only common attention & capacity, to put such knowledge steadily in practice, to give the rules which it dictates & to superintend the execution of them by servants, requires method, diligence, watchfulness, patience, forbearance, & above all that constant thoughtfulness for the good of others which is the best exercise of the heart & temper.

Excuse me this long lecture, my dear, dictated as it is by the most affectionate anxiety for your good....

4. Lucy Aikin to Rev. Dr. Channing, 28 May 1828, Hampstead (*Memoirs* 187)

...You will not wonder after [*my recent illness*] to hear that King Charles has been at a complete stand; yet I am not without doubts that the future work may have been gaining by an interval in which I have found opportunity for some general reading in history, and much meditation. Everything imprints more and more deeply on my mind the importance of the great historic virtue which I thank you for exhorting me to—that of impartiality. Certainly, instead of doing a service to the great cause of liberty by veiling the errors of its champions, we do it in fact the greatest injury, especially where we have failures to relate; for if the great fault was not in the men, it seems a just conclusion that it must have been in the cause. On the other hand, by representing its opponents as worse men than they really were, we lighten arbitrary power itself of the reproaches justly its due, to discharge them on the vices accidentally adhering to its supporters. But certain principles have a tendency to produce certain effects, good or bad, on the minds and manners of their advocates; and the chief utility of introducing biographical details largely into works of history is, that these tendencies may be impressed and illustrated by examples; that both the rule and the exceptions to it may be fully understood, and thence just inferences may be drawn regarding principles themselves—and how can these *just* inferences, so important to virtue and happiness, be drawn from any but *true* premises? ...

5. Lucy Aikin to Anna [Letitia] (Aikin) Le Breton, 12 August 1830, Hampstead (Aikin Family Papers, Department of Rare Books & Special Collections, University of Rochester Library)

... Who, I wonder, is thinking of any thing else but the glorious *new* French revolution—it comes to put you young folks on a level with your elders—you too have now seen a revolution—but never I trust will you witness a new reign of terror.[1] Hitherto all seems to proceed with wisdom & moderation, & I hope these principles may continue to preside. Many things are far more propitious than forty years ago: First, there is much less to be swept away. Feudal rights, exclusive privileges, exemptions from taxation for the noblesse—the exorbitant wealth & power of the clergy, the right of arbitrary imprisonment in the crown, then destroyed, have never been restored. Secondly, there is much more political knowledge diffused through the people by free newspapers: Thirdly, what is of inestimable consequence, the people have now known, & tried & worthy leaders; partly the first revolution, partly the representative government of the last fifteen years, has taught the nation whom to trust; formerly all men were equally untried in public life, because there had been no public life but that of the minister of state, & therefore the people of Paris, who called themselves the nation, tamely surrendered up all power over the lives of men & the destinies of their nation, to every bold bad man who stretched forth a hand to seize it.—Now they have their veteran patriot Lafayette, & the novel leader of the two chambers, & there will be no career, I hope, for ruffians. A long political lecture you may think—but I write as I should talk to you, of which is uppermost.

As for my own little private self, to turn from great things to small, I have one capital symptom of mental & bodily health to report—that the days are too short for me—what with a good deal of reading, a

---

1 In the French Revolution of 1830, also known as the July Revolution, King Charles X, the French Bourbon monarch, was overthrown and replaced by his cousin Louis-Philippe, who would in turn be overthrown in the 1848 revolutions.

little working, marketing,[1] accounts, the superintendence of my large family, walking, morning calls & evening visits, & the great standing dish of King Charles, I really am occupied from morning to night, & should be so if the days were a good deal longer.

Hampstead is very full at present with strangers as well as residents, & I enjoy the society it affords me. There is a most bewitching little woman come to live at Downshire Hill whom I really think I must visit, even there; the daughter of poet Coleridge, married to her cousin Henry Coleridge, who wrote an amusing & rather clever, though flippant book on the West Indies.[2] I met them one evening at the Baillies. She has the ease of one who has seen a good many people, which at Southey's she must have done,[3] but with it the simplicity of one who has not seen London life, or the great world; & she speaks of nature like one who has seen it with poetic eyes....

6. Lucy Aikin to Rev. Dr. Channing, 28 June 1831, Hampstead (*Memoirs* 228–29)

... It is from intimate views of private life in various ages and countries that the *moral* of political history is alone to be derived—and without this what is the value of long tales of wars and conquests, and one king deposing and succeeding another, and republics changes into monarchies, and monarchies into republics? This principle has been always in my view in writing my "King Charles," and will impart, I think, its chief merit to my book; that is, should health and vigour be lent me for its completion....

7. Lucy Aikin to Rev. Dr. Channing, 6 September 1831, Hampstead (*Memoirs* 230–31)

... Just now my feelings are more cosmopolite than usual; I take a personal concern in a *third* quarter of the globe, since I have seen the excellent Ram-Mohun-Roy.[4] I rejoice in the hope that you will see him

---

1 Buying goods at a market.
2 Henry Coleridge (1798–1843), was a barrister and writer. His *Six Months in the West Indies* (1836), according to the *Oxford Dictionary of National Biography* "upset some members of his family by its flippant tone and lively anecdotes." He married Sara Coleridge (1802–52), writer and literary editor and daughter of Samuel Taylor Coleridge, in 1829.
3 Sara Coleridge was raised by her uncle, the poet Robert Southey (1774–1843), in Keswick.
4 Ram-Mohun-Roy, also referred to as Rammohun Roy by Aikin (1774–1833), in 1828 founded an influential Indian socio-religious reform movement. His remarkable influence was apparent in the fields of politics, public administration and education as well as religion.

some time, as he speaks of visiting your country, and to know you would be one of his first objects. He is indeed a glorious being,—a true sage, as it appears, with the genuine humility of the character and with more fervour, more sensibility, a more engaging tenderness of heart than any *class* of character can justly claim. He came to my house, at the suggestion of Dr. Boott, who accompanied him, partly for the purpose of meeting Mrs. Joanna Baillie, and discussing with her the Arian tenets of her book. He mentions the Sanscrit as the mother language of the Greek, and said that the expressions of the New Testament most perplexing to an European, were familiar to an Oriental acquainted with the language and its derivations, and that to such a person the texts which are thought to support the doctrine for the pre-existence, bear quite another sense. She was a little alarmed at the erudition of her antagonist, and slipped out at last by telling him that his interpretations were too subtle for an unlearned person like herself. We then got him upon subjects more interesting to me—Hindoo laws, especially those affecting women. He spoke of polygamy as a crime, said it was punishable by their law, except for certain causes, by a great fine; but the Musulmans did not enforce the fine, and their example had corrupted Hindoos; *they* were cruel to women, the Hindoos were forbidden all cruelty. Speaking of the abolition of widow-burning by Lord W. Bentinck,[1] he fervently exclaimed, "May God *load* him with blessings!" His feeling for women in general, still more than the admiration he expressed of the mental accomplishments of English ladies, won our hearts. He mentioned his own mother, and in terms which convinced us of the falsehood of the shocking tale that she burned herself for his apostasy. It is his business here to ask two boons for his countrymen—trial by jury, and freedom for British capitalists to colonise among them. Should he fail in obtaining these, he speaks of ending his days in America....

8. Lucy Aikin to Rev. Dr. Channing, 7 April 1832, Hampstead (*Memoirs* 257–59)

... We modestly esteem ourselves the first of womankind for knowledge, for accomplishments, for purity of manners, and for all the domestic virtues. I am not sure that we are mistaken in supposing that the *union* of these recommendations is more frequent in England than

---

1   Known as sati or suti, a funeral practice among some Hindu communities in which a recently widowed woman would immolate herself on her husband's funeral pyre. In 1829, the practice was formally banned in Bengal by the governor, Lord William Bentinck. From 1812, Roy had actively campaigned against sati.

elsewhere; but even granting us the whole, there is much, much to be added and to be corrected. Amid all that is put into the head, the soul, and very often the *reason*, starves.

Women are seldom taught to *think*. A prodigious majority never acquire the power of reasoning themselves or comprehending the force of arguments advanced by others. Hence their prejudices are quite invincible, their narrowness and bigotry almost inconceivable, and amidst a crowd of elegant accomplishments, their thoughts are frivolous and their sentiments groveling. Exceedingly few of them have any patriotism, any sympathy with public virtue. Private feelings, private interests engross them. They are even more insensible than you charge our public men with being of "the greatness of the times in which we live." Rammohun Roy has been justly scandalized at the want of zeal for the reform bill[1] amongst the ladies ... You look with some jealousy on the principle of patriotism as hostile to universal philanthropy; but I am sure you will agree with me that it is better to love our country even partially and exclusively than to love nothing beyond our own firesides; and when public good and private interest interfere, to feel no generous impulse to sacrifice the less to the greater. I wish that more women were nurtured in, at least, the Latin classics, because from them they might imbibe *this* elevating senti- ment, without which they can never deserve the *friendship*, whatever thay [sic] may obtain of the *love*, of noble-minded men. If you turn to one of Mrs. Barbauld's "Characters," beginning—"Such were the dames of old heroic days" ... you will fully understand what kind of spirit I long to inspire in my own sex. Almost all my life this desire has been one of my strongest feelings. When a little girl I used to battle with boys about the Rights of Woman. Many years ago, I published "Epistles on Women," all to the same effect; and though I now think I dare say as ill as anybody of the *poetry* of that work, it contains many sentiments which I still cherish, and would give much to be enabled to disseminate....

9. Lucy Aikin to Rev. Dr. Channing, 15 October 1832, Hampstead (*Memoirs* 271–72)

... I wonder whether you have seen a small book published by Ram- mohun Roy containing translations of several of the Hindoo Veds? I

---

1 The *Reform Act*, passed in 1832, extended the franchise and abolished the "rotten boroughs," electoral districts with tiny populations that nevertheless sent members to Parliament. It was the most controversial of the three elec- toral reform bills passed in the nineteenth century (the other two were passed in 1867 and 1884).

have found a good deal of interest in this view of theology and meta-physics of a nation so remote in every respect from us and our way of thinking. The great point which the true friend of his country and his race has had in view in his various controversies with his own countrymen, has been to show that, although some idolatrous rites are sanctioned by their sacred books, yet it has always been the doctrine of the most authentic of these, that the highest future happiness was only attainable by a pure and austere life, and the worship of the invisible, universal Spirit—that idolatry was for the gross and ignorant, rites and observances for them only. Thus he shows that eternal felicity—that is, absorption into the supreme spirit, is promised to women who after the death of their husband lead devout and holy lives; and only a poor lease of thirty-five million years of happiness with their husbands to such as burn with them, after the expiration of which their souls are to transmigrate into different animals. This you will say is mighty puerile, but it is at least meeting his antagonists on their own ground. Afterwards he details the many cruelties and oppressions to which females in his country are subjected by the injustice and barbarity of the stronger sex, and pleads for pity towards them with such a powerful, heartfelt eloquence as no woman, I think, can peruse without tears and fervent invocations of blessings on his head....

10. Lucy Aikin to Rev. Dr. Channing, 14 October 1837, Hampstead (*Memoirs* 362-63)

...With regard to [Harriet Martineau's][1] notions of the political rights of women, I certainly hold, and it appears to me self-evident that, on the principles that there should never be taxation without representation, women who possess independent property *ought* to vote; but this is more the American than the English principle. Here it is, or was rather, the doctrine that the elective franchise is a trust given to some for the good of the whole, and on that ground I think the claim of women might be dubious. Yet the reform bill, by affixing the elective franchise only, and in all cases, to the possession of land, or occupancy of houses of a certain value, tends to suggest the idea that a single woman possessing such property as unrestrictedly as a man, subject to

---

1 Harriet Martineau (1802–76), writer and journalist. Aikin's comments are in response to Martineau's *Society in America* (1837), a critique of America's failure to live up to its democratic principles. Aikin clearly disagreed with some of Martineau's assessments about women, and also disliked her generalizations about America: "what presumption," she writes in the same letter, "in any individual to speak of the tempers of a whole nation!" (*Memoirs*, 363).

the same taxes, liable even to the some burdensome, though eligible to no honourable or profitable, parish offices, ought in equity to have, and might have without harm or danger, a suffrage to give. I vote for guardians of the poor of this parish by merely signing a paper, why might I not vote thus for members of parliament? As to the scheme of opening to women professions and trades, now exercised only by men, I am totally against it, for more reasons than I have time to give....

11. Lucy Aikin to Rev. Dr. Channing, 18 April 1838, Hampstead (*Memoirs* 368)

...Your rector who said the English whipped their wives, I take to have been regardless of the truth; at least, in my whole life, I never either read or heard of one single instance of that infliction; though of many, alas! of husbands injuring, or even killing, their wives by kicks and blows of the fist. In ninety-nine cases out of the hundred, intoxication—either of the man, the woman, or both—is the occasion of these brutalities. If, or let us say *when*, we grow more temperate, we shall mend in this point. Our law does what it can for beaten wives, by binding husbands over, on complaint to keep the peace; and I am told that the merest clown feels deeply the disgrace of this, and seldom offends again....

No!—born champion of my sex as I may almost call myself—I say deliberately, on good knowledge and careful consideration, that there are only two points in which it seems to me that our laws bear hard on women. The first is, in the want of a stricter hand against the inveiglers of girls for wicked purposes; the second, in the full power which the father is still allowed to retain over his children when *his* offences have compelled an innocent wife to obtain a divorce from him. It is surely most monstrous that a woman should be restrained from separating herself, under circumstances of the most aggravated offence, from a brutal and unfaithful husband, by his inhuman threats of never letting her see her children more—of placing her daughters under the very care of his mistress—a menace which I know to have been uttered!

On carefully comparing the Code Napoleon with ours, I am convinced that we have the advantage of French women. Yet, understand me, not as admitting that we have nothing to complain of. Society wrongs us where the laws do not. The *life* of a woman is esteemed of less value than that of a man. Juries of men are very reluctant to punish the slayer of his wife as a murderer. Her *testimony* is undervalued; men-juries often discredit her evidence against a worse than murderer. She is wounded by the privileged insolence of masculine discourse. "Woman and fool," says spiteful Pope, and dunces echo him. Any feeble-minded man is an "old woman"; fathers cry out to their boys in petticoats not to care what their elder sisters say to them. These and the like insults, when my blood was hotter than it is, have cost me many a *bitten lip*. One of our legal exemptions signally offends me. It is that which grants impunity even for felony committed by a wife in presence and under control of her husband. Has a married woman, then, no moral freedom? Must her vow of obedience include even crime? Surely this disgraceful exemption ought now, at least, to be withdrawn, when that immoral vow is no longer an essential of the marriage rite. On the whole, however, I think the present age is more favourable to our sex than any former one. Women are now, with us at least, free of the whole circle of arts and sciences; they have neither ridicule nor obloquy to encounter in devoting themselves to almost any department of knowledge. All men of merit are forward in cheering them on; they are more free than ever. Alas! I speak of women, but you may say I only mean gentlewomen. In truth, I *can* speak of none else with personal knowledge—the miserable drudges, the beaten, and half-famished wives, and a class still more miserable, are never seen, never heard of by me in my tranquil home....

Appendix B: Selected Reviews of Epistles on Women

1. *European Magazine*, July 1811, 35–39

A lady undertaking to assert female rights, and to do honour to the female character, places herself in a rather delicate situation. She must expect criticism, and criticism not always of a pleasant kind. She must expect to be informed, by some male critics, that the subject, if thoroughly examined, leads to discussions in which no young lady can engage with propriety, and in which no female could preside. Nor must she be surprised if some critics of her own sex should be the first to take alarm, and to bestow, if not direct censure, not very liberal praise. She must expect more. She must be prepared to be told by some, that the subject itself cannot support so much argument as some persons imaginations have led them to suppose: that if it seems glorious to be an advocate, it should be in a cause where there is much to dispute and much to be gained: that it can be contested only by the illiberal; the enlightened part of mankind being at all times ready to allow the women every power of intellect, and all advantages for improving it: but that Nature, who has placed boundaries in all her works, has also limits and laws, by which each sex is distinguished and characterized, as well in the rational as irrational world: so that the subject, they will say, in its due length, does not go far: and if carried to the length some persons would wish, it would conduct only to the world of shadows. [The reviewer quotes extensively from the Preface.]
...

These Epistles, then, have in view to combat such opinions, and practices, as seem to controvert these claims, and to militate against female improvement. This the author does by marking the effects of various institutions and states of manners on the virtue and happiness of man, and the concomitant proportional elevation or depression of woman in the scale of existence. We readily allow, as a preliminary concession, that the author possesses some advantages for such a work: she has evidently a well-furnished mind, and her theme is susceptible of poetical embellishment; and that it also carries an air of sufficient novelty, at least considered in its poetical aspect. For though it has been treated of in verse by some Italian and French writers, and discussed in prose in foreign languages, as well as in our own, under the various forms of "vindications," "Female Biographies," and the like, yet no poet, to the best of our knowledge, has professedly handled the subject, except in occasional hints, or complimentary epistles, or, as in one instance, where the female character has been displayed in the exercise of energies which more properly and allowedly character-ize the other sex.

The work consists of four Epistles, addressed to her sister-in-law, Mrs. Charles Rochemont Aikin; and the form is appropriate enough; liable, however, to objection from those who admire the present taste for popular tales, or the fashionable embellishments of chivalry and romance. Had this indeed been avowedly a didactic or descriptive poem, we should certainly have looked for some occasional story; but it would have been ill-placed in Poetical Epistles, or it may rather be said its place is well supplied by touches of nature which interest the feelings, by much historical allusion which fixes the attention and enlivens the narrative....

... Miss A.'s lines [in the first Epistle] lead us to suppose, that as Adam was a moping ideot before he saw Eve (though Moses finds plenty of work for him), so Eve, previously to her actually seeing Adam, had been a great baby, *accustomed* to range by the side of the brooks, and to listen to the music of birds....

In the next Epistle, our author takes a view of savage life in general, and maintains that the sex have always been oppressed by slaves and barbarians: and here she displays considerable and a well-selected reading. ...

This Epistle certainly possesses much true poetry, and manifests very fine feelings. All the facts adduced bear on Miss A's argument; but they seem not sufficiently, or at least exclusively; applicable as general arguments against the manners of savage life. We do not mean to be the advocates of uncivilized life. But in nations deemed civilized, and in some that were highly so, customs and laws have existed equally destructive of female improvements as any that have existed among North American savages. Thus, in the East, the Persian women were immured like slaves, according to the account given by Plutarch. In the scripture account by Moses, we find the most humble and servile employments, assigned to the women, and of the best quality, in Arabia. The Turkish and Chinese women, to this day, are kept in the most painful subjection. In Sparta, indeed, the women were held in due consideration; and therefore it was said, that they only begat men; but in Athens, they were in a manner imprisoned in a remote part of the home, and subjected to employments very unfavourable to mental improvement....

And [*Aikin's description of Athenian wives as "fetter'd and debas'd"*] was true of the sex in general; high and low, free-born and slaves, not excepting even the ladies of the first distinction; to which we find fre-quent allusion in Homer and the Greek tragedians. The Romans in general treated their women more liberally: but even among the

Romans there was a time when, by law, no woman could possess any inheritance. With respect to some horrors charged on savage life, we may remark, that other people beside savages have destroyed their infants; as the Chinese, a civilized, though an idolatrous nation, and the states of Greece, in all of which infanticide, either by exposure or direct killing, was tolerated, and in some actually imposed by law. Portuguese and Spanish Christians were the authors of the horrors in South America, and civilized Christians in Europe are the great promoters of the slave trade. In savage life, the greater strength will assume the greater power, and claim more than its just portion of rights over the weak. In civilized life, law itself may produce similar effects; and some civilized governments have practised all the tortures and oppressions of barbarians.

The third Epistle describes the dawn of civilization, freedom, and the virtues. Miss Aikin's spirit rises with the subject. Her argument is illustrated by many apposite examples, and her ideas are strongly conceived; though, for epistolary writing, there is, perhaps, too much attempt at polish....

What Miss A. says of the Roman women is animated and just: but we submit to her, whether, as she afterwards takes a distinct view of the effects of Christianity in reference to female improvement, she had not better have deferred her allusions to what, probably, she would call its corruptions, to that head? As to the freedom of Christianity, at least of many professing Christians, this must be admitted with great limitations. The Vandals were tolerant as conquerors, except when a certain description of Christians became a state faction; so was Rome Pagan, but not so Rome Christian. As to the Africans, whether Pagan or Christian, they were always a land of slaves; the only party that ever aspired at freedom were treated as heretics, obliged to become vagrants, and to seek in the interior wilds of Africa, among Pagans, that liberty which they could never find among professing Christians; and, according to Miss A's own doctrine, where the men are themselves slaves, the women are never free.

In the fourth Epistle, our author recurs to her subject, and unfolds many varieties of female condition which she had hitherto left unnoticed. To this epistle we most willingly give our unqualified approbation.... [H]er allusions to several distinguished ladies in the English-history with her address to cotemporary ladies, gives a natural and very interesting close to the whole....

From what has been said, some idea may be formed of the character of these epistles. With respect to the *subject*, it has been admitted, that it is capable of poetical embellishment, nor is the poem defective, at least in this respect, in execution: part of the *philosophy*, perhaps, may be objected to by some readers, by such as admit the testimony of Miss A's prophetic angels, that woman was made of "a form more fragile and a tenderer mind," and who maintain, indeed, that mind is the effect of a mere organization of matter; they, on *their* principles, may object to the doctrine that "Souls have no sex"; and, while submitting to the superiority of particular women, and while acknowledging that the customs of savage and civilized society have greatly interrupted female improvement, may yet contend for a *general* inferiority; though it is not intended, as before hinted, to discuss metaphysical subjects here. With respect to the species of *poetry*, it has been admitted, that as Miss A. has adopted the epistolary rather than the didactic or descriptive, she has done right in not adorning it with a story in the manner of Virgil in his Georgics, and Thomson in his Seasons.[1] It should, however, be added, that, as a didactic or descriptive poem allows of much ornament, epistolary writing is rather characterized by simplicity and ease. Miss A. has erred, we think, in this respect, and has displayed sometimes rather too much pomp of thought and luxuriancy of diction. We are aware that Miss A. presents herself as an opponent to Mr. Pope in his attack on the sex, and in some sort as a rival to him in his own style of poetry.[2] But we should rather have seen more of Pope's manner in his Moral Essays in Four Epistles to several Persons, and in his Imitations of Horace, and less of his manner in his Essay on Man. But where, as in this instance, we perceive so much to approve and admire, we are more inclined, both from principle and choice, to praise than to censure. These epistles possess much merit, considered either as a poetical or literary performance; and therefore the patronage from the public to which they are entitled, we hope they will obtain.

2. *Monthly Review*, April 1811, 380–90

... To these detached extracts from Miss Aikin's sensible preface, we might add others, illustrative of her design, and deprecatory of that too probable misunderstanding to which the composition of a woman, advocating the cause of her sex, may be exposed. We are as anxious to assist the present fair writer in removing this obstacle to the success of

---

1 Publius Vergilius Maro (70 BCE–19 BCE), known in English as Virgil, classical Roman poet and author of *Aeneid* and in 29 BCE, *Georgics*, a didactic poem on rural life and farming; James Thomson, 1700–48, Scottish poet and playwright, known for his masterpiece and best-selling nature poem, *The Seasons* (1730).
2 See Pope's "Epistle II: To a Lady on the Characters of Women" (1735), in Appendix C4.

her moral intentions, as we were lately to aid another lady[1] in the same noble design;—namely, that of convincing man how "impossible it is for him to degrade his companion without degrading himself; or to elevate her without receiving a proportional accession of dignity and happiness";—and moreover, we know not one feminine attraction or accomplishment which may not coexist with the greatest cultivation of the female mind; nor one duty, peculiarly belonging to the softer sex, of which the fulfillment will not be farther secured by such cultivation. If we remove but the fear of neglecting the Graces by a closer worship of the Muses,[2] we shall have removed the chief impediment in the way of an enlarged and more liberal education of our females. Let us consider the excellent arguments adduced for such an improvement by every enlightened writer on the subject, and add to those arguments the examples of the best educated women in every age and country. We shall hear them all with one voice confess the proper sphere for the exercise of their abilities, namely the sphere of domestic duty;—and then let us be ashamed to reply with unmanly ridicule, or still more disgraceful calumny, to such accumulated claims on the justice, policy, and generosity of man in giving every artificial aid to those abilities which, Nature seems to whisper, were not originally constituted inferior to his own.

The general style of Miss Aikin's poem is elegant and correct: but it contains passages, undoubtedly, which deserve neither of these characters; and as we shall select some of the best specimens of the fair writer's manner, so we shall feel it incumbent on us to point out her defects. ...

We find but little to censure and much to praise in the second epistle, where the author draws a comprehensive sketch of savage life, and shews how hostile that life is, in all its forms, to female happiness. We must, however, object to some expressions which a little care would have avoided, and which tend to disfigure the general appearance and effect of a composition, more than most writers are willing to believe.

"Where untaught Nature *sports* her fancies rude," (page 17) is a mere vulgarism; and "Nature's *tough* Son" (page 19) is scarcely better....

---

1   See our Review of the posthumous volumes of Miss Elizabeth Smith, Number for January last. [M.R.]

2   The three Graces, generally known in Greek myth as the goddesses of such things as charm, beauty, and creativity; the nine Muses, Calliope (epic poetry); Clio (history); Erato (lyric poetry, especially love and erotic poetry); Euterpe (music and lyric poetry); Melpomene (tragedy); Polyhymnia (sacred poetry); Terpsichore (dance); Thalia (comedy); and Urania (astronomy).

The third epistle opens in a vigorous strain, and worthy of its object,—the dawn of civilization, of freedom, and of the virtues. A striking sketch of the manners of Greece and Rome succeeds; and the present degraded state of the antient seas of glory and of genius is forcibly depicted. The condition of woman throughout is shewn to follow and to imitate the course of man. The promulgation of Christianity is justly hailed as a new security for the interests of woman: but the light which breaks in on her prospects from this quarter is suddenly obscured by the frightful appearance of Superstition, and all her dark train of monastic privations and penances....

We will not lessen the effect of this conclusion by recording any of the little verbal criticisms which occurred to us in re-perusing the last epistle; and we dismiss the poem by expressing the warmest wish that the good, the philosophical, and the patriotic design of its writer may not wholly be frustrated: but that the great truth, to the support of which her pen has devoted itself, may impress some few out of the many who will peruse these epistles, with its importance: stamping the moral of her song on every intellect that is vigorous enough to receive and tenacious enough to retain it:

"Man, stamp the moral on thy haughty mind:
Degrade the sex, and thou degrad'st the kind!"

3. *Belfast Monthly Magazine*, August 1810, 131–35

The question respecting the equality of the sexes has been often debated, but a great diversity of opinion still prevails on this subject. Some contend that literary pursuits, by cultivating and improving the mind, renders a female unfit for the occupations of domestic life. A little knowledge may certainly have a dangerous effect, but the more real knowledge we possess the more fully we feel our deficiency, and how much is yet to be learned.

"A little learning is a dangerous thing;
Drink deep, or taste not the Pierian spring:
There shallow draughts intoxicate the brain,
And drinking largely sobers us again."

It is not good policy to wish the female sex to remain in ignorance, as we always find an ignorant person the most untractable. A judicious education and habits of study have a tendency to strengthen the faculties of the mind, and to promote the advancement in the scale of rational existence....

The admiration of sentimentality, and the sarcasms of those who are afraid of the approach to rationality in the female sex, have tended to increase the frivolity so common among the uninstructed. Some may think that females have no higher destination to attain. Triflers may please for a time by the graces of youth, but when age comes they will regret that the time spent in irrational pursuits was not employed in acquiring solid improvement. These triflers, as well as the mere domestic drudges whose views never rise to just ideas of intellectual excellence, are well depicted by this writer:

"O! vapid summary of a slavish lot!
They sew, they spin, they die and are forgot."

Those who cultivate their minds, and lay in a store of useful knowledge, will never feel ennui. It is education alone which makes the difference in the intellectual capacity between the sexes; if women always had the advantages of a liberal education, and were not afraid to avow their acquirements lest they should be ridiculed by the thoughtless, they would be fully equal to the other sex in every valuable and useful attainment. The difference in the manner of educating the sexes, commences in infancy, and occasions much of the diversity of character, exemplified in their pursuits through life. The boy frequently is forced to apply to his tasks, and to acquire habits of study, while the education of the girl is neglected either through the ignorance or mistaken notions of the parents. Trifling accomplishments are taught, at large boarding-schools, or by a fashionable governess, and the attention of the female is solely turned to seek to please at the expense of neglecting the most important parts of education. Education thus mis-directed has a tendency to make women mere pleasing toys for the passing hour, and music, drawing, and dancing, are made the chief objects of study. With boys they are only secondary objects, but with some women every thing. Hence we may see the difference between the sexes thus instructed. Where women have been well educated, they have shown no inferiority of intellect, and instances of many women breaking through all the obstructions to improvement, and vindicating the dignity of their sex are frequent. In the energetic language of this able vindicator of women.

"Souls have no sex; sublimed by virtue's lore
Alike they scorn the earth, and try to soar;
Buoyant alike on daring wing they rise,
As emulation nerves them for the skies." ...

Queen Elizabeth is described in rather too flattering terms. She was a *great Queen*, but she was not an amiable character. The greatness of her mind on many occasions, could not exempt her from the despicable rivalship of beauty and the desire for admiration, which she suffered to display themselves on many occasions, particularly in her conduct towards Mary Queen of Scots. She was insincere, and vain of her literary talents; yet there are many allowances to be made to her when we consider that she was perpetually assailed by servile homage on the throne, and it requires more than common strength of mind to remain uninjured by the combination of flattery and power. The truth, especially disagreeable truth, could seldom reach her ears.[1] She had, however, great talents for governing, she possessed courage and activity, and she patronized men of talents....

We highly recommend this book to the perusal of our readers, confident that they cannot read it without having a more exalted idea of the female sex, and on this account we have made long extracts of the miscellaneous poems, which compose the remainder of the volume; "the Ode to Cambria," excels in fine painting, and the lines "to the memory of the late Rev. Gilbert Wakefield," in true sensibility and feeling. The whole of the poems have the characteristic of genuine poetry, "Thoughts that breathe, and words that burn," and are unlike those ephemeral poems which leave little impression on the memory after the book is closed.

4. *Poetical Register*, 1810–11, 553–54

We have received great pleasure from the perusal of these epistles. They are, in no common degree, pointed, polished, and energetic. The versification, too, is of the best kind. It is flowing, without being insipid, and varied, without being harsh.

5. *Critical Review*, August 1811, 418–26

We have two reasons for noticing this book, independent of its merits, viz. that the author is a lady, and that the subject relates to her own sex. It is not from a feeling of gallantry, a motive which can scarcely be supposed to influence a spectacled reviewer, that we are induced to pay our compliments to the literary fair, but because we are happy to see a woman asserting the proper dignity of her sex, and evincing by her own example that female pretensions are well founded. It is quite time that the doctrine of the natural inequality of the sexes should be

---

1 In her *Memoir* of Elizabeth, Aikin addressed many of these criticisms in her representation of the monarch.

exploded: indeed we imagine that most sensible people are of this opinion, especially when they recollect, among many others, the names of Seward, Bailey, Edgworth, Barbauld, Opie, and Hamilton:[1] at any rate we are disposed to allow feminine claims to the utmost extent that Miss Aikin requires: our only business at present is to investigate the precise nature of Miss A's individual claim, and to determine with that authority which the self-created judges of letters exercise in as much plentitude as the more regularly appointed judges of the law, in what rank of female worthies Miss A. is to be placed....

The first epistle opens the subject in some very respectable lines, and presents us with the following ironical, and we think silly piece of reasoning, which does not much accord with the professions in the preface:

"No, heaven forbid! I touch no sacred thing,
But bow to right divine in man and king;
Nature endows him with superior force,
Superior wisdom then I grant of course;
For who gainsays the despot in his might,
Or when was ever weakness in the right?"

We are sorry that Miss A's indignation at the supposed humiliated condition of her amiable sex should have led her into this pert and inconclusive style of argument, which evinces anger without power: she should have recollected that there is no spectacle more ridiculous than impotent rage.

Miss A. then proceeds to give an account of Adam and Eve before and after their meeting. Those who recollect Milton's beautiful description of our first parents will feel something worse than disappointment, they will be inclined to laugh at Miss A's very different portraiture of the same personages. She describes Adam as a mere moping idiot, and Eve as a mere baby before their tête-à-tête. As we are not inclined to dispute the poet's well-known privilege of "quidlibet audendi,"[2] handed down to them from the magna charta of Horace, we shall not demand on what authority this delineation so unsupported by Moses and Milton is founded, but shall content ourselves with saying that it is in very bad taste....

---

1 Anna Seward (1742–1809), poet; Joanna Baillie (1762–1851), playwright and poet; Maria Edgeworth (1768–1849), novelist and educationalist; Anna Barbauld (1743–1825) poet and essayist, Amelia Opie (1769–1853), novelist and poet; and Elizabeth Hamilton (1756?–1816), novelist and essayist, were all well-known female authors of the period.
2 "Poetic license."

The second epistle, which gives an animated and poetical sketch of savage life is in our opinion much superior to the first. We shall quote two passages which appear to us particularly good.

The first is a high-wrought and poetical description of the lawless Otaheitans....

The language of the above quotation is rich and poetical, and the style is at the same time spirited and tasteful.

The next passage, which depicts the horrors of the slave-trade, we give not only for its own merits, but because we think we cannot too often impress on the public mind the abominations of that inhuman traffic....

The third epistle contains a description of women in the different periods of civilized life. There are many passages of considerable merit in this section, but there are many also which are reprehensible for their obscurity and tasteless expression....

The fourth epistle is a poetical excursus on the various conditions, yet unnoticed, of women in different ages, from ancient Germany to modern England. It is the longest, and we think the best....

We suppose, that Miss A's admiration for chivalry and chivalrous men, those ridiculous compounds of unprovoked ferocity towards their fellows and childish fondness towards the ladies, is confined to her poetry; indeed she hints so herself, else we should be compelled, with great regret, to observe, that a literary lady who wishes to exalt the dignity of her sex, feels all the unmeaning rapture for prancing horses, and their more pompous riders, or, as Mrs. Sneak, in Foote's farce,[1] more humbly expresses it, for *milintary men*, which the merest romance and novel reading miss of fourteen can be supposed to feel when she first dances with a sentimental ensign, or a "gay boldfaced cornet." ...

Upon the whole, however, we think very highly of Miss A's talents. Her mind is evidently well cultivated, and stored with elegant and useful information: she has all the good sense and justness of thinking on moral and political subjects which we should expect in the daughter of Dr. Aikin, and though her poetical powers are not of the higher order, she is fully entitled to the praise of an elegant and accomplished versifier.

---

1   Samuel Foote (bap. 1721, d. 1777), actor and playwright, who became well known in the mid-eighteenth century for his satirical revues mimicking well-known people.

6. *Eclectic Review*, November 1810, 418–26

It is difficult to say what a poem on Women should include. It appears to us, that the fair and ingenious author of the Epistles, has too much circumscribed her theme, by confining her attention almost wholly to woman, as she has been, and as she is, in various ages and nations, in her relationship to man—as the weaker part of the species, oppressed by his tyranny among barbarians, and raised by his courtesy to her due rank, in proportion as he became civilized. Woman in her more abstract and universal character,—woman as she is with respect to herself, as well as with respect to her helpmate,—woman in her individual sphere, fulfilling her duties as daughter, sister, wife, and mother—is only incidentally mentioned; and scarcely celebrated with the commendation that is due to her, even from one of her own sex, who has most laudably and successfully undertaken to vindicate her dignity—and to prove both by argument and illustration, that as man himself sinks or rises in society, by the ascendancy which belongs to him, he depresses or elevates his partner. But we are not disposed to find fault with the plan of this work. Had a hundred writers, male and female, chosen the same subject, each would have taken a different view of it. In every one we might have found peculiar traits excelling the corresponding traits in all the rest; in none perhaps harmoniously and perfectly assembled all the beautiful features and enchanting graces that belong to woman,—to woman as she is in our country, at our home, by our own fire-side. Where it may be asked, should the poet find a prototype for such a delineation? Truly we know not where a lady ought to look for it,—unless where she who *might* find it there, would certainly *not* look for it, in her glass. But where the poet of the *other* sex—young—in love—and full of hopes, chastised by fears that make even hope more exquisitely precious,—then we would tell him to shew us the woman of his heart, as she appears to him in those entrancing moments, when he thinks on future happiness; and with happiness, in every state, and under every form, associates her dear idea, as the companion of his life, the friend of his bosom, the mother of his children, his position on earth, his partner even in the joys of heaven. Woman thus lovely and virtuous, thus amiable and exalted would surely be the most inspiring Muse, the most delightful theme, that ever prompted the numbers, or warmed the fancy of a poet worthy to be her admirer and panegyrist. We have had enough in verse, of the agonies and raptures of love, in youth and before marriage: but love in all the holy, sweet, and generous forms which it assumes when the exchanged affections of two are centered on a third object, equally near and dear to each—when a family of children grow up together—and connubial, filial, parental, and fraternal feelings are so divided and diffused, and in one small circle at least to

> "form with artful strife
> "The mingled harmony of life";—

love thus enlarged, refined, and ennobled, has been but rarely, and at least but imperfectly sung by poets. The poet therefore, who should chuse woman for his theme, and represent her as the mother of such multiplied and abiding blessings to her species, might produce a work of far deeper interest, if not of far higher merit, than any that we have seen on the subject, in our own or other languages. It is at present, however of no consequence to enquire how the subject might have been adorned by another: it only behooves us to inform our readers, how the sex has been exhibited in these elegant epistles by one of its living ornament; and for this purpose we select, from the introduction the following candid and curious avowal of the scope of the fair author's reasoning, "on the character and condition of women in the various stages of society, among the principal nations of the earth."

7. Henry James, "Review of Correspondence of William Ellery Channing and Lucy Aikin 1826–1842," *Atlantic Monthly*, March 1875, 368–71

[Aikin met Channing, the leading American Unitarian preacher and author of his day, at her aunt's home during his only visit to England in 1822. Channing initiated the correspondence in 1826. Over the next sixteen years, Aikin and Channing—born only a year apart—exchanged hundreds of letters, at times written nearly monthly and at other times with longer gaps of up to six months. Their correspondence was published together in 1874, and what follows are excerpts from a review by the great American novelist and critic, Henry James, whose writing frequently centered on transatlantic cultural exchanges.]

Dr. Channing's and Miss Aikin's letters belong to the ante-telegraphic period, and to an epistolary school diametrically opposed to the postal card manner. They have a sort of perfume of leisure; you feel that the writers could hear the scratching of their pens. Miss Aikin lived at quiet Hampstead, among suburban English lanes and garden-walls, and Dr. Channing dwelt in tranquil Boston, before the days of street-cars and semi-annual fires. It took their letters a month to come and go, and these missives have an air of expecting to be treated with respect and unfolded with a deliberate hand. They have other merits beside this agreeable suggestiveness....

He made Miss Aikin's acquaintance during a short visit to England prior to 1825, when the correspondence opened. She was a literary lady, a niece of Mrs. Barbauld, and member of a Unitarian and liberal circle in which Dr. Channing's writings were highly prized.... They continued to exchange letters until the eve of Dr. Channing's death in 1842, and their correspondence offers a not incomplete reflection of all the public events and interests of these sixteen years. It deals hardly at all with personal matter and has nothing for lovers of gossip. Except for alluding occasionally to his feeble health, Dr. Channing writes like a disembodied spirit, and defines himself, personally, almost wholly by negatives. Politics and banks are his principal topics, and in Miss Aikin he found an extremely robust interlocutor. The letters were presumably published for the sake, mainly, of Dr. Channing's memory, but their effect is to throw his correspondent into prominent relief. This lady's extremely sturdy and downright personality is the most entertaining thing in the volume. Clever, sagacious, shrewd, a student, a blue-stocking, and an accomplished writer, one wonders why her vigorous intellectual temperament has not attracted independent notice. She wrote a Life of Charles I. and a Life and Times of Addison (which Macaulay praises in his Essay); but she did a great deal of lively thinking which is not represented by her literary performances. Much of it (as of that of her correspondent) is of a rather old-fashioned sort, but it is very lucid and respectable, and, in a certain way, quite edifying. Both she and Dr. Channing were strongly interested in their times and the destiny of their respective countries, and there is a sort of antique dignity in the way they exchange convictions and theories upon public affairs and the tendencies of the age.... She had no love for the French, and they were rather a bone of contention between her and the doctor, who admired them in a fashion that strikes one as rather anomalous. But his admiration was intellectual; he was in sympathy with their democratic and *égalitaire* theories; whereas Miss Aikin's dislike was inherent in her stout British temperament. By virtue of this quality she gives one a really more masculine impression than her friend. She had a truly feminine garrulity; pen in hand, she is an endless talker; but her style has decidedly more color and force than Dr. Channing's, and whatever animation and point the volume contains is to be found in her letters. She was evidently a woman of temper, and her phrase often has a snap in it; but the only approach to absolute gayety in the book, perhaps, is on her side.... Miss Aikin's early letters have a tone of extreme deference and respect, but as the correspondence lasts, her native positiveness and conservatism assert themselves. Her letters indeed have throughout a *manner*, such as may very well have belonged personally to a learned British gentlewoman; she professes much, and she fulfills to the utmost all the duties of urbanity. But she speaks frankly, when the spirit moves her, and her frankness reaches a sort of dramatic climax in the last letter of the series, which Dr. Channing did not live to answer. She was willing to think hospitably and graciously about American people and things, but the note of condescension is always audible. She says of Prescott's style that it is "pretty well for an American," but regrets that, not having "mingled with the good society of London" he should be guilty of the vulgarity of calling artisans "*operatives,* the slang word of the Glasgow weavers." It illustrates her literary standard that she could see nothing in Carlyle but pure barbarism.

Dr. Channing's letters are briefer and undeniably less entertaining.... His optimism savors a trifle of weakness; it seems rather sentimental than rational, and Miss Aikin, secluded spinster as she is, by virtue of living simply in the denser European atmosphere, is better aware of the complexity of the *data* on which any forecast of the future should rest ... We have said that the correspondence moves toward a kind of dramatic climax. The late Miss Sedgwick had expressed herself disparagingly on the subject of the beauty and grace of Miss Aikin's countrywomen,[1] and Dr. Channing, with a placid aggressiveness which must certainly have been irritating to his correspondent, attempts to lay down the law in defense of her dictum.... He had flung down the glove and it was picked up with a vengeance. Miss Aikin comes down upon him, in vulgar parlance, with a cumulative solidity which he must have found rather startling. If he wishes the truth he shall have it! She proceeds to refute his invidious propositions with a logical and categorical exhaustiveness at which, in the light of our present easy familiarity with the topic, we feel rather tempted to smile. Miss Aikin is not complimentary either to American beauty or to American manners, and the most she will admit is that so long as Dr. Channing's countrywomen sit in a corner and hold their tongues, they avoid giving positive offense; whereas she proves by chapter and verse that English comeliness and English grace ought to be, must be, shall be, of the most superlative quality. The English ladies "walk with the same quiet grace that pervades all their deportment, and to which you have seen nothing similar or comparable." Dr. Channing died almost immediately after the receipt of her letter.

---

1   Catherine Sedgwick (1789–1867), American novelist and author of *Letters from Abroad to Kindred at Home, in Two Volumes* (1841), based on her fifteen-month tour of Europe.

Appendix C: Contexts for Epistles on Women

1. From Juvenal, *Satires*, Satire VI: "The Ways of Women," *The Satyrs of Decimus Junius Juvenalis: And of Aulus Persius Flaccus. Translated into English Verse by Mr. Dryden, and Several Other Eminent Hands*. Sixth edition. J. Tonson: London, 1735. 74-76

[Juvenal was a Roman satirist living in the second century. His sixteen satires address the immediate foibles of Rome as well as larger issues relating to the problems and frailties of humankind. Each satire has a particular theme; the sixth satire examines and critiques womankind. The following selections are taken from a translation by John Dryden (1631–1700), a leading poet, playwright, and critic of the later seventeenth century.]

If then thy Lawful Spouse thou canst not love,
What Reason should thy Mind to Marriage move?
Why all the charges of the nuptial feast,
Wine and desserts, and sweetmeats to digest??
Th' endowing Gold that buys the clear Delight,   290
  Giv'n for their first and only happy Night?
If thou art thus uxoriously inclin'd,
To bear thy Bondage with a willing Mind,
Prepare thy Neck, and put it in the Yoke:
But for no Mercy from thy Woman look
For tho', perhaps, she loves with equal Fires,
To absolute Dominion she aspires;
Joys in the Spoils, and triumphs o'er thy Purse;
The better husband makes the Wife worse.
Nothing is thine to give, or fell, or buy,   300
All offices of ancient Friendship die;
Nor hast thou leave to make a Legacy.
By[1] thy imperious Wife thou art bereft
A privilege, to Pimps and Pandars[2] left;
Thy Testament's her will; where she prefers
Her Ruffians, Drudges, and Adulterers.

---

1 All the *Romans*, even the most inferior, and most infamous sort of them, had the Power of making Wills. [Dryden]
2 Pandars: panderers.

Adopting all thy Rivals for thy Heirs.

      Go[1] drag that Slave to Death:[2] You Reason, why
Shou'd the poor Innocent be doom'd to die?
What Proofs? For, when Man's Life is in debate,   310
The Judge can ne'er too long deliberate.
Can'st[3] thou that Slave a Man? the Wife replies:
Prov'd, or unprov'd, the Crime, the Villain dies.
I have the Soveraign Pow'r to save or kill;
And give no other Reason but my Will.
Thus the she-tyrant reigns, till pleas'd with Change,
Her wild affections to new Empires range:
Another Subject-Husband she desires;
Divorc'd from him, she to the first retires,
While the last Wedding Feast is scarcely o'er,   320
And Garlands hang yet green upon the Door.
So still the Reck'ning rises; and appears
In total Sum, Eight Husbands in Five Years.
The Title for a Tomb-stone might be fit;
But that it wou'd too commonly be writ.

      Her Mother living, hope no quiet Day;
She sharpens her, instructs her how to Flea[4]
Her Husband bare, and then divides the Frey.
She takes Love-Letters, with a crafty Smile,
And, in her Daughter's Answer, mends the Style.   330
In vain the Husband sets his watchful Spies;
She cheats their Cunning, or she bribes their Eyes.
The Doctor's call'd; the Daughter, taught the Trick,
Pretends to faint; and in full Health is sick.
The panting Stallion, at the Closet-door,
Hears the Consult, and wishes it were o'er.
Can'st thou, in Reason, hope, a Bawd[5] so known,
Shou'd teach her other Manners than her own?
Her int'rest is in all th' Advice she gives:
'Tis on the Daughter's Rents[6] the Mother lives.   340

      No Cause is try'd at the litigious bar,
But Women Plaintiffs or Defendants are.

---

1 Go drag that Slave, &c: These are the Words of the Wife. [Dryden]

2 Your Reason why, &c: The Answer of the Husband. [Dryden]

3 Can'st thou that slave a man? The Wife again. [Dryden]

4 Flea: as a verb flea means "to rid of fleas, remove fleas from." (*OED*)

5 A procuress, or a woman who procures people, usually women, as prostitutes
    or illicit sexual partners for others. (*OED*)

6 Income or revenue.

They form the Process, all the Briefs they write;
The Topics furnish, and the Pleas indite;
And teach the toothless Lawyer how to bite.

2. From Publius Cornelius Tacitus, *Germania*, Chapters 7–8, 18–20; *A Treatise on the Situation, Manners, and Inhabitants of Germany; and the Life of Agricola*, translated by John Aikin. J. Johnson: Warrington, 1777. 21–27; 53–64

[Tacitus (ca. 56–ca. 117), was a Roman senator and historian. He chronicled the reigns of several Roman Emperors, and also wrote an important ethnography of the Germanic tribes. He held the strict monogamy and chastity of Germanic women in high regard, and in contrast to the profligacy of Roman society. *Germania* enjoys a special place in women's history, and to Aikin, in that it relates an ancient society in which women had considerable sex equality and political influence. The work was well known to Aikin, having been translated by her father in 1777. The following excerpts are taken from his translation; most of his copious footnotes have been removed.]

In the election of kings they have regard to birth; in that of military commanders, to valour. Their kings have not an absolute or unlimited power;[1] and their generals command less through the force of authority, than of example. If they are daring, adventurous, and conspicuous in action, they procure obedience from the admiration they inspire. None, however, but the priests are permitted to chastise delinquents, to inflict bonds or stripes; that it may appear not as a punishment, or in consequence of the general's order, but as the instigation of the god whom they suppose present with warriors. They also carry with them to battle, images and standards taken from the sacred groves. It is a principal incentive to their courage, that their squadrons and battalions are not formed by men fortuitously collected, but by the assemblage of families and clans. Near them are ranged the dearest pledges of their affection; so that they have within hearing the yells of their women, and the cries of their children. These, too, are the most respected witnesses, the most liberal applauders, of the conduct of each. To their mothers and wives they bring their wounds; and these are not shocked at counting, and even requiring them. They also carry food and encouragement to those who are engaged.

Tradition relates, that armies beginning to give way have been brought again to the charge by women, through the earnestness of

---

1   An attractive feature of their government for the Aikins, who were opposed to any concept of divine right or absolute power.

their entreaties, the opposition of their bodies,[1] and the pictures they have drawn of imminent slavery; a calamity which these people bear with more impatience on their women's account than their own; so that those states who have been obliged to give among their hostages the daughters of noble families, are the most effectually engaged to fidelity. They even suppose somewhat of sanctity and prescience to be inherent in the female sex; and therefore neither despise their counsels,[2] nor disregard their responses. We have beheld, in the reign of Vespasian, Veleda long reverenced by many as a deity. They formerly also venerated Aurinia, and several others; but without adulation, or as if they intended to make them goddesses....

The matrimonial bond is, nevertheless, strict and severe among them; nor are their manners in any respect more deserving of praise.[3] Almost singly among the barbarians, they content themselves with one wife; a very few of them excepted, who, not through incontinence, but because their alliance is solicited on account of their rank, practice polygamy. The wife does not bring a dowry to her husband, but receives one from him. The parents and relations interpose, and pass their approbation on to the presents—presents not adapted to please a female taste, or decorate the bride; but a yoke of oxen, a caparisoned steed, a shield, spear and sword. By virtue of these, the wife is espoused; who on her part also makes a present of armour to her husband. This they consider as the firmest bind of union; these, the sacred mysteries, the conjugal deities. That the woman may not think herself excused from exertions of fortitude, or exempt from the casualties of war, she is admonished by the very ceremonial of her marriage, that she comes to her husband as a partner in toils and dangers; an equal both to suffer and to dare, in peace and in war: this is indicated by the yoked oxen, the harnessed steed, the offered arms. Thus she is to live; thus to die. She receives what she is to return inviolate[4] and

---

1 They not only interposed to prevent the flight of their husbands and sons; but, in desperate emergencies, themselves engaged in battle.... [J.A.]

2 See the same observation with regard to the Celtic women, in Plutarch *On the Virtues of Women*. The North Americans pay a similar regard to their females. [J.A.]

3 The chastity laws of the Germans, and their strict regard to the laws of marriage, are witnessed by all their antient codes of law. The purity of their manners in this respect afforded a striking contrast to the licentiousness of the Romans in the decline of the empire ... [J.A.]

4 Thus in the Saxon law, *concerning dowries*, it is said "The Ostfalli and Angrarii determine, that if a woman have male issue, she is to possess the dower she received in marriage during her life, and transmit it to her sons." [J.A.]

merited to her children; what her daughters-in-law are to receive, and again transmit to her grand-children.

They live, therefore, in a state of well guarded chastity; corrupted by no seducing spectacles, no convivial incitements. Men and women are alike ignorant of the secret methods of corresponding by letters. Adultery is extremely rare among so numerous a people. Its punishment is instant, and at the pleasure of the husband. He cuts off the hair of the offender, strips her, and in presence of her relations expels her from his house and pursues her with stripes through the whole of the village. Nor is any indulgence shewn to a prostitute. Neither beauty, youth, nor riches can procure her a husband: for none there looks on vice with a smile, nor calls mutual seduction the way of the world. Still more exemplary is the practice of those states in which none but virgins marry, and the expectations and wishes of a wife are at once brought to a period. Thus they take one husband and one body and one life; that no thought, no desire may reach beyond him; and he may be loved not only as their husband, but as their marriage.[1] To limit the increase of children, or put to death any of the husband's blood, is accounted infamous: and virtuous manners have there more efficacy than good laws elsewhere.

In all their houses they grow up in nakedness and filth to that bulk of body and limb which we behold with wonder. Every mother suckles her own children, and does not deliver them into the hands of servants and nurses. The master and slave are not to be distinguished by any delicacy in bringing up. They lie together amidst the same cattle, upon the same ground, till age separates, and valour marks out, the free-born. The youths partake late of venereal pleasures, and hence pass the age of puberty unexhausted: nor are the virgins brought forward; the same maturity, the same full growth, is required; the sexes unite equally matched,[2] and robust; and the children inherit the vigour of their parents. Children are regarded with affection by their maternal uncles as by their fathers: some even consider this as the more sacred bond of consanguity, and prefer it in the requisition of hostages, as if it held the mind by a firmer tye, and the family by a more extensive obligation. A person's own children, however, are his heirs and suces-

---

1 Some nations carried this idea so far, that the wife refused to survive her husband, but killed herself in order to be burnt on the same funeral pyre with him. St Boniface, in the epistle above cited, relates this of the Winedi; and Procopius of the Heruli. Some of the East-Indian tribes, it is well known, practice the same to this day. [J.A.]

2 Equal not only in age and constitution, but in condition. Many of the German codes of law annex penalties to those of both sexes, who marry persons of inferior rank. [J.A.]

sors; and no wills are made. If there are no children, the next in order of inheritance are brothers, paternal and maternal uncles. The more numerous are a man's relations and kinsmen, the more comfortable is his old age; nor is it any advantage to be childless.

3. From John Milton, *Paradise Lost*, ed. Thomas Newton. London: J. and R. Tonson and S. Draper, 1750. Book IV, lines 288–311; 634–38

[John Milton (1608–74), poet and polemicist, completed his most famous poem, *Paradise Lost,* in 1663. It was written over a span of many years late in his life during the political upheavals of the Restoration, and the personal difficulties he faced including increasing blindness. The basic structure of the poem is an Epic depiction of the fall of Adam and Eve, beginning with the fall of the angel Lucifer. The initial response to the poem was tempered, the first edition selling only a modest number of copies until a very deluxe folio fourth edition was printed in 1688. The following excerpts are those most relevant to Aikin's revision of Milton's telling.]

Book IV

[The following passage describes Satan's first sight of Adam and Eve.]

Two of far nobler shape erect and tall,
Godlike erect, with native honor clad
In naked majesty seem'd lords of all,   290
And worthy seem'd, for in their looks divine
The image of their glorious Maker shone,[1]
Truth, wisdom, sanctitude severe and pure,
Severe but in true filial freedom plac'd;
Whence true authority in men; though both
Not equal, as their sex not equal seem'd;
For contemplation he and valor form'd,
For softness she and sweet attractive grace,

---

1   Genesis 1.26–27 "26. And God said, Let us make man in our image, after our likeness: and let them have dominion over the fish of the sea, and over the fowl of the air, and over the cattle, and over all the earth, and over every creeping thing that creepeth upon the earth. 27. So God created man in his own image, in the image of God created he him, male and female created he them."

He for God only, she for God in him:[1]
His fair large front[2] and eye sublime declar'd   300
Absolute rule; and hyacinthin locks
Round from his parted forelock manly hung
Clustr'ng, but not beneath his shoulders broad:
She as a veil down to the slender waste
Her unadorned golden tresses wore
Dishevel'd, but in wanton ringlets wav'd
As the Vine curls her tendrils, which imply'd
Subjection, but requir'd with gentle sway,
And by her yielded, by him best receiv'd,
Yielded with coy submission, modest pride,   310
And sweet reluctant amorous delay....

[Eve responds as follows to Adam's instructions about the Sabbath.]

To whom thus Eve with perfect beauty adorn'd.
My Author and Disposer, what thou bid'st   635
Unargued I obey; so God ordains,
God is thy Law, thou mine:[3] to know no more
Is woman's happiest knowledge and her praise.

4. **From Alexander Pope, *Epistles to Several Persons*, "Epistle II: To a Lady on the Characters of Women," *The Poetical Works of Alexander Pope*, Vol. 3. London: J. French, 1777. 73, 79-80, 82[4]**

[Alexander Pope (1688–1744) was the leading poet of the early eighteenth century. His "Epistle II: To a Lady on the Characters of Women" (1735) is addressed to Pope's closest female friend, Martha Blount (1690–1763). There was much gossip that she was his mistress and even that he had secretly married her, but there is no convincing evidence to support such speculation. His devotion to Martha remained unbroken and in his will he left her a considerable fortune. The poem

---

1 He for God only, she for God in him: Genesis 1.21–23 "21. And the LORD
   God caused a deep sleep to fall upon Adam, and he slept: and he took one of
   his ribs, and closed up the flesh instead thereof; 22. And the rib, which the
   LORD God had taken from man, made he a woman, and brought her unto
   the man. 23. And Adam said, This is now bone of my bones, and flesh of my
   flesh: she shall be called Woman, because she was taken out of man."
2 Forehead; a large forehead was thought to indicate intelligence.
3 God is thy Law, thou mine: similar to line 299 above.
4 This Epistle is part of a tradition of Epistles on women along with Juvenal's
   Epistle VI above.

is the most satirically scathing of Pope's ethic epistles. The reader eaves-drops as Pope, the painter-poet, and his companion, Martha Blount, stroll round an imaginary portrait gallery and the poet points out the most prominent (and usually negative) characteristics of the portraits of different women.]

Nothing so true as what you once let fall,
"Most Women have no Characters at all."
Matter too soft a lasting mark to bear,
And best distinguish'd by black, brown, or fair.

How many pictures of one nymph we view,
All how unlike each other, all how true!
Arcadia's Countess, here, in ermin'd pride,
Is, there, Pastora[1] by a fountain side.
Here Fannia, leering on her own good man,
And there, a naked Leda with a Swan.[2]   10
Let then the Fair one beautifully cry,
In Magdalen's[3] loose hair and lifted eye,
Or dress'd in smiles of sweet Cecilia[4] shine,
With simp'ring angels, palms, and harps divine;
Whether the charmer sinner it, or saint it,
If folly grows romantic, I must paint it....

But grant, in public men sometimes are shown,
A woman's seen in private life alone: 200
Our bolder talents in full light display'd;
Your virtues open fairest in the shade.
Bred to disguise, in public 'tis you hide;
There, none distinguish twixt your shame or pride,
Weakness or delicacy; all so nice,
That each may seem a virtue, or a vice.

In men, we various ruling passions find;
In women, two almost divide the kind;
Those, only fix'd, they first or last obey,
The love of pleasure, and the love of sway.   210

---

1 A shepherdess.
2 Leda was a character from Greek mythology who became the mother of Helen of Troy after Zeus seduced her in the form of a swan.
3 Mary Magdalen from the New Testament was often conceived of as a reformed prostitute.
4 Saint Cecilia was a Roman martyr and patroness of music.

That, Nature gives; and where the lesson taught[1]
Is still to please, can pleasure seem a fault?
Experience, this; by man's oppression curs'd,
They seek the second not to lose the first.

    Men, some to bus'ness, some to pleasure take;
But ev'ry woman is at heart a rake:
Men, some to quiet, some to public strife;
But ev'ry Lady would be queen for life.

    Yet mark the fate of a whole sex of queens!
Pow'r all their end, but beauty all the means.   220
In youth they conquer, with so wild a rage,
As leaves them scarce a subject in their age:
For foreign glory, foreign joy, they roam;
No thought of peace or happiness at home.
But wisdom's triumph is well-tim'd retreat,
As hard a science to the fair as great!
Beauties, like tyrants, old and friendless grown,
Yet hate repose, and dread to be alone,
Worn out in public, weary ev'ry eye,
Nor leave one sigh behind them when they die....   230

    And, yet, believe me, good as well as ill,
Woman's at best a contradiction still.   270
Heav'n, when it strives to polish all it can
Its last best work, but forms a softer man;
Picks from each sex, to make the fav'rite blest,
Your love of pleasure, our desire of rest:
Blends, in exception to all gen'ral rules,
Your taste of follies, with our scorn of fools:
Reserve with frankness, art with truth allied,
Courage with softness, modesty with pride,
Fix'd principles, with fancy ever new;
Shakes all together, and produces—You.   280

    Be this a woman's fame: with this unblest,
Toasts live a scorn, and queens may die a jest.
This Phœbus[2] promis'd (I forget the year)

---

1 "This is occasioned partly by their Nature, partly by their education, and in
   some degree by necessity." [Pope]
2 Apollo.

When those blue eyes first open'd on the sphere;
Ascendant Phœbus watch'd that hour with care,
Averted half your parents' simple pray'r,
And gave you beauty, but denied the pelf[1]
Which buys your sex a tyrant o'er itself.
The gen'rous God, who wit and gold refines,
And ripens spirits as he ripens mines,   290
Kept dross[2] for duchesses, the world shall know it,
To you gave sense, good humour, and a poet.

5. From Mary Wollstonecraft, *A Vindication of the Rights of Woman*. London: J. Johnson, 1792. 92-93, 96-97, 98-101, 102, 103-07.

[Mary Wollstonecraft first began writing after her family had suffered a series of financial misfortunes. The over three hundred pages of *A Vindication of the Rights of Woman* was written in approximately three months. The first and second *Vindications* are written as a response to Burke and Rousseau respectively. The ambitious and confident stance Wollstonecraft assumed put her at the center of debates regarding her text. While more conservative readers admonished Wollstonecraft's assertions regarding women's oppression, the *Vindication* was soon translated into German and French and was very well received.]

... It is time to effect a revolution in female manners—time to restore to them their lost dignity—and make them, as a part of the human species, labour by reforming themselves to reform the world. It is time to separate unchangeable morals from local manners.—If men be demi-gods—why let us serve them! And if the dignity of the female soul be as disputable as that of animals—if their reason does not afford sufficient light to direct their conduct whilst unerring instinct is denied—they are surely of all creatures the most miserable! and, bent beneath the iron hand of destiny, must submit to be a fair defect in creation. But to justify the ways of Providence respecting them, by pointing out some irrefragable reason for thus making such a large portion of mankind accountable and not accountable, would puzzle the subtilest [sic] casuist....

---

1 "Riches, material possessions. Could refer to stolen goods, or to riches with a corrupting influence." (*OED*)

2 "Generally, refuse; rubbish; worthless, impure matter, though here there is an allusion to the more specific usage, which is the extraneous matter thrown off from metals in the process of melting." (*OED*)

... It were to be wished that women would cherish an affection for their husbands, founded on the same principle that devotion ought to rest upon. No other firm base is there under heaven—for let them beware of the fallacious light of sentiment; too often used as a softer phrase for sensuality. It follows then, I think, that from their infancy women should either be shut up like eastern princes, or educated in such a manner as to be able to think and act for themselves.

Why do men halt between two opinions, and expect impossibilities? Why do they expect virtue from a slave, from a being whom the constitution of civil society has rendered weak, if not vicious?

Still I know that it will require a considerable length of time to eradicate the firmly rooted prejudices which sensualists have planted; it will also require some time to convince women that they act contrary to their real interest on an enlarged scale, when they cherish or affect weakness under the name of delicacy, and to convince the world that the poisoned source of female vices and follies, if it be necessary, in compliance with custom, to use synonymous terms in a lax sense, has been the sensual homage paid to beauty:—to beauty of features; for it has been shrewdly observed by a German writer, that a pretty woman, as an object of desire, is generally allowed to be so by men of all descriptions; whilst a fine woman, who inspires more sublime emotions by displaying intellectual beauty, may be overlooked or observed with indifference, by those men who find their happiness in the gratification of their appetites. I foresee an obvious retort—whilst man remains such an imperfect being as he appears hitherto to have been, he will, more or less, be the slave of his appetites; and those women obtaining most power who gratify a predominant one, the sex is degraded by a physical, if not by a moral necessity.

Besides, if women are educated for dependence; that is, to act according to the will of another fallible being, and submit, right or wrong, to power, where are we to stop? Are they to be considered as vicegerents allowed to reign over a small domain, and answerable for their conduct to a higher tribunal, liable to error?

It will not be difficult to prove that such delegates will act like men subjected by fear, and make their children and servants endure their tyrannical oppression. As they submit without reason, they will, having no fixed rules to square their conduct by, be kind, or cruel, just as the whim of the moment directs; and we ought not to wonder if sometimes, galled by their heavy yoke, they take a malignant pleasure in resting it on weaker shoulders.

But, supposing a woman, trained up to obedience, be married to a sensible man, who directs her judgment without making her feel the servility of her subjection, to act with as much propriety by this reflected light as can be expected when reason is taken at second hand, yet she cannot ensure the life of her protector; he may die and leave her with a large family.

A double duty devolves on her; to educate them in the character of both father and mother; to form their principles and secure their property. But, alas! she has never thought, much less acted for herself. She has only learned to please men, to depend gracefully on them; yet, encumbered with children, how is she to obtain another protector—a husband to supply the place of reason? A rational man, for we are not treading on romantic ground, though he may think her a pleasing docile creature, will not choose to marry a family for love, when the world contains many more pretty creatures. What is then to become of her? She either falls an easy prey to some mean fortune-hunter, who defrauds her children of their paternal inheritance, and renders her miserable; or becomes the victim of discontent and blind indulgence. Unable to educate her sons, or impress them with respect; for it is not a play on words to assert, that people are never respected, though filling an important station, who are not respectable; she pines under the anguish of unavailing impotent regret. The serpent's tooth enters into her very soul, and the vices of licentious youth bring her with sorrow, if not with poverty also, to the grave.

This is not an overcharged picture; on the contrary, it is a very possible case, and something similar must have fallen under every attentive eye....

It does not require a lively pencil, or the discriminating outline of a caricature, to sketch the domestic miseries and petty vices which such a mistress of a family diffuses. Still she only acts as a woman ought to act, brought up according to Rousseau's system. She can never be reproached for being masculine, or turning out of her sphere; nay, she may observe another of his grand rules, and cautiously preserving her reputation free from spot, be reckoned a good kind of woman. Yet in what respect can she be termed good? She abstains, it is true, without any great struggle, from committing gross crimes; but how does she fulfil her duties? Duties!—in truth she has enough to think of to adorn her body and nurse a weak constitution....

I must relieve myself by drawing a different picture.

Let fancy now present a woman with a tolerable understanding, for I do not wish to leave the line of mediocrity, whose constitution, strengthened by exercise, has allowed her body to acquire its full vigour; her mind, at the same time, gradually expanding itself to comprehend the moral duties of life, and in what human virtue and dignity consist.

Formed thus by the discharge of the relative duties of her station, she marries from affection, without losing sight of prudence, and looking beyond matrimonial felicity, she secures her husband's respect before it is necessary to exert mean arts to please him and feed a dying flame, which nature doomed to expire when the object became familiar, when friendship and forbearance take place of a more ardent affection.—This is the natural death of love, and domestic peace is not destroyed by struggles to prevent its extinction. I also suppose the husband to be virtuous; or she is still more in want of independent principles.

Fate, however, breaks this tie.—She is left a widow, perhaps, without a sufficient provision; but she is not desolate! The pang of nature is felt; but after time has softened sorrow into melancholy resignation, her heart turns to her children with redoubled fondness, and anxious to provide for them, affection gives a sacred heroic cast to her maternal duties. She thinks that not only the eye sees her virtuous efforts from whom all her comfort now must flow, and whose approbation is life; but her imagination, a little abstracted and exalted by grief, dwells on the fond hope that the eyes which her trembling hand closed, may still see how she subdues every wayward passion to fulfil the double duty of being the father as well as the mother of her children. Raised to heroism by misfortunes, she represses the first faint dawning of a natural inclination, before it ripens into love, and in the bloom of life forgets her sex—forgets the pleasure of an awakening passion, which might again have been inspired and returned. She no longer thinks of pleasing, and conscious dignity prevents her from priding herself on account of the praise which her conduct demands. Her children have her love, and her brightest hopes are beyond the grave, where her imagination often strays.

I think I see her surrounded by her children, reaping the reward of her care. The intelligent eye meets hers, whilst health and innocence smile on their chubby cheeks, and as they grow up the cares of life are lessened by their grateful attention. She lives to see the virtues which she endeavoured to plant on principles fixed into habits, to see her children attain a strength of character sufficient to enable them to endure adversity without forgetting their mother's example.

The task of life thus fulfilled, she calmly waits for the sleep of death, and rising from the grave, may say—Behold, thou gavest me a talent—and here are five talents.

I wish to sum up what I have said in a few words, for I here throw down my gauntlet, and deny the existence of sexual virtues, not excepting modesty. For man and woman, truth, if I understand the meaning of the word, must be the same; yet the fanciful female character, so prettily drawn by poets and novelists, demanding the sacrifice of truth and sincerity, virtue becomes a relative idea, having no other foundation than utility, and of that utility men pretend arbitrarily to judge, shaping it to their own convenience.

Women, I allow, may have different duties to fulfil; but they are human duties, and the principles that should regulate the discharge of them, I sturdily maintain, must be the same.

To become respectable, the exercise of their understanding is necessary, there is no other foundation for independence of character; I mean explicitly to say that they must only bow to the authority of reason, instead of being the modest slaves of opinion....

6. From Anna Lætitia Aikin Barbauld, "The Rights of Women" in Lucy Aikin, ed., *The Works of Anna Lætitia Barbauld*. London: Longman, Hurst, Rees, Orme, Brown and Green. 2 vols., 1825. Vol. 1. 185-87

[First published posthumously by Lucy Aikin in *The Works of Anna Lætitia Barbauld*, the title of the poem and its subject matter has led to its association with Wollstonecraft's *Vindication of the Rights of Woman*. Most commentators have read the poem as a challenge to Wollstonecraft's strident feminism, and it is likely for this reason that Lucy Aikin felt comfortable in publishing it. More recent readings of the poem recognize its tonal complexity, and her ambiguous use of irony. If the poem was written in response to Wollstonecraft, it is interesting that Barbauld declined to include it in her 1792 edition of *Poems*, the last lifetime edition of her verse.]

Yes, injured Woman! rise, assert thy right!
Woman! too long degraded, scorned, opprest;
O born to rule in partial Law's despite,
Resume thy native empire o'er the breast!

Go forth arrayed in panoply divine;
That angel pureness which admits no stain;
Go, bid proud Man his boasted rule resign,
And kiss the golden sceptre of thy reign.

Go, gird thyself with grace; collect thy store
Of bright artillery glancing from afar;   10
Soft melting tones thy thundering cannon's roar,
Blushes and fears thy magazine of war.

Thy rights are empire: urge no meaner claim,—
Felt, not defined, and if debated, lost;
Like sacred mysteries, which withheld from fame,
Shunning discussion, are revered the most.

Try all that wit and art suggest to bend
Of thy imperial foe the stubborn knee;
Make treacherous Man thy subject, not thy friend;
Thou mayst command, but never canst be free.   20

Awe the licentious, and restrain the rude;
Soften the sullen, clear the cloudy brow:
Be, more than princes' gifts, thy favours sued;—
She hazards all, who will the least allow.

But hope not, courted idol of mankind,
On this proud eminence secure to stay;
Subduing and subdued, thou soon shalt find
Thy coldness soften, and thy pride give way.

Then, then, abandon each ambitious thought,
Conquest or rule thy heart shall feebly move,   30
In Nature's school, by her soft maxims taught,
That separate rights are lost in mutual love.

7. From Richard Polwhele, *The Unsex'd Females: A Poem.* London: Cadell and Davies, 1798. 6-7, 13-15

[Richard Polwhele (1760–1838) was a poet, theologian and literary chronicler. His most notorious composition, and the only one he is known for today, is *The Unsex'd Females*, in which Polwhele attacks the radical feminism of Mary Wollstonecraft, whom he casts as Satan, in contrast to the more socially conservative Hannah More, whom he styles as a Christ figure. Published in the year after Wollstonecraft's death and in the same year as William Godwin's sexually frank *Memoir* of her life, Polwhele's poem demonstrates the vehement hostility directed towards her, and the more general backlash against all forms of female ambition and unconventionality.]

... Survey with me, what ne'er our fathers saw,
A female band despising NATURE's law,
As "proud defiance" flashes from their arms,
And vengeance smothers all their softer charms.
I shudder at the new unpictur'd scene,   15
Where unsex'd woman vaunts the imperious mien;
...
See Wollstonecraft, whom no decorum checks,
Arise, the intrepid champion of her sex;

O'er humbled man assert the sovereign claim,
And slight the timid blush of virgin fame.

"Go, go (she cries) ye tribes of melting maids,
"Go, screen your softness in sequester'd shades;
"With plaintive whispers woo the unconscious grove,
"And feebly perish, as depis'd ye love.   70

"What tho' the fine Romances of Rousseau
"Bid the flame flutter, and the bosom glow;
"Tho' the rapt Bard, your empire fond to own,
"Fall prostrate and adore your living throne,
"The living throne his hands presum'd to rear,
"Its seat a simper, and its base a tear;
"Soon shall the sex disdain the illusive sway,
"And wield the sceptre in yon blaze of day;
"Ere long, each little artifice discard,
"No more by weakness winning fond regard;   80
"Nor eyes, that sparkle from their blushes, roll,
"Nor catch the languors of the sick'ning soul,
"Nor the quick flutter, nor the coy reserve,
"But nobly boast the firm gymnastic nerve;
"Nor more affect with Delicacy's fan
"To hide the emotion from congenial man;
"To the bold heights where glory beams, aspire,
"Blend mental energy with Passion's fire,
"Surpass their rivals in the powers of mind
"And vindicate the Rights of womankind."   90
She spoke: and veteran BARBAULD caught the strain,
And deem'd her songs of Love, her Lyrics vain ...

Appendix D: Contexts for Aikin's Feminist Historiography

1. From Catherine Macaulay, *Observations on the Reflections of the Right Hon. Edmund Burke, on the Revolution in France, in a Letter to the Right Hon. The Earl of Stanhope.* I. Thomas and E.T. Andrews: London and Boston, 1791. 22–23

[Macaulay (née Sawbridge; later married name Graham) (1731–91), historian and political polemicist, was the leading female historian of the eighteenth century. Her eight-volume *History of England*, published over twenty years (from 1763 to 1783), was a remarkable achievement. It won immediate critical praise—though many reviewers were of the view that history was not a suitable pursuit for female authors. The *History* demonstrates Macaulay's meticulous scholarship as well as her radical politics. She was also a staunch supporter of female education. The following excerpt is taken from her response to Burke's hostile account of the French Revolution, and addresses his famous lament that "the age of chivalry is gone."]

The age in which the spirit of chivalry was triumphantly prevalent, would indeed have been a very *improper* time to have attempted a regeneration of constitutions on a *popular* principle; but I have always regarded the necessity which gave birth to the orders of chivalry, as a mark of *disgrace* to the times in which they were formed. They were indeed a proper remedy to the evils arising from *ferocity, slavery, barbarism*, and *ignorance*; but now, when the causes no longer exist which rendered them useful, we should rather think of *freeing* society of all the evils inherent in those *false* notions of honour which they have given rise to, than endeavour to call back their spirit in its full force. That enthusiastic military fire, that *methodized sentimental barbarism*, which instigates men to deprive their fellow citizens of life for *supposed* personal affronts, in *defiance* of the laws of *religion* and *society*, are the offsprings of chivalry, and unknown to *all* the nations of the *ancient civilized* world. But it is the *simplicity* of all *abstract principles* against which Mr. Burke makes an *eternal* war; all the *devices* of pride, all the *fond conceits* of vanity, all the train of *pompous* ostentation, by which *naked* virtue is put *out* of her *rank*, to give way to the more imposing glare of external magnificence, are represented as useful ideas, "furnished from the wardrobe of a *moral* imagination, which the heart owns, and the understanding gratifies, as necessary to cover the defects of our naked shivering nature, and to raise it to dignity in our own estimation."

It is not, according to *these* ideas, recommended by Mr. Burke, that the Scripture teaches us to *respect ourselves*; and although the maxims of the sacred writings are exploded by all politicians as *incompatible* with their views, yet certainly the *excellency* of their precepts consists in their being *exactly* fitted to a *temporal* as well as to a *spiritual* happiness. Neither in a *moral* view of things, can I perceive how the *ornaments* of artificial greatness, which are found to answer all the purposes of *human pride*, should assist us in acquiring that *true* dignity of character which *alone* ought to constitute distinction; nor how we can truly respect ourselves, by *idolizing* the *mere phantom* of greatness, whether it be attached to our own persons, or the persons of others.

2. From Mary Hays, *Female Biography; or, Memoirs of Illustrious and Celebrated Women, of All Ages and Countries, Alphabetically Arranged.* 6 vols. London: Richard Phillips, 1803. Preface, iii–vi

[Mary Hays (1759–1843), was a journalist, novelist, children's writer, essayist, polemicist, and historian. Her most radical work, the *Appeal to the Men of Great Britain in behalf of Women* (1798), was written in 1792, the same year as Mary Wollstonecraft's *A Vindication of the Rights of Woman*, though it was not printed for another six years; in her *Appeal*, Hays claims that there is no basis for the continued subjection of women. In *Female Biography*, Hays includes a series of 290 lengthy biographical sketches. She provides extensive accounts of the lives of, among those specifically discussed by Aikin, Boadicea, Queen of the Britons, Ethelfleda, Elizabeth I, Lady Jane Grey, Margaret More Roper, Lady Rachel Russell, Charlotte Corday, Portia, daughter of Cato, and Cornelia, mother of the Gracci.]

PREFACE

To give an account, however concise, or general, of every woman who, either by her virtues, her talents, or the peculiarities of her fortune, has rendered herself illustrious or distinguished, would, notwithstanding the disadvantages civil and moral under which the sex has laboured, embrace an extent, and require sources of information, which few individuals, however patient in labour or indefatigable in research, could compass or command. Yet no character of eminence will, in the following work, I trust, be found omitted, except among those who have come nearer to our own times; of whom, for reasons unnecessary to be detailed, but few have been brought forward.

My pen has been taken up in the cause, and for the benefit, of my own sex. For their improvement, and to their entertainment, my labours have been devoted. Women, unsophisticated by the pedantry of the schools, read not for dry information, to load their memories with uninteresting facts, or to make a display of a vain erudition. A skeleton biography would afford to them but little gratification: they require pleasure to be mingled with instruction, lively images, the graces of sentiment, and the polish of language. Their understandings are principally accessible through their affections: they delight in minute delineation of character; nor must the truths which impress them be either cold or unadorned. I have at heart the happiness of my sex, and their advancement in the grand scale of rational and social existence. I perceive, with mingled concern and indignation, the follies and vices by which they suffer themselves to be degraded. If, through prudence or policy, the generous contention between the sexes for intellectual equality must be waived, be not, my amiable country-women, poorly content with the destination of the slaves of an Eastern haram, with whom the season of youth forms the whole of life! A woman who, to the graces and gentleness of her own sex, adds the knowledge and fortitude of the other, exhibits the most perfect com-bination of human excellence. Let not the cold sarcasms of the pedant stifle your generous ardour in the pursuit of what is praise-worthy: substitute, as they fade, for the evanescent graces of youth, the more durable attractions of a cultivated mind; that, to the intoxicating homage of admiration and love, may succeed the calmer and not less gratifying tribute of friendship and esteem. To her who, sacrificing at the shrine of fashion, wastes her bloom in frivolity; who, trained but for the purposes of vanity and voluptuousness, and contemning the characteristic delicacy of her sex, dauntless obtrudes her charms on the public eye, the jest of the licentious, and the contempt of the severe; dreadful must be the approach of age, that season of collected thought and of repose to the passions, that will rob her of her only claim to distinction and regard.

To excite a worthier emulation, the following memorial of those women, whose endowments, or whose conduct, have reflected luster upon the sex, is presented more especially to the rising generation, who have not grown old in folly, whose hearts have not been seared by fashion, and whose minds prejudice has not yet worked.

Unconnected with any party and distaining every species of bigotry, I have endeavoured, in general, to serve the cause of truth and of virtue. Every character has been judged upon its own principles; the reflections, sparingly interwoven, have been such as naturally arose out of the subject; nor have I ever gone out of my way in favour of sex or systems.

3. From Elizabeth Benger, *Memoirs of the Life of Anne Boleyn, Queen of Henry VIII*. London: Longman, Hurst, Rees, Orme, and Brown, 1821. Preface iii–v

[Elizabeth Benger (bap. 1775, d. 1827), historian and novelist, wrote biographies and historical memoirs of Elizabeth Hamilton, John Tobin, Mary Queen of Scots and Elizabeth of Bohemia. As her preface to the *Memoirs of the Life of Anne Boleyn* suggests, Benger was inspired by her close friend, Lucy Aikin, to emphasize the influence of woman upon the politics of her day. Further, her "historical biography is surprisingly critical in approach to its sources; Benger's emphasis on the queen's support of early protestant reformers such as Latimer has been vindicated by later research" (*Oxford Dictionary of National Biography*). After Benger's death in 1827, Aikin wrote a brief "Memoir of Miss Benger," which was included in all subsequent printings of Benger's *Memoirs*.]

PREFACE

In the records of biography there is perhaps no character that more forcibly exemplifies the vanity of human ambition than that of Anne Boleyn: elevated to a throne, devoted to a scaffold, she appears to have been invested with royalty only to offer an example of humiliating degradation, such as modern Europe had never witnessed. But, abstracted from those signal vicissitudes of fortune, which, in every age and country, must awaken curiosity and sympathy, there are various circumstances connected with the history of Anne Boleyn, which are calculated to create peculiar interests in the English reader. It would be ungrateful to forget that the mother of Queen Elizabeth was the early and zealous advocate of the Reformation, and that by her efforts to dispel the gloom of ignorance and superstition, she conferred on the English people, a benefit, of which, in the present advanced state of knowledge and civilization, it would be difficult to conceive or to appreciate the real value and importance. But the most prominent feature of her destiny is, that the abolition of papal supremacy in this country must be referred to her influence: and that the only woman ever permitted to effect a change in our national and political institutions, has been instrumental in introducing and establishing a better system of things, whose effects have altered the whole fabric of society. On this single circumstance, perhaps, is founded the diversity of opinion which to this day prevails respecting the moral qualities of Anne Boleyn, alternately the subject of unqualified censure and extravagant praise. Catholic bigots and protestant enthusiasts, calumniators and encomiasts, historians and poets, have alike conspired to create and transmit of her an unfaithful and even a distorted portraiture. It is, however, worthy of remark, that whilst she is reproached for real virtues by Bayle, and by Marot stigmatised for pretended vices, Calderon, the great dramatic poet of Spain, leaves her chastity unimpeached. In his fine play, "The Schism of England," she is invested with the ambition of Lady Macbeth; but her ruin is attributed to Henry's fantastic and impetuous jealousy.

4. **From William Alexander, M.D.** *The History of Women, from the Earliest Antiquity, to the Present Time, Giving Some Account of Almost Every Interesting Particular Concerning that Sex, Among All Nations, Ancient and Modern.* **2 vols. London: Strahan and Cadell, 1779. I: 1–4; I: 102–04**

[William Alexander (bap. c. 1742, d. c. 1788), physician and author, was an experimental scientist and is best known for his *History of Women*. For his narrative of women's history, Alexander drew widely from many sources, including biblical history, theology, classical and medieval texts, and travel literature. He wrote about women's everyday lives throughout history, including topics such as women's work, marriage, child-rearing patterns, and customs and ceremonies, as well as their public status and power. Alexander anticipates many of Aikin's arguments in this history, while diverging from Aikin in his insistence on female "decorum" through the ages.]

INTRODUCTION

Although there is nothing in nature that so much engages our attention, so forcibly draws our inclinations, or with which our interests are so intimately blended, as with the other sex, yet so strong is our partiality to ourselves, that we have never in any period, nor in any country, sufficiently attended to the happiness and interests of those beings, whom in every period, and in every country, we have professed to love and to adore: and while the charms which they possess, have every where extorted from us the tribute of love, they have only in a few places extorted from us good usage.

Almost every man is full of complaints against the sex, but hardly do we meet with any one who seriously endeavours to rectify the evils against which he exclaims so bitterly. He who consider women only as objects of his love, and of his pleasure; complains, that in his connections with them, he finds them inconstant, unfaithful and ever open to flattery and seduction. The philosopher, who would wish to mingle the joys of friendship and of conversation with those of love, complains that they are destitute of every idea, but those that flow from gallantry and self-admiration; and consequently incapable of giving or receiving any of the more refined and intellectual pleasures. The man of business complains, that they are giddy and thoughtless, and want the plodding head, and the saving hand, so necessary towards thriving in the world. And almost every man complains, of their idleness, extravagance, disregard to every kind of admonition, and neglect of the duties of domestic and social life.

Without examining how far these general complaints are well or ill founded, we shall only observe, that in cases where they are well founded, when we trace them to their source, we find the blame ultimately fall on ourselves. Does not the man of love and gallantry commonly set the example of infidelity and inconstancy to the females with whom he is connected? And do not men in general, but too obviously, chalk out to the other sex, the way that leads to every levity and folly? What made the philosopher so susceptible of the rational and the intellectual pleasures? doubtless, the education bestowed upon him; and the same education might have given his wife or his daughter, an equal, or even a superior relish for them; it is folly in him therefore to expect the fruit without the culture necessary to bring it to perfection. The plodding and steadiness of the man of business, he has acquired in his early years; and they are augmented by his being sole master of what he can amass, and having a power to spend or dispose of it as he thinks proper. But his wife was brought up in no such school, and has no such motives to industry; for should she even toil with the utmost assiduity, she cannot appropriate to herself what she acquires; nor lay out any part of it without leave of her husband. Nor is the idleness, extravagance, and neglect of domestic duties, which we so commonly charge upon the sex, so much the fault of nature as of education. Can we expect that the girl whom we train up in every fashionable levity and folly, whom we use our utmost efforts to flatter and to amuse, shall, the moment of her marriage, totally change her plan, and become the sober and oeconimcal housewife? as well might we sow weeds and expect to reap corn.

If this be, as we persuade ourselves it is, a candid and impartial state of the source of female folly and of female weakness; if the whole may be traced either to the total want of, or to an improper education; and if the power of neglecting this education altogether, or bestowing it improperly, be lodged in our hands, as having the sole management and direction of the sex; then it will follow, that we should act a much better and more becoming part, in trying to amend their faults by a more judicious instruction, than to leave them ignorant, and complain that they are so; or teach them folly, and rail at them for having learned what we taught them. But instead of doing this, in every age, and in every country, while the men have been partial to the persons of the fair, they have either left their minds altogether without culture, or biased them by a culture of a spurious and improper nature; suspicious, perhaps, that a more rational one would have opened their eyes, shewn them their real condition, and prompted them to assert the rights of nature; rights, of which the men have perpetually, more or less, deprived them.

But we do not only neglect the sex, or mislead them in point of education; while youth and beauty is on their side, the scene which we open to them is all delusion, flattery, and falsehood; for while we take every opportunity of telling them when present, that their persons are all beauty, and their sentiments and actions all perfection; when absent, we laugh at the credulity of their minds, and splenetically satirise and exhibit to view every fault and every folly. Nor is it till they have become wives, or till the wrinkles have furrowed their brows, that the other sex hear the voice of truth from ours.

Nor are the follies and foibles of the sex, only the subject of verbal sneer, and of verbal criticism; such of our sex as have been soured by disappointments of any kind, and more particularly those who have been unfortunate in the pursuit of lawful, and still more so, in that of unlawful love; like cowards who attack everyone who, they are assured, will make no resistance, have in all ages dipped their pens in gall, and for the supposed faults of a few, illiberally vomited out spleen and ill-nature against the whole sex....

CHAPTER V

Of the Treatment and Condition of Women, and the various Advantages and Disadvantages of their Sex, in savage and civil Life.

There is in the fate of women something exceedingly singular; they have at all periods, and almost in all countries, been, by our sex, constantly oppressed and adored. And what renders their case still more extraordinary, is, that we have not oppressed, because we hated, but because we loved them. We have not in Asia and Africa confined them; because, like the lion and the tyger, we were afraid of their depredations; but because we were unwilling that any body should share with us the pleasure and enjoyment of their company. We have not in Europe assumed almost the sole management of affairs, because we were afraid that they would manage them to our prejudice, but only to save them the trouble of thought and of labour, and to enable them to live in ease and elegance.

Such, however, is not the condition of women in those states approaching the nearest to savage barbarity; there, they have not attained consequence enough even to merit confinement; and far less, to merit that exemption from labour and perpetual guardianship, by which, in Europe, they are complemented and chained. As strength and courage are in savage life the only means of attaining to power and distinction, so weakness and timidity are the certain paths to slavery and oppression: on this account, we shall almost constantly find women among savages condemned to every species of servile, or rather, of slavish drudgery; and shall as constantly find them emerging from this state, in the same proportion as we find the men emerging from ignorance and brutality, and approaching to knowledge and refinement; the rank, therefore, and condition, in which we find women in any country, mark out to us with the greatest precision, the exact point in the scale of civil society, to which the people of such country have arrived; and were their history entirely silent on every subject, and only mentioned the manner in which they treated their women, we would, from thence, be enabled to form a tolerable judgment of the barbarity, or culture, of their manners.

There is hardly any thing more natural to the rude and uncultivated mind, than to consider strength as giving unlimited right to whatever it can conquer; it is one of the first ideas which is derived from attention to the whole of the brute animals; every one of which constantly appropriates to itself, any thing it can take from a weaker being of the same, or of any other species. Whether the human mind has in its rude and barbarous state the same innate idea of right, or whether it has borrowed that idea from the other animals, it is uncertain; but it appears from history, that every savage people either have it from nature or from imitation; and thence undoubtedly arose at first the barbarous custom of enslaving and treating with the utmost severity that sex which nature had formed, not to force, but to charm us into a proper behavior towards them; but though among people of savage and uncultivated manners, this natural weakness of the sex, has subjected them to almost every species of indignity and ill usage; among the civil and polite, it has had a very different effect: these, disdaining to take the advantage of weakness, and rather considering it as intitled to their protection and indulgence, have, from generosity of principle, raised women to a rank and condition, in many cases superior even to that enjoyed by themselves; and this merely in condescension to their weakness: but as we shall have occasion afterwards to mention the causes of the ill treatment of the sex, we shall at present proceed to take a view of their progress from slavery to freedom, and to mark the various causes which have more or less accelerated or retarded that progress.

Select Bibliography

Works by Lucy Aikin

Poetry

Epistles on Women, Exemplifying Their Character and Condition in Various Ages and Nations. With Miscellaneous Poems. London: J. Johnson, 1810. [First American Printing 1810.]
"The Balloon." *The Annual Register for 1812,* 217–18.
Poetry for Children: Consisting of Short Pieces, to Be Committed to Memory. Selected by Lucy Aikin. London: R. Phillips, 1801. [Eight editions by 1820. Repeatedly reprinted in London until the 1840s.] Aikin contributed around ten original poems to this volume.
"Written in an Alcove at Allerton." Mary Ann Humble's Autograph Album. New York Public Library, Misc. 4023.

History

Memoirs of the Court of Queen Elizabeth. London: Longman, Hurst, Rees, Orme, and Brown, 1818. [This book was in its fourth edition in 1819, and its eighth printing by 1869. First American printing 1821, with four more printings by 1870. Translated into Dutch (1821), French (1827), and German (1819).]
Memoirs of the Court of King James the First. London: Longman, Hurst, Rees, Orme and Brown, 1822. [This book saw its third English edition in 1823. It was printed in Boston in 1822, and was translated into Dutch in 1824–26.]
Memoirs of the Court of King Charles the First. London: Longman, Rees, Orme, Brown, Green, Longman, 1833. [Second edition, 1833. First American printing, 1833.]

Fiction

Lorimer: A Tale. London: Henry Colburn, 1814. [American edition, 1816. Second English edition, 1818.]

Family Memoirs and Editions

Memoir of John Aikin, M.D.: With a Selection of His Miscellaneous Pieces, Biographical, Moral, and Critical. London: Baldwin, Craddock and Joy, 1823. [American edition, 1824.]

Literary Criticism and Biography

Review of William Wordsworth, *Poems in Two Volumes*, *Annual Review*, 6 (1807). 521–29.
Review of Lord Byron, *Hours of Idleness*, *Annual Review*, 6 (1807). 529–31.
Review of *The Life of William Roscoe*, *Edinburgh Review*, 58:117 (July 1833). 65–86.
The Life of Joseph Addison. London: Longman, Brown, Green, and Longman, 1843. [American edition, 1843.]
"Recollections of Joanna Baillie." In Philip Hemery Le Breton (ed.), *Memoirs, Miscellanies, and Letters of the Late Lucy Aikin, Including those Addressed to the Rev. Dr. Channing from 1826–1842*. London: Longman, Green, Longman, Roberts and Green, 1864.

Essays

"Words upon Words." In Le Breton (ed.), *Memoirs, Miscellanies, and Letters*.

Children's Literature

Poetry for Children: Consisting of Short Pieces, to Be Committed to Memory. Selected by Lucy Aikin. London: R. Phillips, 1801. [Eight editions by 1820. Repeatedly reprinted in London until the 1840s.]
Juvenile Correspondence, or, Letters, Designed as Examples of the Epistolary Style, for Children of Both Sexes. London: J. Johnson and Co., 1811. [This book saw two more London editions (1816 and 1826), an American printing (1822), and an English language edition published in Paris (1837).]
An English Lesson Book for the Junior Classes. London: Longman, Rees, Orme, Brown, and Green, 1828. [Reprinted in 1833.]
The Juvenile Tale Book: A Collection of Interesting Tales and Novels for Youth. London: Truchy at the French and English library, 1837. [Includes contributions by Aikin.]
Holiday Stories for Young Readers. London: Groombridge, 1858. [A reissue of *An English Lesson Book*.]

Books in Words of One Syllable by Mary Godolphin

[The attribution of Mary Godolphin's one-syllable books to Aikin is not universally accepted. These books were overwhelmingly published and republished, in large numbers, in the United States, rather than England, and many were undated. The following list is therefore incomplete and may not reflect first publication dates. For further discussion of and a selection from these works, see the online edition.]

Aesop's Fables in Words of One Syllable. New York: Felt & Dillingham, 1868.

Aikin, John. *Evenings at Home: In Words of One Syllable*. New York and Philadelphia, 1869.

Bunyan, John. *The Pilgrim's Progress in Words of One Syllable*. London: Routledge, 1869.

Day, Thomas. *Sandford and Merton in Words of One Syllable*. 1868.

Defoe, Daniel. *Robinson Crusoe in Words of One Syllable*. 1868.

The One Syllable Sunday Book. London and New York: Routledge, c. 1870.

Wyss, Johann David. *The Swiss Family Robinson in Words of One Syllable*. 1869.

Translations

Hess, Jean Gaspar. *The Life of Ulrich Zwingle*. Trans. Lucy Aikin. London: J. Johnson, 1812. [Reprinted in 1813.]

Jauffret, L.F. *The Travels of Rolando: Containing, in a Supposed Tour Round the World, Authentic Descriptions of the Geography, Natural History, Manners and Antiquities of Various Countries Translated from the French of L.F. Jauffret*. London: Richard Phillips, 1804. [Preface signed L.A. This book saw five editions in less than 20 years, and five more in the 1850s.]

Aikin as Editor and Contributor

Aikin, John. *The Arts of Life. A New Edition, with Additions and Alterations by Lucy Aikin*. London: Longman, Brown, Green, Longman and Roberts, 1858.

Aikin, John and Anna Lætitia Barbauld. *Evenings at Home, or, The Juvenile Budget Opened, by Dr Aikin and Mrs Barbauld. Sixteenth Edition, the Whole Carefully Revised, Corrected Throughout, and Newly Arranged by Arthur Aikin, Esq ... and Miss Aikin, with Some Additional Pieces by the Authors*. London: Longman, 1846. [Includes a preface by Lucy Aikin]

——. *Selected Works of the British Poets with Biographical and Critical Prefaces. A New Edition with a Supplement by Lucy Aikin*. London: Longman, 1845.

Barbauld, Anna Lætitia. *The Works of Anna Lætitia Barbauld: With a Memoir by Lucy Aikin.* London: Longman, Hurst, Rees, Orme, Browne and Green, 1825.

——. *A Legacy for Young Ladies: Consisting of Miscellaneous Pieces in Prose and Verse. Edited with a Preface by Lucy Aikin.* London: Printed for Longman, Hurst, Rees, Orme, Brown, and Green, 1826.

Benger, Elizabeth Ogilvy. *Memoirs of the Life of Anne Boleyn, Queen of Henry VIII. With a Memoir of the Author, by Miss Aikin.* Third edition. London: Longman, Rees, Orme, Brown and Green, 1827. [Elizabeth Ogilvy Benger died in 1827, and Aikin's memoir was included in all subsequent printings of Benger's *Memoirs* as well as in an 1828 London collection, *Historical Works.*]

The Juvenile Tale Book: A Collection of Interesting Tales and Novels for Youth. London: Truchy at the French and English library, 1837. [Includes contributions by Aikin.]

Le Breton, Anna Letitia, *Memoirs of Mrs. Barbauld.* London: George Bell and Sons, 1874.

——. (Martin, Mrs. Herbert.) *Memories of Seventy Years, by One of a Literary Family.* London: Griffith & Farran, 1883.

Correspondence

Le Breton, Anna Letitia (ed.). *Correspondence of William Ellery Channing, D.D., and Lucy Aikin, from 1826–1842.* London: Williams and Norgate, 1874; Boston: Roberts Brothers, 1874.

Le Breton, Philip Hemery (ed.). *Memoirs, Miscellanies, and Letters of the Late Lucy Aikin, Including those Addressed to the Rev. Dr. Channing from 1826–1842.* London: Longman, Green, Longman, Roberts and Green, 1864.

Secondary Literature on Aikin's Works

Reviews of Aikin's Works

Obituary of Aikin
Annual Register (1865): 181.

Epistles on Women
Belfast Monthly Magazine (August 1810): 131–35.
Eclectic Review (November 1810): 1003–07.
New Annual Register (1810): 368.
Poetical Register (1810–1811): 553–54.
Monthly Review (April 1811): 380–90.

European Magazine (July 1811): 35–39.
Critical Review (August 1811): 418–26.

Memoirs of the Court of Queen Elizabeth
  Monthly Review (November 1818): 225–50.
  Eclectic Review (February 1819): 105–26.
  The Ladies' Monthly Magazine (March 1820): 155–56.

Memoirs of the Court of King James I
  Monthly Review (March 1822): 225–47.
  Eclectic Review (August 1822): 97–119.

Memoir of John Aikin
  Gentleman's Magazine (November 1823).
  Monthly Review. Reprinted in *Museum of Foreign Literature, Science, and Art* 4.22 (1 April 1824): 313.

Works of Anna Lætitia Barbauld: With a Memoir by Lucy Aikin
  Monthly Review. Reprinted in *Museum of Foreign Literature, Science, and Art* 7.41 (1 November 1825): 391.
  Christian Examiner and Theological Review 3.4 (July/August 1826): 299.
  North American Review 23.2 (1826): 368.

Memoirs of the Court of King Charles I
  Monthly Review (August 1833): 449–56.
  Eclectic Review 10 (December 1833): 461–79.
  Edinburgh Review 58.118 (January 1834): 398–422.
  The Knickerbocker, or, New York Monthly Magazine 3.2 (February 1834): 145.

Life of Joseph Addison
  Monthly Review 2.1 (May 1843): 261–67.
  The Irish Sketchbook. Reprinted in *The Eclectic Museum of Foreign Literature, Science, and Art* 2:3 (July 1843): 429.
  [Macaulay, Thomas]. "The Life and Writings of Joseph Addison." *Edinburgh Review* 78.157 (July 1843): 193–260.
  [Peabody, William Bourne Oliver]. *The North American Review* 64.135 (April 1847): 314–73.

Memoirs, Miscellanies and Letters of the Late Lucy Aikin
  The Spectator. Reprinted in *Littell's Living Age*. 3 December 1864: 520.

The Saturday Review. Reprinted in *Littell's Living Age.* 24 December 1864: 657.

"Letters of Lucy Aikin." *Theological Review: A Quarterly Journal of Religious Thought and Life* 2 (1865): 92.

Correspondence

Dall, C.H. *Unitarian Review and Religious Magazine* 2 (1874): 598.

Dicey, A.V. "Letters of Lucy Aikin." *Nation: A Weekly Journal Devoted to Politics, Literature, Science, and Art* 65 (1874): 270.

James, Henry, Jr. *The Atlantic Monthly* 35.209 (March 1875): 368–71.

"Three Women of Letters." *North British Review* 42 (1865): 327–56. [Also reviews Joanna Baillie's *Fugitive Verses*; and *Selections from the Letters of Caroline Frances Cornwallis.*]

The Academy 6 (1874): 65.

Lippincott's Magazine of Popular Literature and Science 14 (November 1874): 647.

New Englander and Yale Review 34:130 (January 1875): 188–90.

Others

Review of *The Fortunes of Nigel*, by Walter Scott. *Edinburgh Review* 37.73 (June 1822): 204–25. [Contains a footnote that gives high praise to *Memoir of the Court of King James the First.*]

Review of *Memoirs of the Life of Anne Boleyn, Queen of Henry VIII*, by Elizabeth Ogilvy Benger. *The Southern Quarterly Review* 2.4 (November 1850): 536. [Mentions Aikin.]

Encyclopedia Entries

B., A.A. "Lucy Aikin." *Dictionary of National Biography.* Ed. Leslie Stephen. Vol. 1. London: Smith and Elder, 1885. 186–87.

Cousin, John William. "Lucy Aikin." *Short Biographical Dictionary of English Literature.* London: J.M. Dent and Sons, 1910.

Knapp, Elise F. "Lucy Aikin." *Dictionary of Literary Biography: Nineteenth-Century British Literary Biographers.* Ed. Steven Serafin. Vol. 144. Detroit: Gale, 1994. 3–11.

Schnorrenberg, Barbara Brandon. "Aikin, Lucy (1781–1864)." *Dictionary of National Biography*, Oxford: Oxford UP, 2004. <http://www.oxforddnb.com>.

Turzynski, Linda J. "Lucy Aikin." *Dictionary of Literary Biography: British Children's Writers, 1800–1880.* Ed. Meena Khorana. Vol. 163. Detroit: Gale, 1996.

Contemporary Criticism

Behrendt, Stephen C. "The Gap That Is Not a Gap: British Poetry by Women, 1802–1812." *Romanticism and Women Poets: Opening the Doors of Reception*. Ed. Harriet Kramer Linkin and Stephen C. Behrendt. Lexington: U of Kentucky P, 1999.

Graver, Bruce. "Lucy Aikin's Marginalia to Biographia Literaria." *European Romantic Review* 14.3 (2003): 323–43.

Guest, Harriet. *Small Change: Women Learning Patriotism, 1750–1810*. Chicago: U of Chicago P, 2000.

Janowitz, Anne. "Memoirs of a Dutiful Niece: Lucy Aikin and Literary Reputation." *Repossessing the Romantic Past*. Ed. Heather Glen and Paul Hamilton. Cambridge: Cambridge UP, 2006.

Kelly, Gary. "Romanticism and the Feminist Uses of History." *Romanticism, History, Historicism: Essays on an Orthodoxy*. Ed. Damian Walford Davies. New York: Routledge, 2009. 163–80.

Kucich, Greg. "Romanticism and Feminist Historiography." *The Wordsworth Circle* 24.3 (Summer 1993): 133–40.

——. "Women's Historiography and the (Dis)Embodiment of Law: Ann Yearsley, Mary Hays, Elizabeth Benger." *Wordsworth Circle* 3.1 (Winter 2002): 3–7.

Laurence, Anne. "Women Historians and Documentary Research: Lucy Aikin, Agnes Strickland, Mary Anne Everett Green, and Lucy Toulmin Smith." *Women, Scholarship and Criticism: Gender and Knowledge c. 1790–1900*. Ed. Joan Bellamy, Anne Laurence and Gillian Perry. Manchester: Manchester UP, 2000.

Levy, Michelle. "'The Different Genius of Woman': Lucy Aikin's Historiography." *The Dissenting Mind: The Aikin Circle, c. 1740s– c. 1860s*. Ed. Felicity James and Ian Inkster. Cambridge: Cambridge UP, forthcoming.

——. "The Radical Education of Evenings at Home." *Eighteenth Century Fiction* 19.1 & 2 (2006): 123–50.

McCarthy, William. "A 'High-Minded Christian Lady': The Posthumous Reception of Anna Lætitia Barbauld." *Romanticism and Women Poets: Opening the Doors of Reception*. Ed. Harriet Kramer Linkin and Stephen C. Behrendt. Lexington: U of Kentucky P, 1999.

——. *Anna Letitia Barbauld: Voice of the Enlightenment*. Baltimore: Johns Hopkins UP, 2008.

Mellor, Anne. "The Female Poet and the Poetess: Two Traditions of British Women's Poetry, 1780–1830." *Studies in Romanticism* 36 (1997): 261–76.

Mitchell, Rosemary. "The Busy Daughters of Clio: Women Writers of History from 1820–1880." *Women's History Review* 7.1 (1998): 107–34.

Ready, Kathryn. "Dissenting Sociability and the Anglo-American Context: The Correspondence of William Ellery Channing and Lucy Aikin." *Symbiosis: A Journal of Anglo-American Literary Relations* 9.2 (2005): 117–33.

——. "The Enlightenment Feminist Project of Lucy Aikin's *Epistles on Women* (1810)." *History of European Ideas* 31 (2005): 435–50.

White, Daniel E. "The "Joineriana": Anna Barbauld, the Aikin Family Circle, and the Dissenting Public Sphere." *Eighteenth-Century Studies* 32.4 (1999): 511–33.

Works Inspired by Aikin's Writings

Linley, George. *Catherine Grey: A Grand Opera in Three Acts.* 1837. [Aikin's *Memoirs of Elizabeth* "have furnished the groundwork of this opera" (2).]

Sacred and Miscellaneous Poetry Selected for Young Children: Intended as a Sequel to Miss Aikin's Poetry for Children. London: Souter, 1829.